The
Parables
of
Jesus

*"And He spake many things
unto them in parables"*

A BOOK OF SERMONS BY:
J. WAYNE McKAMIE

Second Edition
Published By
Robinson Digital Publications
P.O. Box 2634
Weatherford, TX 76086

All scripture quotations are taken from the Holy Bible, King
James Version unless otherwise noted.

For additional copies contact:
Gary Robinson
P.O. Box 2634
Weatherford, TX 76086
parables@sbcglobal.net

Table of Contents

Sermons

Chapter

Introduction to First Edition

In July of 1978, Brother J. Wayne McKamie conducted a series of Gospel Meetings in the city of Wichita, Kansas. This meeting provided him with the opportunity to fulfill a goal he had thought about for many years: to preach an entire series on the Parables of Jesus. His selected theme not only edified the church and brought out many visitors but brought favorable results before the week-long meeting came to a close.

While sitting in the assembly and hearing these sermons preached, I realized what a blessing it would be to give them a much wider audience. We made plans to publish them in a book and thereby allow readers to benefit from such inspiring messages for years to come.

The first seven sermons in this book are those presented during the Gospel Meeting in Wichita, Kansas. We have added other sermons on the Parables to the book, sermons that Wayne has presented to congregations across the nation.

Reducing these sermons to the printed page forces us to remove much of the life-giving substance, the animating force behind the sermons. We lose the man himself. The spoken word may be preserved in writing, but the sparkle in the eye, the emotion of the delivery, the sweep of the hand, the thunder of the voice—these we cannot print. The excellence and the message within these discourses command their preservation. Perhaps those among us who know Wayne will be able to feel his soul-stirring energy and to hear his thunderous voice. More importantly, perhaps we can hear the Son of God himself as he "taught them many things by parables" (Mark 4:2).

A number of people have devoted their time, talents, and energy to help us produce such a work, and we stand in their debt.

Sister George A. (Louva) Hogland of Lubbock, Texas, spent countless hours transcribing, typing, and reviewing each sermon. Her task was a tedious one, and we wish to express deep appreciation for her interest and indefatigable dedication.

We also wish to thank Brother Joe Norton of Hurst, Texas, who was responsible for the reading and revision of the manuscript as well as the writing of the biography. His proficiency has given this work a merit of excellence.

Brother Virgil Hogland of Kansas City, Missouri, provided the financial assistance necessary for such a project, without which this work would not have been possible.

And now, this book is launched with the prayer that it may be used of the Lord to inspire hope and dedication in the lives of Christians everywhere. In Brother McKamie's own words, "My main attempt has been to make these grand sermons live anew in the hearts of our people. They have lived for me; I want them to live for others." May the Lord bless this work to that end!

Bob C. Loudermilk
12917 W. Harvest Ct.
Wichita, KS 67235
Bob@quantumexpo.com

In Dedication to . . .

… my wife, Jean, without whose influence I would have never come to a knowledge of the truth.

… my four sons who have heard these lessons since their earliest recall and in whom I hope most to see them come alive as a beautiful blending of the human and the divine as Jesus teaches in His parables.

… my home congregation, in McGregor, Texas, whose members have listened patiently through the years.

… the Cause of Him from whose lips these great truths first fell.

J. Wayne McKamie

Acknowledgments

I salute Bob Loudermilk for sharing his vision of publishing this work and for the patience he exhibited while it was being written. My utmost gratitude to Mrs. George A. (Louva) Hogland, whose clerical skills and tremendous tenacity made possible the transcription and completion of the first edition of this work: without her it would not have been done. My deep appreciation to Joe Norton who contributed his superb instinct for the real character of the target and for his technical scholarship.

My gratitude also goes out to Gary Robinson of Weatherford, Texas, for coming up with the idea of reprinting this book and then for following the project through to completion.

The story of this book is best said in the words "other men have labored, the author has entered into their labors." One thing immediately evident is that this work was written neither by a scholar nor for scholars. It was designed for those who love the Lord and His Word and for those who love to hear again and again "Him who spake as man never spake."

J. Wayne McKamie

J. Wayne McKamie

Biography

God's kingdoms have always included men who rose above the ordinary and became exemplary in performing the responsibilities God had for them to do. In each case, they had a deep and abiding love for God and developed a close relationship with Him. During the First Age, the patriarchs worked closely with God and led the people as God directed them. During the Mosaic Age, the same happened as God used men like the prophets, priests, and judges to lead His people. These men had the advantage of direct communication with God and, many times, the use of the miraculous in fulfilling their tasks.

During the opening years of the Christian Age, God set in place a system in which men would no longer have the use of the miraculous. Rather, God wanted men who would rise up and perform service for Him because of their love and dedication to Him and the Cause of His Son—men who would perform their responsibilities without the use of the miraculous. The church has always been blessed with such men—and J. Wayne McKamie is such a man.

Background

Having been born into a staunch Baptist family, Wayne grew up in a rural environment, faithfully attending a Baptist church in Moody, Texas. He was born April 26, 1933, near Moody in McLennan County. His father was Dudley Clarence McKamie, and his mother was Mary Ellen McKamie. He was the youngest of four children.

From his earliest remembrance, his parents taught him to believe in and love God. As well, they maintained extremely high moral standards and taught him to do the same, warning him against drinking, gambling, dancing, and immorality. He heard some of the strongest sermons he has ever heard against such from his home and from the pulpit during his early years. He has related that he grew up with the conviction that a bottle of beer or a deck of cards would be as welcome in his home as a rattlesnake.

Wayne's first exposure to the New Testament pattern of worship was in 1949 when he attended a service of the Jones Hill Church of Christ about seven miles south of McGregor, Texas, at the invitation of a classmate, Jean Cherry (they later married). Billy Jack Ivey, a young preacher from Oklahoma, spoke that day. Wayne remembers being quite taken by the uniqueness of the building as well as simplicity of the worship:

> The building was a small typical one-room country school house. Gray weathered walls supported a steep wood-shingled roof. The well that served the school for so many years was still near the old front porch. Two doors opened in from the porch. Once inside a choice of short benches or ancient desks afforded one a seat. A raised section completely across the opposite end of the building, which once served as the teacher's vantage point, had been converted into the preacher's platform.

From that time, Wayne continued to visit the Jones Hill congregation as well as other congregations in the area. One such place was the Whitehall Church of Christ just outside of Moody, only about eight miles from the community where he grew up. He also visited the services of various other congregations in the vicinity of Waco, Temple, and Belton, all in Texas, hearing gospel sermons preached by such men as Homer A. Gay, James R. Stewart, Irvin Waters, E.H. Miller, Lynwood Smith, Homer L. King, C.S. Holt, Gillis Prince, Isom Hayes, Billy Jack Ivey, Fred Kirbo, and Barney Welch. He remembers well some of the gospel meetings at the Jones Hill congregation when the brethren set up lights outside and had an open-air service because of the hot Texas summers. Crowds were always good during those times because "people came to church back then."

During one of the first gospel meetings he attended, he heard Lynwood Smith preach at the 29th Street congregation in Temple. One of the first debates he heard was between Irvin Waters and John Staley about whether the church could use fermented wine in the Lord's Supper. Another debate he remembers was by E.H. Miller and John O'Dowd discussing whether it was scriptural to use individual communion cups in the Lord's Supper and whether they could divide the assembly into Bible classes.

In February 1950, after much searching and Bible study, Wayne decided to leave the Baptist Church and obey the plan of salvation as taught in the New Testament. He was almost seventeen years old at the time. Barney Welch, who was conducting a gospel meeting at the Vaughn Blvd. congregation in Fort Worth, Texas, baptized him into Christ.

Wayne was married to Jean Cherry June 29, 1951. To them, four sons were born: Charles Wayne, Carlis James, David Neal, and Brian Dudley.

Evangelistic Work

Receiving much encouragement from brethren who had been in the church for a long time, Wayne began to speak publicly. He preached his first sermon at the old 4th Street congregation in Waco in early 1951. Because of his obvious understanding of the scriptures, his exceptional talent as a public speaker, and his booming resonant voice, brethren continued to encourage him to become a full-time preacher of the gospel. Making the decision to follow their advice, Wayne's first opportunity to do evangelistic work came August 8, 1951, when he began working with the congregation in Harrodsburg, Indiana; thus, he has served the Lord as an evangelist for sixty-three years. Wayne and his wife, Jean, loaded up all of their possessions and their wedding gifts and headed for Indiana in a car that was a gift from Jean's father.

Wayne remembers the tremendous spiritual rewards of those years but also the difficulties that accompanied those rewards. He was extremely busy, and he realized the sacrifices his new wife was having to make. He says, in fact, that few really realize the great sacrifices preachers' wives must make so that their husbands can preach the gospel. Their situation was an extreme case. They were eighteen years old and they had been married only two months when they moved into this work that had taken them more than one thousand miles from their home.

While living in Harrodsburg, Wayne was ordained as an evangelist by Homer L. King in 1952. During the two years he and Jean spent there, he undertook a tremendous workload for a young Christian and a new evangelist. In fact, for the first six months, they did not stay at home for even one evening because they were busy with visitation and other responsibilities for the church. In addition to edifying and building up the church there, he also began a radio work, conducted home studies, began mission work at nearby points, and performed numerous other duties connected with a located evangelistic effort. Preaching three times a week and preparing a radio sermon for every Sunday morning plunged Wayne into an intensive study of the Bible that kept him busy almost day and night. Out of that study, however, came a knowledge of the Bible that has served him well throughout his years of preaching.

Jean reminisces, too, about their move to Indiana when they settled into the little house behind the historic big red-brick church building: "The church in Harrodsburg was the largest Church of Christ we had ever seen or had been a part of. There were about one hundred members. I will never forget our first Sunday there. A huge bell was rung at 10 o'clock and again at 10:30, calling the worshipers to come in. The singing was beautiful." She commented on how extremely friendly all of the people at Harrodsburg were and how much she appreciated that. "Even so, I got so homesick I thought I would die."

"We actually grew up in Harrodsburg," she said. "It was hard times, money was scarce, but we were happy." She becomes philosophic when she reflects on her years as a preacher's wife: "The Lord had something special planned for me. He had Wayne McKamie waiting and a life of preaching. Since I was a little girl, I wanted to be a preacher's wife." She says they never gave much thought for the future when they first began their spiritual journey together: "We wanted to be together, and together we were for the next eleven years more than most couples would be." She made this statement in reference to those years of traveling and preaching across the United States before they settled back in Texas to rear their family. They celebrate sixty-three years together in 2014.

While in Indiana, Wayne endeared himself to the Christians there and established a reputation that has stayed with him. He is still loved and highly respected wherever he works or conducts meetings. The fact that he is called back over and over to some of the same congregations for meetings testifies to the regard his fellow Christians have for him.

The first wedding he performed was in Harrodsburg in 1951, and the first funeral was also there in 1952.

Returning to the site of his first sermon, Wayne conducted his first gospel meeting at the 4th Street congregation in Waco in 1951.

While living in Indiana, Wayne took voice lessons and studied music under Dr. Ross at Indiana University. He also attended the Stamps Quartet School of Music in Dallas in 1959 where he studied under Videt Polk and Bobby Burnett. He has sung with and made records with the Sunny South Quartet, The Lamplighters, Celebration, and various other gospel singing groups.

After completing his work in Indiana, Wayne spent the next eleven years doing located work in a number of other states and conducting gospel meetings in many parts of the United States. Even after that time when he settled back in McGregor, Texas, to rear his family, he continued to conduct gospel meetings all across the U.S. as time allowed. The places where he did located work include Wayne, West Virginia; Memphis, Tennessee; Greenville, South Carolina; and in Andrews, Midland, Odessa, Waco, McGregor, and the congregation on Green Oaks in Arlington, in Texas.

Wayne has preached and/or conducted gospel meetings in every state where we have faithful congregations except the state of Alaska. He remembers the "hey day" of gospel meetings in the 1950's and 1960's when brethren would arrange to use "brush arbors" or set up tents for mission meetings either in their own city or in cities where there was no faithful congregation, and they would attract large numbers of people from a community to hear the gospel. These meetings were usually highly successful as evidenced by the large number of responses. Wayne recalls that brethren would find a vacant lot, clean it up, string lights or hang lanterns, get some funeral home fans, and advertise the meeting. During one such meeting in 1956 in Greenville, SC, Wayne and Bro. E.H. Miller preached what he called a "double header": both of them preached every night of the meeting. His wife Jean recalls, "they preached and preached while we sat for hours on metal folding chairs." Gospel meetings were longer back then, some lasting two full weeks and over three Sundays. Some went even longer if people continued to show an interest in the gospel. Buildings were filled to capacity many times with people standing outside and listening through open windows.

During those years, he and his fellow evangelists preached in any venue to which a crowd could be gathered: in country schoolhouses, court houses, prisons, municipal auditoriums, old store fronts, and others. And many people responded to the gospel. He remembers that during some of those meetings his "baptizing clothes never got dry." For Wayne, the largest number ever responding during any gospel meeting was forty-one, and the largest number baptized in a new work was thirty-five. Gospel meetings were really a big occasion during those times. Preachers could go into any community and begin preaching, assuming that people already believed in God and in the Bible as the word of God. Many times young men who wanted to become preachers of the gospel showed up to help with the singing, to assist in other ways during the services, and just to learn as much as they could.

"Preaching was our life, our work, our world," Wayne said. He remembers one tour in California when he preached thirty-five nights without a break, going from one meeting to another—that tour was in 1956. There were others when he preached from one end of that state to the other to enthusiastic audiences eager to hear the gospel.

Besides assisting countless souls in obeying the Lord and in remaining faithful, Wayne has conducted numerous weddings and funerals for fellow Christians across the nation. He has also participated in many brotherhood preachers' studies in this country.

Educational and Professional Career

All of Wayne's public school education was completed in the Moody Public School System. After several years as a well-known and respected evangelist, he moved back to his home in McGregor and continued his education at Temple Junior College, receiving his Associate in Arts degree in 1962. While at Temple, he was selected to be a member of Phi Theta Kappa, a national junior college honor society. Transferring to Baylor University, he completed the requirements for a Bachelor of Arts degree with a major in education in 1964. He was an honor student at both Temple and Baylor.

Having completed his bachelor's degree, Wayne decided in the fall of 1964 to teach school during the winter months and preach during the three summer months plus over weekends and during holiday periods. His goal was to provide a stable environment for his four boys while they were in school. He actually continued that rigorous schedule for the next twenty-four years. His first position was as a sixth grade teacher in the Waco Public Schools as well as helping in special education as needed.

In 1966, he became a master teacher with the Hallsburg schools, assisting other teachers and helping with some of the responsibilities of the principal, who was looking toward retirement. After the principal retired, Wayne did some teaching but also took on the responsibilities of the principal. In preparation for this position, he had begun working on a Master of Science degree in education at Baylor University, a degree he completed in 1970. Soon his position was upgraded to a combination of superintendent and principal, a position he held until his retirement in 1988. At that time, he returned to full-time preaching, the work he loved the most.

Radio Work

Having begun his radio work in Indiana, Wayne has also had programs in several other states. He has had extended broadcasts across the state of Texas, including Midland, Hillsboro, and San Antonio. At this time he has a program broadcasting from Waco, Texas, and from Lubbock, Texas, which has been on the air continually for the past thirty-five years. Radio was as effective in earlier days as television and the Internet are today.

In 2002, Wayne spent a little more than a year going to a professional studio in Dallas to make a recording of the entire New Testament. The congregation located on Grauwyler Road in Irving, Texas, sponsored this work.

Mission Work

For the past forty-seven years, Wayne has been involved in missionary work in Mexico, having made his first trip in 1967, accompanied by this writer. He has made many trips to visit congregations and mission points in Mexico, has accompanied native preachers into areas to explore the possibilities of new mission points, and has observed native preachers in their performance of evangelistic responsibilities. He has also conducted countless numbers of studies for preachers in the villages and has conducted many major studies for preachers in Saltillo, in Monterrey, and in Mexico City with all of the Mexican evangelists in attendance.

Studying the Spanish language at both Temple Junior College and Baylor University facilitated his work among the Spanish-speaking brethren in Mexico. He also became involved in the Texas Bilingual Institute in Waco.

Wayne continues to communicate with Juan Rodriguez, Jr., about the work there and occasionally with other native preachers. He also communicates with brethren in this country about the work in Mexico.

As well, Wayne has been involved in mission work in South America in the countries of Peru and Ecuador. He has made two mission trips to the continent of Africa: one was to Ghana with this writer where he assisted in conducting intensive Bible studies for the local preachers and the other was to Zambia where he worked with Roger Boone and Duane Permenter. In the 1980s, he and this writer made a good-will trip to England and Scotland to visit brethren and to establish ties with faithful churches there.

Conclusion

An asset that has stood well with Wayne in preaching is his phenomenal memory. Having been an avid reader not only of the scriptures but also of the classic literature of the church, Wayne's memory has allowed him to have at his disposal vast amounts of information that he can insert on the spot, enhancing his preaching and making the scriptures really come alive for his audiences. Because of his memory, he has always been able to preach his sermons from abbreviated notes rather than manuscripts.

Few who have heard the masterful persuasiveness of Wayne's sermons have gone away untouched in some way—saint or sinner. No sincere Christian has ever sat in the audience and listened to the gospel preached with Wayne's deep resounding voice without feeling a need to live a little more closely to the Lord.

Aside from the fact that his preaching is informative and inspirational, Wayne has always set before the people a model of a Christian witness in every aspect of his life. He is always diligent in doing the work of an evangelist and has proved to be a most congenial work fellow to many. He loves the souls of men and puts forth every effort toward their salvation. It has been while listening to Wayne preach that many, young and old, have made decisions that put them back on a stable course in their Christian lives. It is perhaps the message of penetrating practicality that causes people to be moved to action more than any other one characteristic of Wayne's preaching.

Wayne's basic philosophy really sums up the foundation upon which he has built his years of service to the Lord: "I believe in the inspired, inerrant, once-for-all-time handed down Word of God."

Joe L. Norton
Mansfield, Texas
June 2014

Preface

"Never man spake like this man." And when we consider that almost all that our Lord spoke to the masses He spoke in parables, it is only fitting that generation after generation rise up with heart, tongue, and pen to make these great sermons live anew. The parables of Jesus are, and will always remain, the heart of His teachings.

The concept of parabolic teaching was not new even in the time of Christ. It was He, however, who shined the light of perfection upon it.

A simple word regarding parables may be in order at this point. Without attempting to delve into theological attributes, it can be safely observed that a parable is neither fable, metaphor, simile, nor allegory. A parable is a laying alongside, a comparison, a parallel drawn between basic earthly truth and heavenly truth. Not specifically, but generally, the popular "earthly story with heavenly meaning" is true.

The Master's lessons were of the earth, earthly. The common tongue, the ordinary, the believable, were His stock in trade as He translated life into religion and religion into life. We shall never understand, I think, these great lessons until we learn to feel this comparing, this compounding of the human and the divine. Human experiences were the windows through which He poured the Sunlight of truth divine.

The dynamics of a parable are best seen in what our Lord did with this human-divine mixture. We cannot long dwell on the touching picture of a shepherd seeking his sheep because in a flash the truth of God seeking lost men is upon us. The pathos of five virgins with cold, darkened lamps frantically searching for oil in the still marketplace cannot long hold our view as we envision a time when unready souls run fruitlessly through the closed markets of mercy! Ah, in the parables His simple arguments are unanswerable; His appeal is inescapable!

Through every page the universal King
From Eden's loss unto the end of years,
From East to West, the Son of Man appears ...

Truth through the sacred volume hidden lies,
And spreads from end to end her secret wing,
Through ritual, type, and storied mysteries.

— Isaac Williams

Sermon One

The
Parables
of
Jesus

"And He spake many things
unto them in parables"

2

Matthew 13:1-9

"The same day went Jesus out of the house, and sat by the sea side. And great multitudes were gathered together unto him, so that he went into a ship, and sat; and the whole multitude stood on the shore. And he spake many things unto them in parables, saying, Behold, a sower went forth to sow; And when he sowed, some seeds fell by the way side, and the fowls came and devoured them up: Some fell upon stony places, where they had not much earth: and forthwith they sprung up, because they had no deepness of earth: And when the sun was up, they were scorched; and because they had no root, they withered away. And some fell among thorns; and the thorns sprung up, and choked them: But other fell into good ground, and brought forth fruit, some an hundredfold, some sixtyfold, some thirtyfold. Who hath ears to hear let him hear."

1. The Sower

We welcome you to the evening assembly, and we would say in the beginning that we are extremely grateful to be in Wichita tonight. We trust that it is for our good and to God's glory that we are here. We do welcome you to the beginning service of this series of Gospel Meetings; and we trust that before this time is over, we can feel that this week has been well spent. We trust that in the course of one week's time, great good can be accomplished. I realize that we will be speaking but relatively a short period in the course of the day, but a great deal can be done during this time.

We are grateful for your invitation to come to this place to study with you the Lord's Word and in particular this format that we have before us. I have been preaching some twenty-seven years and I have never had the opportunity, or at least I have never taken the opportunity, to speak only on the parables of Jesus. It is something that I have long desired to do, but you are the first ones to have invited me to do that particular thing. You may feel the parables of Jesus are nothing more than some stories from the Bible. I will assure you that such is not the case.

As I come to begin this series of Gospel Meetings, I think of what a person some time ago said that a preacher ought to be. He listed several things: a preacher ought to be an administrator, a promoter, a business manager, and a public relations man. But I will tell you, tonight, that I do not come as any of these. I come to this place believing that a gospel preacher just simply ought to be that—a preacher of the gospel. And that is all that I plan to do while I am in your

4

presence in Wichita, Kansas—I plan to preach the Gospel of the Lord Jesus Christ. We are here to call men back to Jesus Christ, to tell, as we have sung tonight, "the old, old story of Jesus and His love." You remember the second stanza of that song says, "I love to tell the story. For those who know it best, seem hungering and thirsting to hear it like the rest." So I hope that will be the case as we study from night to night.

When I first thought of presenting this series, my first concern was which parables would I teach. There are so many that the Lord used to show the many beautiful sides and the many facets of the great kingdom of God. I wondered which ones to use, but I did not have any problem deciding which one I would use first. There is a particular reason we have chosen to begin with "The Parable of the Sower" or "The Parable of the Soils."

I want you to notice first of all as we begin to study that we shall say a few things tonight that we probably will not say every night. We will lay some groundwork, explaining why the Lord began to speak in parables. When we consider the personal ministry of Jesus Christ, we notice it moves along a true continuum from the time He was born until it became evident He must be about His Father's business. Then there was a period of time in which the Lord openly and freely laid down the principles of the kingdom of God. And then there came the day when the Lord began to speak to them in parables.

Someone has said—someone who has taken the time to study such—that Matthew is forty-three percent parabolic—that forty-three percent of the Gospel of Matthew would fall into this category. So what we have is a new form and a new content in the teaching of Jesus Christ, so much so that His disciples came to Him and said, "Why speakest thou unto them in parables?" They were amazed that Jesus had so switched His method that He spoke to them on this occasion only in parables.

This particular parable is somewhat of a key, if I may call it so, to all the others. In fact, in Mark 4:13, when our Lord had finished the Parable of the Sower, He said, "Know ye not this parable? and how then will ye know all parables?" So I must understand that there is something in particular about this parable that we need to understand. If we don't know this parable, then there are some things, the Lord would suggest, that we may not know about the others. We have some priority or some emphasis that is laid by the Lord upon this particular study, and so we begin with it.

I would like to say in the beginning that parables are not easy. We tend to think of parables as being some lovely stories that we read to our children, and that's true. But I want to tell you, that's not all the truth. The parables of Jesus sometimes become difficult, I am persuaded, because we are concerned with the mysteries of the kingdom of Heaven. When we use the word "mystery," now or in the course of this study throughout this week, we will be using it in this sense—and I believe this is the sense in which the Bible uses it—mysteries in the Bible are not things that are unraveled by science but things that are unfolded by revelation. Our Lord is saying, I will unfold to you, through this means, some of the great mysteries of the kingdom of Heaven.

I do know this: we are living in the age of the sowing of the seed of the kingdom. Our Lord has departed from our presence; He has gone into a far country, (Luke 19; Daniel 7). He has gone "into a far country to receive for himself a kingdom, and to return." He has received that kingdom: He has been crowned as King. We have received the kingdom: we are in the age of the sowing of the seed of that kingdom. And this process will continue until the end. If it is the age of the sowing of the seed of the kingdom, it is also the age of growth.

What is a Parable?

The word "parable" comes from two words: one that means to "throw or cast" and the other means "beside." The idea is that the Lord is taking something that we understand, to some degree, and laying along side it something that otherwise we would not understand. They are simple stories, and yet they are always true. At no time should we ever look at a parable as being a myth or a fable because it was always something true—and from this point, the Lord proceeded with His great spiritual truths. It is as someone once said, "A parable of Jesus is an earthly story with a Heavenly meaning." There is a great deal of truth in that statement.

Something that I have noticed in preparing for this study is that Jesus always draws on the memory of His hearers when He speaks in parables. He refers to things they knew, and it is only through the memory of something familiar to them, that His stories begin to take on real meaning.

I would like to say, too, that the parables of Jesus are not the basis for doctrine. They are the illustration of the doctrines—the greatest doctrines you know. If Mr. Spurgeon's words be true, and I think in this case they are, he says, "A sermon is the house—the illustrations are the windows that let the light into the house." We know about the great doctrines of the kingdom of God, and these parables are the means through which the Lord sheds light and illustrates those great doctrines.

Now, tonight, and every night, we are going to proceed from the simple to the complex. We are going to move from the known to the unknown, from the seen to the unseen. There are going to be some amazing prophecies. I am no prophet, but the Lord was: and He lays down some amazing prophecies in some of the parables that have, or will, come true because He said so. We will try to point these out as we come to them night after night.

If you have your Bible open this evening, please turn to Matthew 13, and let's just think about what is being said. I want you to notice, in verse 10, they come to the Lord quite amazed that the Lord has departed from His form of teaching and has turned to a new way. "Why speakest thou unto them in parables?" When the Lord gives His reason, He gives us a justification for the teaching in parables in His day; and whatever the justification was in HIS day, it is the same in OUR day. So, I feel quite secure, although I might say this—I think it is quite an awesome undertaking any time we presume to say that we are going to preach Jesus' sermon. It is no little thing we are doing. It is with a great deal of awe and responsibility that we should approach this teaching. When they ask, "Why do you speak in parables?" He responds with two reasons: parables give truth to the receptive and hide it from those who are unreceptive. He is saying, to use the framework of this lesson, that a parable can yield truth for those who want to know His will, but it will add nothing to the store of the unbeliever or the person who could care less about learning the truth of God.

Notice in verse 11, He says, "It is given unto you to know the mysteries of the kingdom of heaven, but to them it is not given." Now that may seem a little harsh to us, but the Lord is saying, "To you ... IT ... IS ... GIVEN"—"To them ... IT ... IS ... NOT ... GIVEN." You may think that is a strange thing, but it really isn't because the Lord is laying out spiritual truth. Those who want to know that truth, He says, may know it; those who could care less will never have anything from a parable added to their store of learning.

I am persuaded there is still a great deal of truth in that when it comes to studying it even in our day. In fact, the Lord emphasizes it so heavily in verse 12, that He says, "Whosoever hath" ... listen ... "Whosoever hath, to him shall be given." "He who has ... gets!" "Whosoever hath, to him shall be given." Now that sounds strange. We would say in our day, "Whoever doesn't have is the one that ought to have it." Well, there is some truth in that, but what our Lord is saying to us is—to use spiritual truth is to possess that spiritual truth. And I believe it is still true tonight that the only way we will ever possess spiritual truth, is to be receptive and to USE that truth. "Whosoever hath, to him shall be given." As we measure attention to the Lord, so He will measure knowledge to us through His Word.

I don't want to weary you with the introduction, but I do want you to think about what He is saying in verse 13: "Therefore" ... (or, for this reason) ... "Therefore speak I to them in parables: because they seeing see not; and hearing they hear not, neither do they understand." Now what has happened? As we mentioned, there are those who have refused and rejected and simply turned aside from the Lord. They have even proceeded to the place that He says it is like "casting pearls before swine." They are totally unappreciative of what He is saying, and so He is simply saying of these individuals—"They see, but they do not see; and they hear." I will guarantee you, tonight, that in the Twentieth Century, we still have many people who can sit in an audience and see, and not see; they hear, and they never hear. As the Apostle Paul says, they are people who are "ever learning, and never able to come to the knowledge of the truth" (2 Timothy 3:7).

And then our Lord goes on to say something I think is really beautiful. He quotes from Isaiah chapter 6 about these people and about their hearts; then in verse 16, He says:

> Blessed are your eyes, for they see: and your ears, for they hear. For verily I say unto you, That many prophets and righteous men have desired to see those things which ye see, and have not seen them; and to hear those things which you hear and have not heard them.

What He is saying is that the prophets had to content themselves with simply what they were prophesying, ever trying to understand what they were prophesying. But He is saying, while they had the visions, YOU have the Messiah. While they had visions of the church to come, YOU possess the church. They were prophesying of the blessings of God: we are sitting in their very midst.

The Lord says, "He that hath ears to hear ... let him hear." What is He saying? Don't they all have ears to hear? Yes, they do! At the very least, the Lord is saying that mere recitation of a parable doesn't mean you are going to get something out of it. They all heard Him in that sense. When He speaks the parable, they audibly pick it up. But, He says, I want people who have ears with the capacity to understand—to UNDERSTAND.

Look at verses 51 and 52 now. He says to His disciples:

> Have you understood all these things? They say unto him, Yea Lord. Then said he unto them, Therefore every scribe which is instructed unto the kingdom of heaven is like unto a man that is an householder, which bringeth forth out of his treasure things new and old.

I think this is a beautiful thing that He gives us here. Our Lord says, "Have you understood it?" Our goal tonight, people, is to understand these things about the kingdom of God. He says, "EVERY scribe," not some, but "EVERY scribe" was "instructed unto the kingdom of heaven," and that is our goal. We want to be "instructed unto the kingdom of heaven." He is like a man who is a householder, and he is able to bring out of his treasure things both new and old. Our goal: to be instructed. Our goal: to be able to bring out of what we know about the kingdom of God so that others may hear and they may learn—that we can refresh our hearers out of both past and present experience and knowledge of His truth. "Old lessons in new garments," the Lord is saying, "so that people can know and understand My will."

Now we come down to this particular parable, and you will notice in Matthew 13:1 that, "The same day went Jesus out of the house." We could turn over to Mark chapter 3, if we had time, and find that the Lord on this occasion was in the house and there was such a press—such a multitude there that day—that the Lord could hardly walk.

The scripture states that He went "out of the house," and this is evidently the time when He went down "to the beach" as we would say it today—to the shore; and He gets into a boat and He pushes out just a little. It must have been a beautiful setting that day, with the rolling fields of Galilee out there in the distance, sloping gently down to the water's edge. It was about October or November, the time of the sowing of the winter seed.

As our Lord looks out upon those people, He begins to say, "Behold, a sower went forth to sow," and those people could immediately pick up on that because this is life to them. This is what they do day after day.

Incidentally, you can follow the study of this particular parable from Matthew 13, Mark 4, or Luke 8; and in all three of those accounts, you have the identical story. I will be attempting, in the course of this lesson, to draw all three of these together. Should you not see exactly the word I use, please look in the other accounts because it should be there.

The Sowing

Notice what we have: we have a message to the soils and a message to the sowers. And I want us all to get the full impact of what the Lord is saying. I am persuaded that in this parable, we have an answer to many of the problems that confront us individually and collectively. We have an answer to our weak and to our anemic ways—an answer that can give us real life.

Jesus says, "Behold a sower went forth to sow." I think what makes the sowing so important, is that which the man sowed. When we talk about sowing, we are simply talking about teaching or preaching the Word of God. As we think about that which he sowed, it was the seed; and the Bible calls that seed the "word of the kingdom." Doesn't it make it a meaningful thing—to know that we are people who have some small part in sowing the "word of the kingdom" in the hearts of men today, just as it was in that day?

Our Lord uses the idea of a seed; and I suppose there is nothing that has greater relative potential than a seed. I think none of us, regardless of how long we have lived in the city, are so far removed from the agrarian way of life—I will assure you, I am not—that we will not understand this lesson. We know what He is talking about. We know there is tremendous potential within a seed. But so long as it is not sown in the field—which is the heart of man—it remains potential and only potential. It must be sown before we really reap anything from it.

You know, as we think about the potential of a seed, I think about an acorn. You can take a tiny acorn, which is so insignificant, and plant it out there beside your house; and if all goes well, the day will come when the produce of that tiny seed will rival the house itself. So there is tremendous potential within a seed, and the Lord is using it as He talks about His kingdom.

We must have the correct seed. Paul says, "I certify you, brethren, that the gospel which was preached of me is not after man. For I neither received it of man, neither was I taught it, but by the revelation of Jesus Christ." We are not to sow just anything; but we are to sow, Paul says, a "certified" seed. This makes the sowing that we are attempting to do here in Wichita, and throughout the world, so important. Preaching of the Lord's Word is number one. It holds priority over everything else. I guess one of the best examples of this point is found in Acts chapter 6. You remember that in the early church, when everything seemed to be going so lovely and so smooth, all of a sudden ... they faced a real problem! Some began to complain. The Grecians began to complain against the Hebrews because, they said, "Our widows are neglected in the daily ministration." A real problem! But you remember, the apostles didn't let this matter go; they called them and said, "Look ye out among you seven men of honest report, and full of the Holy Ghost and wisdom, whom we may appoint over this business. But we will give ourselves continually to prayer, and to the ministry of the word." He is saying that regardless of how important some things may be, there is nothing as important to the church of our Lord as the sowing of the seed. It's something that simply must be done.

You know, every place you go, you find a field. Anytime it is said, "The sower went forth to sow," He wants us to understand that this is in the field and, of course, the field is what?—the hearts of men. I think sometimes we tend to think of the field as ever being somewhere over yonder. People, the age of romanticism is not dead. We still tend to think that somewhere over yonder—"If I were only there, I'd do great things for God! If I were there, what a great sower of the seed I would really be!"

You know, I have learned this, that whatever we are doing here in Wichita, Kansas, tonight, with whatever we have to do with, is about what we would do if we were over yonder. Because those people down yonder are thinking that if they were in Wichita, Kansas, they would do some great things for God. "It's bound to be different in Wichita, Kansas!" So, we tend to think, "Well, if we were only over there, we would get some great, great things done." I think we must just realize that wherever we find a field—a heart—we hold the seed of the kingdom ... drop it there! Only eternity will reveal the real results.

Preachers get together sometimes, and they talk about meetings. I guess they are like people who go fishing and they talk about—"How many did you catch?" The preachers get together sometimes, after they have held meetings, and they'll say, "How did you do? How did your meeting go over at that last place?" I remember reading some years ago about two who were talking about the last place they had been, and one said, "How did you do?" "Well," he said, "I didn't do much. I baptized one little freckle-faced girl." But the man went on, as he reflected on this—looking back down through the years—and said they had not realized that that one little freckled-faced girl went on to become the mother of four gospel preachers. So you must never think, "Well, there is really not much to do here." Because any place you find a human, you have found a field, you have found a world, and you should sow the seed. Drop it there and let God take care of the results.

Preparation

Sometimes we insist on doing all of it ourselves. When you think about this matter of going out to sow the seed, and you think about the field—which, of course, is the heart—I am persuaded that one of the real things that we need to understand is the preparation of the field. When I was a child at home, down on the farm in Texas, we used to spend countless hours and days and days and days out there in the field preparing it. We hadn't sown one seed, and I used to become a little upset about that. My father didn't. When we talked about it—"Why do we work and work and work, and we have not planted a single seed?"—he would insist that it makes all the difference how you make the seed bed, how you prepare the place. Jesus Christ had already said, two thousand years ago in this parable, that such is so important! He said we need some good, honest-hearted people in which to sow the seed of the kingdom.

Do you know what one of our greatest opportunities is? One of our greatest opportunities is in the hearts of our own children. For you have, this evening, if you have children, hearts that have been given to you that are not filled with the rocks of sin and the stumps of iniquity. Jesus says, "Of such is the kingdom of heaven." (Matthew 19:14)

I was up in Huntington, West Virginia, many years ago knocking on doors around the church building and met a little lady; as she came to the door, she had several children clinging to her skirt. I invited her out to the meeting. I said, "Please come. We are simply here to preach the Gospel of Jesus Christ, and we want you to come." She said, "Well, I will try to do that." And I insisted, "Please do! And when you come, will you please bring those little children with you?" And she said, "No, I probably won't do that. I am of the opinion that you ought to let children just grow up and let them decide for themselves, when they are grown, what they want to be and what they want to believe." That's exactly like saying, "See my garden spot? This year I'm not going to plow it; this year I'm not going to plant it; this year I'm not going to cultivate it. I'm going to let it decide for itself whether it wants to grow cockleburs or strawberries." I will promise you it won't grow any strawberries! But it will surely grow some weeds! And so we must realize that we have a marvelous opportunity in the hearts of our own children. Here is simply a wonderful place in which we can sow the seed of the kingdom.

Our people talk to me about what we need; I will tell you what we need. We need just some plain good old honest-hearted people who will hear the gospel. It doesn't matter how good the sower may be ... . this One was perfect. And the seed may be perfect; but unless you have an honest heart in which to sow it, you really can't accomplish much.

Some years ago, I worked in a northern state. Shortly after arriving, two young people began to attend the services. They were interested and attended faithfully; they continued to listen to the gospel preached. It wasn't long until the young man obeyed the gospel—I mean just a short time. That young man had never been taught anything religiously, except that he should be a good person, that there was a God in Heaven, and that this Book is His Word. He was just honest; he just simply wanted to obey the gospel. That young lady listened to the preaching for almost a year before she ever obeyed. And she would tell you tonight—there had to be first a rooting out of an awful lot of things that had been planted in her heart that the Bible does not teach. It was sowing seed in a wilderness, and there first had to be a removing of some of those things.

When the pioneers came into this country, they began to push their way westward. When they came into a new area, they didn't take the few precious seed they had and walk out there in that wilderness and throw them out and say, "Now we will have a great harvest." What they would do was to proceed, however back-breaking the toil, to clear a bit of land; and they would sow a little seed. Then next year they would clear a little more, and they would sow a little more. We might do well to take a lesson from that because this method is what the Lord is discussing. In our own hearts, sometimes we need to do some clearing, and we need to do some sowing.

I think it is lamentable to have a congregation where all they ever have is a clearing process; or where all they ever have is sowing. We need somebody to do some clearing, and we need to do some sowing so that we may eventually take our hearts for God—this is what our Lord is saying to us. I learned long ago that it is easier to keep a field clean, little by little, than it is to let it grow up and think, "Well, some day I will clean it all up." Those who are uninitiated to such things might think that all you have to do is let the field go through the years and then go out there and plow it up, and it'll be fine. But I will guarantee you this, you are not through—and you are not going to be through—for those seed will be there, and they will keep coming up year after year and time after time. I think the spiritual lesson is very applicable for us.

The Wayside Soil

But I want us to look at the conditions into which these seed fell. I think this is the main burden and the main thrust of the parable. Jesus says, "Behold, a sower went forth to sow; and when he sowed, some seeds fell by the wayside." This, of course, is a picture of a Galilean farmer as he is walking, broadcasting the seed. And these are the paths that go through the fields, paths that have been baked by the sun day after day and by the passing of feet time after time. And while the seed is falling, some of the seed falls onto that hardened ground, and there is no way that seed can penetrate.

Now is there any problem with the sower? The problem is with the soil; and please remember this—that the soil is the heart of man. Here is where the real problem comes. And so we get a good profile of the heart of man.

I can remember when I was a child, that out at the end of the row, there was a portion we called the "end row." A brother down in Mississippi reminded me it is a "turn row." You can call it what you want, but out on the end is a hard, hard place. Have you ever stopped to reflect that the soil out on the end row, or turn row, or beaten path, is the same texture as the other. It gets the same sun; it gets the same rain; it gets the same everything, except it isn't worked. It isn't plowed, and we just simply run over it time after time, and thus the seed cannot penetrate. Oh, I have seen a few seed fall there, and they just might get in a little crack somewhere, and they produce some little spindly plants that never really amount to anything; but generally, they do not come up at all.

So, our Lord is saying, what makes the difference is in the heart of man. Now one might think, "Well, my heart may be hard underneath, and I may not be what I ought to be in this respect; but some day I am going to open up my heart, and I am going to let the seed of the kingdom come in, and I am really going to be something for God." Don't count on it! Our Lord said, "And the fowls came."

I want you to notice that Satan knows that the Word of God is so dangerous to his cause that he isn't even going to let that seed lay there on THAT kind of soil. And if Satan can ever convince us that we don't need to preach the gospel and we don't need to sow the seed, he has won the battle without firing a single shot. But now, if that seed ever gets inside that soil, or that heart, then he is going to bring many other influences to bear upon it in order to kill it. But, if he can just keep it out in the first place, then it's an easy battle; he has won, and all things are well for him.

I was out in Andrews, Texas, many years ago knocking on doors and I met a young man and began to talk to him about the Lord's plan and ancient order of worship. How that in the beginning, only the church was there; and how it worshiped the Lord; and how there was in his town, at that every moment, a congregation that worshiped and served the Lord as they did so long ago. That young man was interested. He said, "Talk to me more about it; let's discuss it." We studied it; we talked about it. And as I left there that night, he said, "I want my people to know about this." And he said, "I'll call you; I want you to come back." That call never came! And the next time I saw that young man, he would barely speak to me. I understood—the fowls came, they really did. Almost there was a heart opening up to receive the Word, and Satan saw that, and the fowls came and took it away. Like a bird just flitting by, Satan will come and take away any chance, any possibility, of your learning the truths of our God.

Who are these wayside people? Jesus says, "They heard and they understood not." These are the calloused; these are the Pharaohs, the Felixes, the Drusillas. These are those who are unbothered by the presence of the Word of God. I have stood before many an audience of people; and in that audience, so many times, I have seen people who were totally untouched. They were totally unbothered; it didn't make any difference what I was preaching or what I was saying; they were not bothered by the Word of God.

The Stony Ground

In His sermon Jesus says some of the seed "fell on stony ground." He gives us the picture this time of the seed being able to get into this soil, and it begins to grow. He tells us that as this plant begins to grow—that as the sun rises, and this plant seeks to reach down—that it begins to wither. He uses this expression—"because it had no depth of earth." There wasn't any place for it to go because that heart had only a little thin layer of soil—there had been some emotional response to the gospel, but there was nothing there to sustain it. We have all seen soil like that—a soil that is so shallow it's like skin stretched over a bone. Because of its nature, the tiniest bit of moisture and the tiniest bit of heat combined with a little help from underneath will cause the plant to spring up quickly. But it dies about as quickly as it begins. It withers, "because it had no depth of earth."

That is a beautiful picture the Lord is projecting. Can you imagine those people as they are sitting there, listening to our

Lord teach that lesson, and He says, "These are they ... ." He says, "You know who I am talking about." These are they that "anon with joy receive the word" and "endure for a while," but by and by, He says, "they withered away." Here are those excited emotional responses. Here are the superficial hearers of the Word of God. These are those people to whom preaching is like an intoxicant.

One of the old-time preachers said that when a preacher comes to town to preach the gospel, to some it is an intoxicant, to others it is a good tonic and you can tell when the meeting is over whether people have been on a religious spree or whether they have really been helped. These are those to whom the gospel is an intoxicant. It's a beautiful thing, and they are excited for the moment. These are the Big Meeting people. These are the Mr. Temporaries. These are those in John 6 who "walked no more with Him"; they turned and went away.

I would like to tell you that that's not true anymore. But I rather will tell you it's so true that it is amazing to me that anything so old could be that current. I know people with no real conviction. I have seen people who, simply because of some little problem that arises in the church, can be with us today and gone tomorrow. They're gone and you just don't see them anymore. These are those of whom the Lord spoke so long ago.

I remember a situation many years ago out in West Texas where a man wanted to become an elder in the church. In fact, he insisted on being an elder in the church. The man was not qualified in any sense of the term to be an elder, and it was not allowed. The next Lord's Day the man went into digression. He would have made a "great" elder in the church! These are those of whom our Lord spoke. Any opposition makes them partial or total apostates. They have no root; they have no tenacity of purpose.

Notice what happened. Jesus says that everything is going rather well until the sun comes up. And I want you to look at what the sun is. It takes the sunlight to begin the real test. You can see things in the sunlight you can't see at any other time. In this case, the sun comes up, and the plant begins to die.

Jesus says, in putting the three accounts together, that the sun is "tribulation," "persecution," and offense "because of the word." There are those who simply can't stand this idea. And one might say, "Well, that's not the problem of the heart; it's the problem of the sun." That is not true. It dawned on me in the study, that it takes the sun to make the healthy plant grow.

Do you realize what the Lord is saying? He is saying that you will never really grow to be the kind of Christian you ought to be without the sun—that is, without tribulation, persecution, or the necessity to stand for what's right in the sight of God. If a person is a real Christian and has real convictions, he just lets the sun come up—just lets the stormy winds of persecution blow—and all he will do is just simply sink his roots a little deeper into the storehouse of God's love; he will be there, and he will be there to stay.

If I were to quit the church, if I were to walk out tonight and say, "Look people, I'm through." I don't care what I tell you the problem is, Jesus says when I walk out that I am announcing to the world with a trumpet voice, "My heart's not right with God." I can call it whatever I want to call it, but He says what my problem is … what your problem is … it is our heart. You get your heart right, and you can take it, and you'll be what you ought to be. So we must conclude that tribulation establishes real faith while it destroys the counterfeit.

The Thorns

Then our Lord has another part to His sermon; let's look at this one quickly. Our Lord tells us that as this man sowed, some seed "fell among thorns." There is no problem with the seed getting into this soil. It begins to grow, and everything is fine; but as it begins to grow, some other things also begin to grow. That which looks so good at first, finds itself absolutely choked by thorns, the roots of which were there all along.

I want you to think about this for a moment. The soil is not hard. There are no rocks. It can germinate. It can emerge. It can grow … but so can the thorns. And they grow quite well; in fact, they are so prolific that they eventually will choke the plant. Our Lord is saying that you don't have to cultivate evil;

brother, it will work by itself! And He is saying that hearts that are untended will revert to a wilderness, and we know this is so true. You don't let a field go and decide that you are going to clean it up overnight. How many times I have seen situations in which people have just simply let their lives go, and let their family go. Then, many times with tears in their eyes, they come to me and say, "Won't you go talk to this person or talk to that one," And we try, in a few moments, to repair the negligence of many, many years. It just simply doesn't work very well.

Now I want you to look at this particular field because as one brother down home said, "Here is the patch that most of us are working in." Take a good look. What are the thorns? The writers say they are "the deceitfulness of riches," "the cares of this world," "the pleasures of this life," and "the lusts of other things." These are the things that choke us. Is there one person here, tonight, who would arise in this audience and say, "That's not true with my life?" Surely it's true! And we know it's true! These are things that will choke the Word of God.

Notice what they are. In one case we are dealing with enemies from within, so to speak—the problems of the heart. In the other case we are dealing with enemies from without. Here are some extra things in our hearts; maybe the top was cut off those old thorns, but we never really did dig out the roots. The old roots of bitterness are still there, and they begin to grow. These are those things that Peter says in 1 Peter chapter two, "war against the soul." There is not a person sitting here tonight, of any age at all, who does not understand that there are things that war against the soul.

These are like Lot so long ago. Lot wanted the best of two worlds, didn't he? He "pitched his tent toward Sodom." You notice he didn't pitch it IN Sodom, he "pitched his tent TOWARD Sodom." But when you turn over a chapter later, the scripture says, "Lot sat in the gate." He moved in. When you pitch your tent toward Sodom, you generally will then begin to move in.

And there is one thing I want us to see quickly—take a look at that plant. What do you see? Do you see a plant that never did get going? No! Do you see a plant that begins to grow and because of hardness of heart, it withers and begins to die? No! What's the problem with that plant? Is it living? It's living! So we are prone to say, "Lord, what's the problem? The plant is living." Is it not sufficient that we can say, "I have been to the river, I have been baptized, I am a member of the Lord's church. I'm living ... so what's the problem?" The problem is—it is bearing no fruit! So the Lord is saying to those in His vineyard, "I don't need any ornamental trees!" The Lord is saying He wants people who bear fruit for Him.

And do you realize this evening the Lord is strongly telling us that if we are not bearing fruit for Him, things are not well with our soul, though we are both His and here. These are those in whom the Word of God has, at best, a disputed hold on their lives. Doesn't that ring familiar to you? I am not saying this just to you ... to US. Sometimes we find the Word of God has got a little hold in our life; but, brother, it's a disputed hold, and a constant struggle goes on and on.

The Good Ground

Last, tonight, our Lord talks to us about seed that "fell into good ground." This time as the man went forth to sow, it just simply falls into the right place ... no problem. It sinks down into the ground and begins to grow. There is no hard ground under there, but remember there is a sun over there, too. You must have the sun! The plant is there, and it is growing and begins to bear fruit—the scripture says, "some thirtyfold, some sixty, and some an hundred fold." Who are these? Our Lord says these are they that received the Word into a good and honest heart. They heard and they understood. They had ears to hear, and they heard. They understood these things. It would be interesting to hear those who advocate the doctrine of inherent total depravity explain how this was good ground before the Word of God ever touched it. Good ground!

Matthew uses four prepositions that we should look at. Seed fell "BY the wayside," "UPON stony places," "AMONG thorns," and "INTO good ground." All of those so beautifully and perfectly fit. Notice—in the good ground the amount of fruit borne was of varying amounts; and I am glad of that.

When I was a child at home, I used to hear my father come in at the end of the year and talk about that old rocky hill where we planted cotton. It didn't seem to bother him too much that it just made a little bit of cotton. He didn't expect much of that field. But I will tell you this: he was very upset when the little piece of bottom ground didn't really produce. He was bothered because it had the capabilities and the possibilities. The potential was always there.

I just wonder as we sit here in this audience if our Lord doesn't look down upon our lives with great concern as we sometimes say, "Well, I can't do what somebody else is doing; therefore, I'll do nothing." He wants to know what you are doing. What CAN you do? He knows what you can do; He just wants you to do what you can do. And this is what He wants me to do. I wonder, tonight, is my Lord satisfied with me? That's the question. Not, am I doing what you are doing! But, is my Lord satisfied with me?

Well, we are going to close lest we weary you. Let me ask you this—what kind of soil are YOU tonight? Do you realize that two thousand years ago, Jesus Christ preached a sermon that is so perfect, so applicable, that if you ever heard the gospel preached, you are pictured on that board tonight. Your picture is there. We are there.

Either, you have heard the gospel preached time after time after time, but you never really opened up your heart and received it; you heard it, but you didn't understand—you have never received it into a good and honest heart. Or … ?

There was a time when you "with joy received the word"; you can still remember it. You received it and let it begin to sink into your heart. But pretty soon the sun came up and for these many years you have been saying the sun killed you. Tribulations, persecutions, and problems were too much for you. Won't you just simply face the fact—that's not what did it. It was your heart. Your heart was not right. Or … ?

Tonight this is your picture. You are a member of the church. You come every service. You are here, but you know in your heart that you are not bearing any fruit for God—you are just here. You're not really doing anything for God. You're not really doing what you are capable of doing, whatever it is. Is that your picture tonight? Or ... ?

You have received the Word of God in "good ground," and you are bearing fruit for Him. Now remember, Jesus says you are in one of these pictures; I sincerely believe that's the truth. How are you responding to the "word of the kingdom"?

That's our Lord's sermon. Would you obey Him tonight? He is still telling that same story. If you are not a Christian, why don't you come tonight, receiving that Word, repenting of your sins, confessing the Holy Christ, and being immersed in His name for the remission of your sins?

Sermon Two

The
Parables
of
Jesus

"And He spake many things
unto them in parables"

THE GOOD SAMARITAN

Luke 10:23-29

"And he turned him unto his disciples, and said privately, Blessed are the eyes which see the things that ye see: for I tell you, that many prophets and kings have desired to see those things which ye see, and have not seen them; and to hear those things which ye hear, and have not heard them. And, behold, a certain lawyer stood up, and tempted him, saying, Master, what shall I do to inherit eternal life? He said unto him, What is written in the law? how readest thou? And he answering said, Thou shalt love the Lord thy God with all thy heart, and with all thy soul, and with all thy strength, and with all thy mind; and thy neighbour as thyself. And he said unto him, Thou hast answered right: this do, and thou shalt live. But he, willing to justify himself said unto Jesus, And who is my neighbour?"

2. The Good Samaritan

We welcome you to the evening service, the second in this series of meetings, and to another study of the Lord's Word. We are grateful for your presence in that we believe it indicates an interest in things unseen and eternal, those things that are divine. It is through faith, of course, that we see "the things which are not seen" as the apostle expresses in so many places. And so we are grateful tonight for people who are willing to set aside a certain portion of their time to attend to what we believe are the greatest realities of life. As we talk about death and about the judgment, about Heaven and about Hell, about God and about Satan—about the great doctrines of the Bible—we believe it would be the supreme folly of man to ignore these great truths. They are words that are so applicable to us, as we said in the outset of this series. Our Lord, two thousand years ago, preached a sermon that is perfectly applicable tonight in Wichita, Kansas, and is as current as, or perhaps more current than, today's newspaper headlines.

As announced, we will study this parable; and our brother has read the introduction or the occasion for us. Sometimes we view parables as just beautiful stories, things we ought to read to our children—and that we should—but I assure you, a study of the parables is more than that. It's an awesome thing to stand before a group of people, and especially before Heaven itself, and announce that we shall study one of the sermons of Jesus. But we believe He intended for us to do just that. It is not then presumption for us to speak to the people in parables.

Luke chapter ten reveals one of the most beautiful and most meaningful parables of the entire Bible. It has been read by many and yet practiced by so few. It is a parable of universal significance and application. If, tonight, this parable were read and understood and applied, it would remove any semblance of pride or arrogance or envy or selfishness from your heart, and it would cause you to be determined to lay your all upon the altar of service and sacrifice to God. If we properly understood and applied this parable, it would remove all wars, caste systems, and partialities from our world. If there is in all the Holy Scripture a parable of practical benefit and service to mankind, it is this lesson that Jesus taught a long time ago.

There are three divisions in this parable; a question, an answer, and an application. That's about what this sermon entails; yet that perhaps is more than we shall be able to say as we look at these three points.

The Occasion for the Parable

There is an occasion for this parable; in fact, some particular event occasioned every parable that Jesus preached. He did not get up in the morning as I do and say, "What shall I preach tonight?" I assure you that from the time I get up in the morning until I've finished with the sermon that night, my mind is never free of it. I am thinking about what would be the best order or manner of presentation. But I don't think Jesus got up in the morning and thought, "What shall I preach today?" or "What shall I say over in Galilee?" or "What will I preach in Capernaum or such places?" He just met individuals and dealt with them and their needs as they came. He could meet people, and in that He was the Great Physician, heal them with His super-abounding health.

The Question

On this day there is a specific reason for this particular sermon. There is a lawyer who has heard of the fame and knowledge of Jesus. He has heard of this man whose fame has now spread abroad as an unlettered person who possessed tremendous knowledge. "How knoweth this man letters, having never learned?" (John 7:15). Here is a man, it is reputed, who can throw out the question, "Which of you convinceth me of sin?" and no one could answer. The lawyer comes to tempt Him, to test Him, and to try Him. And that is exactly what he does. I want you to notice his question proposed to Jesus: "What shall I do to inherit eternal life?"

There is nothing wrong with his question. In fact, the question is quite good. And if you want to know what a person believes, if you want something revealed to you, the answer given to this question, then or now, is a great revealer. "What shall I do to inherit eternal life?" The lawyer on this occasion was not a legal voice as we think of a lawyer today. A lawyer in that day, or at least this lawyer, was a man who was so well schooled and so well versed in Old Testament Law that he was a professional. He was a person who knew the law. If there were someone who wanted a point clarified, such men could clarify it. I understand that on the Jewish Sanhedrin there were lawyers of this stripe; and should one of the elders call for a clarification or should he say, "What does this particular passage say?" the lawyer could rise in that audience and tell him exactly what it said. He knew it: he was a professional!

This man asks Jesus, "What shall I do to inherit eternal life?" He quickly finds how skilled the Lord is because the Lord immediately turns to him and says, "What is written in the law? how readest thou?" From this response we understand that the Lord, then or now, expects us to read His Word and understand it the way He does. Sometimes we think there are ecclesiastics in this world, who read special things the common masses do not read or that the Lord knows some things that we just couldn't know. On this occasion He just says, I will answer your question of eternal life by asking you to tell me what it says, and the lawyer immediately comes out with it. Now again, I say he is pretty good because he correctly quotes from Deuteronomy 6:5 and Leviticus 19. He comes up with it. It is written, "Thou shalt love the Lord thy God with all thy heart ... soul ... strength ... and mind; and thy neighbour as thyself." Jesus immediately answers; notice that He does not contest his quotation. Jesus is saying, in effect, that is correct. He simply says, "This do and thou shalt live."

The lawyer now finds himself confronted with a practical aspect of this whole matter. He learns it is more than knowledge; here is a Man saying to him, "This do and thou shalt live." Our Lord makes it quite plain that it is obedience that leads to life. Now we can avow a lot of things. We can stand here say how we love Jesus. We could talk about a lot of things. But what really matters, Jesus says, is the very practical point of obedience. "This do and thou shalt live."

Please notice what He is saying, "This do." Here is a man who knew these things because He correctly quotes them, but the Lord is pointing out one of the main points of the parable. He is pointing out the great gulf that exists between what we KNOW and what we DO. Here was a man who knew, he could quote the passages and correctly, too. But the Lord tells him he is not doing what he knows to do. Nowhere does the Lord ever say, "This KNOW and thou shalt live." I am persuaded that the Lord is still saying that to us. And the Lord is still striking at the great gulf that exists between what we know and what we are doing. As little as we may know, people, I am persuaded that we still don't always do what we know to do. The Lord wants us to understand this point.

He is saying that love and life are inseparable, and doing and living are inseparable; because of this teaching, the lawyer finds himself on the defense. How quickly have the tables turned. He came to the place to put Jesus to flight, but he finds himself on the defense. And notice, instead of just doing what Jesus says, "This do and thou shalt live" and that being the end of the matter, he proceeds to justify himself. The scripture states, "But he, willing to justify himself, said unto Jesus, And who is my neighbour?" From Adam until now, we are always trying to justify ourselves. And that is just human. I know that if someone crosses something that I believe, I immediately find myself, right or wrong, coming up with a justification for what I say and for what I do. I guess there is some good about that if we are following the scripture that says, "Sanctify the Lord God in your hearts: and be ready always to give an answer to every man that asketh you a reason of the hope that is in you with meekness and fear" (1 Peter 3:15). But it is one thing to be able to come up with a reason from Holy Scripture for what we are—it is another thing to try to justify ourselves in that that is opposed to the scriptures.

The Second Question

Now let's discuss the second question. It just seems so out of place and out of context at first. Here is a man who "willing to justify himself, said unto Jesus, And who is my neighbour?" Isn't that strange? Why does he come up with a question about his neighbour? Why doesn't he say, "What does it mean to love God with all your heart and with all your soul, your mind and strength?" We moderns could discuss that from now on. We could say, "What does He mean by heart? What does He mean by soul? What does He mean by strength? What does He mean by God?" We could debate that for a long time, but he doesn't discuss any of those things. He doesn't even bring them up. What he does is incriminate himself and blurt out what his problem really is. He does not love his neighbor, and he seeks to justify himself by saying he doesn't know who he is.

Do you know what this man is doing when he says, "Who is my neighbour"? He is splitting some theological hairs. Now sometimes we are pretty good at that, but I don't think we are nearly as accomplished—and I hope we never are—as the Jews were. When it came to deciding who their neighbors were, they could split the hair down the middle, and they could split it again. They would say, "This man is my neighbor, and that man is not my neighbor." And, "These people are my neighbors, and those people are not my neighbors." And I will assure you, a Samaritan was always excluded. At no time would they ever include a Samaritan in any way. Never!

The lawyer is saying, "Now I don't know who he is, but, Jesus, I want you to get busy and define for me my sphere of activity; I want to know who my neighbor is." He is saying he wants to know if his neighbor begins here and ends there. You see what his problem is? He is scared that he might love someone who isn't his neighbor. Unless he can get this point defined, he might do too much—he might love someone he didn't have to love. We are amused at this lawyer; and we think, "Well, that is a strange thing!" But, we shouldn't be too amused at him because we still do the same thing. As I listen, I don't hear, "And who is my neighbour?" but I hear—"Do I have to go to church all the time? Do I have to attend night meetings? Do I have to go to Gospel Meetings? Do I have to visit the sick? Do

I have to do this and that?" And, when we raise these kinds of questions, we are raising the same old question that lawyer raised so long, long ago. We want somebody to define for us our sphere of activity so that we can say, "Duty begins here, and it ends there." We can then get busy and get it done so we can say with certainty, "I ... have ... done ... my ... duty ... and I am through!" The Lord is not going to let you off like that. He doesn't let this man get off like that, and He won't let us off like that. He wants us to understand that the only limit true love knows is its own inability to proceed any farther. True love does not know boundaries like these.

At home we still sing the old song titled, "At The Cross," by Isaac Watts.

> "Alas! and did my Saviour bleed?
> And did my Sovereign die?
> Would He devote that sacred head
> For such a worm as I?"

Do you remember the second stanza?

> "But drops of grief could ne'er repay
> The debt of love I owe:
> Here, Lord, I give myself away,
> Tis all that I can do."

Ah, we owe a debt of love that will never in this world be paid off. Never will! I assure you, when we just take one glimpse at Calvary and what was done there for us on that lonely hill, we are convinced that we will never, never pay the debt of love.

In Romans 13:8, Paul has an amazing little passage: "Owe no man anything, but to love one another." Have you ever thought about that? What a strange thing for Paul to say, and especially to us in this generation: "Owe no man anything." How do you interpret that? Well, you may not wish to deal with it, but we best get busy and begin to interpret it because if there is anybody sitting in this room tonight who owes no man anything, he is the exception and not the rule. Surely Paul is saying that we must fulfill our financial obligations. When I am fulfilling my financial obligations, I owe no man anything. If I say I will meet this obligation on the 15th of the month and

I meet it, I am fulfilling my financial responsibilities. You can interpret that as you will, but he is saying, "Owe no man anything, BUT ... ." Now like a little red flashing light, he is saying, here is something different—"but to love one another." You see, we can fulfill our financial obligations, but there is an obligation of love we will never finish paying. Here is a debt it is all right to owe, so long as we keep on paying. "Owe no man anything, but to love one another." True love would have us to say, "What CAN I do for my Lord?" not say, "What MUST I do?" and "Who is my neighbour?"

The Answer

We, thus, have the occasion for the parable, and this is the point at which the sermon begins: as the Lord answers the lawyer, who is standing before Him. The Lord begins, "A certain man went down from Jerusalem to Jericho, and fell among thieves." I hope that every child here tonight knows the story; I can't remember the day that I didn't know the story. He says, "A certain man ... ." Look at this word if you want to see something interesting: "A CERTAIN" Then notice what He says next: "A certain MAN ... ." Who is that? You talk about being definite and then being indefinite, He does it with that one statement; but there is a reason why He does that. "A certain man went down from Jerusalem to Jericho," and this is so well stated because this road descended over some fifteen miles of rough and rocky terrain and in that fifteen miles descended some three thousand feet. So it truly was going "down from Jerusalem to Jericho," and the scripture declares that somewhere down there the man fell into foul play.

This road is sometimes referred to in religious literature as the Red Way, or the Bloody Way. It was rife with robbers, so infested with highwaymen, that it was a dangerous, dangerous place. But Jesus says this man went down; and somewhere along the way thieves fell upon him, they wounded him, they departed, they left him half dead. They could care less whether he lived or died. But again, look at him. Who is he? "A certain man went down from Jerusalem to Jericho." Would you say he is of a particular race? The Lord does not identify his race, nor his creed, nor his color. Who is he? He could be anyone, couldn't he? And I think that is the point. He is a human who has need of what someone else can do. This is not a contrived need but a person in definite need. You really can't determine who he is, and the Lord leaves it this way for a reason.

The Lord is saying—there is your neighbor; he is not merely the man who lives next door. Mr. Webster says that your neighbor is your "nigh dweller," but I will assure you he is more than that. Our Lord broadens our scope; He wants us to know that our neighbor is not just the man who lives next door or the man who moves in your same socio-economic circle. He is any human who has need of what you can do.

There is a little formula that someone some years ago expressed, and I think it is pretty good. He simply said that ability plus opportunity equals responsibility. I would rather think that if there is any formula we need to memorize, it should be this one. I want you to think about it. If you have an ability and an opportunity confronts you, is there not a responsibility? If you have no ability and you are confronted with an opportunity, it may well be you don't have a responsibility. Or if you have no opportunity while possessing the ability, you may not have responsibility. But, when you get these two together, you automatically have responsibility!

The Lord states this man "fell among thieves." I like the way He puts it. This is one of the marks of inspiration. If you want to read something that shows you the difference between the inspired Word of God and the apocryphal books—and the apocryphal books are well named because the word means of doubtful origin—read the epistle of Barnabas; notice many of them are sort of "living happily ever after" situations—it is so apparent they aren't like THIS Book. This Book just tells it as it is. Who are those people? The scripture says he "fell among thieves." Our Lord does not suggest that he fell into a group of individuals who were economically and culturally deprived. He does not say that here are some poor fellows who, because of their temporary stumbling in their upward progress, are not quite what they ought to be. He just calls them "thieves." And that's what they were. We are the ones who have contrived such fancy expressions about such people. The Bible just calls them what they are: "thieves." And their philosophy of life is they will take what you have if they can get it.

I wonder if you have ever met anybody like that? Surely you have! Our world has not changed to the point that we have outgrown this philosophy. It is still in our world. It bothers me that there are those in this world who look at another human and see only a source of gain and could care less about the person. It's simply, "What can I get out of that person." And we even live in times where legal means are being used to immoral ends. For example, those in the ungodly liquor industry are not in this world to ennoble mankind—and I will assure you that every time I have an opportunity to get in a word against it I shall because I sincerely believe it is ungodly. They are not in the world to ennoble your youth, I promise you. They are here to get what they can get, it matters not what happens to a young man or a young lady or to you or to society in general. Legal means are being used to immoral ends, and it bothers me when I pick up a magazine and it advertises the finished product of the brewers' art. Or I drive down the road and see, not some old-timer, but some young man or young lady in the bloom of life pictured drinking it.

One night many years ago we were in Columbus, Ohio, on our way to Pennsylvania for a meeting; and we stopped about three o'clock in the morning for a rest. We stopped downtown because I thought it would be safe to stop there for a few minutes to walk around and rest in a lighted area. I decided soon that my decision wasn't wise because as we sat there, we saw a number of undesirable things. Down the street a young man and a young lady came out of a bar supporting two people older than they, evidently their father and mother, who were so drunk they couldn't walk. And those two were trying to get Mama and Daddy home. I just wished that it might be possible to capture that moment and say, "Look, World, HERE is the finished product of the brewers' art!" These, too, had fallen among those whose philosophy is, "I'll take what you have if I can get it; and it doesn't matter what happens to you."

The next words in the parable seem like such an odd thing to find in one of the sermons of Jesus. He says, "And by chance there came down ... that way." If you have studied those words, "by chance," you have learned that He is not talking about mere coincidence. He is rather discussing a concurrence of events where emptiness is brought into relationship with fullness, where one person's ability to help is brought into relationship to another person's need of help. "By chance there came down a certain priest that way." You know the story. I have often thought if you didn't know the story so well, I might really do something with this. But you already know the story. You know what is going to happen. You know this man is going to come down the road. It doesn't make any difference if he is a priest, you already know he isn't going to do anything for the wounded man. If we had been standing there and we didn't know that, I'll tell you, we could look up the road and we could take on all kind of courage; that man's a priest of God! Here is a man of the ancient Levitical priesthood. Here is a man who worships the Lord, here is a man who serves on dress parade in the city of Jerusalem; he'll help. But I can't do much with that tonight because you know he didn't help him. He walked right on by and left that man to die. He left that quivering piece of humanity to die! He walked on by.

Again we look up the road; and if you didn't already know, I could give you great hope in that a Levite is coming down the road. Now, a Levite is not a priest, but a helper around the Temple; and while a priest may be too busy, a Levite can help. But you already know that he is worse than the priest because Luke says he "looked on him" and walked off to let him die.

Now, how do we explain that? How do we explain that kind of activity to an already cold and calloused world that is saying, "How do you know whether to trust people or not? How do you know whether to trust the person who is down the pew from you tonight? How do you know what kind of people they are?" You know what? I don't even try to explain that. I think we ought to do just what Jesus is doing, just flatly say—there they are. Our Lord wants us to understand that here are people in whom there is a form of religion, but the power is gone. He wants us to know these people didn't do what they ought to have done. Now I don't know what they thought. When they came down and saw that man in that pitiful shape, I don't know what they thought. In fact, I am not authorized to give you any excuses because Jesus doesn't give any. But I can't believe they walked right on by and didn't think anything. I will tell you some excuses we could have thought of had we been there: "This might happen to us. After all, everybody knows what kind of place this is; and if we stay around, it may happen to us; and after all, the robbers may still be nearby; or it may well be that if we stop to help this man, someone may accuse us of it; and how in the world would we ever prove that we weren't involved in it!" And to be more current than that, we can simply say, "Brother, that's his problem. We didn't get him into it. He should have known better than to come this way. That's his problem, let him handle it."

You know what our Lord is doing with the story of that priest and Levite? He is saying that He wants us to see them as they really are. I don't really think the priest, while serving on dress parade in the city of Jerusalem, would have ever done what he did. I cannot believe that the Levite, in his duties about the Temple, would have ever done such in the city of Jerusalem, But out on this lonely stretch of road, who would ever know? Out of this incident must evolve a good thought that is a powerful lesson. Our Lord is saying, what we really are is best revealed in how we act in places where we are not known.

All of us can think back to times and places where we have been, and felt, "Nobody knows me here." I have decided there is not any place like that! I have been in crowded airports far from home and met people I know. Take a real long, hard look at yourself in such a setting. Think how you thought, how you acted, how you dressed. Take a long hard look because that's the real you. What we are is best revealed in how we act in places where we are not known.

What is the philosophy of the priest and the Levite? It wasn't that they were going to take something that belonged to another. They would never have caused such injury. Their view was just, "I am going to hang on to what's mine. I didn't do him any harm. That's his problem." This is negative thought and negative religion. These are the negatives we often hear, "Well, Christianity is NOT doing certain things. I DIDNT do it, I WOULDN'T get into this arrangement, I WOULDN'T do that kind of thing." This is the negative side. They are just saying, "I will keep what is mine." People, we are living in a world that is becoming increasingly selfish. And we are going to have to be extremely careful lest we come to the place where we begin to think and act like the world about us. The scripture states in 1 Corinthians 13:5, love "seeketh not her own" to say nothing about seeking what belongs to another. It doesn't even insist upon its own. In Romans 12:10 Paul says, "Be kindly affectioned one to another with brotherly love; in honor preferring one another." Think what he is saying.

The scripture says that after they saw the poor beaten man, they "passed by on the other side." We must understand then that every road has what Jesus calls this side and the other side. And one might project this idea and say "this side" is the Lord's side and "the other side" is the devil's side. And you might go a little farther and say that this is the difficult side and that is the easy side. They "passed by on the other side."

I am sure the priest and the Levite would have done their duty in the city of Jerusalem. But on this lonely stretch of road, though they may have paid their tithe of mint and annis and cummin, they omitted justice and faith and mercy. They were orthodox, but they had cold and uncaring hearts.

Strange would be the person who could really think about this teaching without being rebuked by it. As we look back down the road of life, and some of us have come a long way down the road now, we can look back and lamentably see times when we could have done more. We could have traveled a little farther. We could have studied more. We could have preached with greater diligence. Ah, but it is so easy to take the other side. Let's remember that the Lord is unfolding these great truths to the lawyer, and I think the thing that really crushes him is the person introduced next in the parable. He has named a priest and a Levite and now He says, "A certain Samaritan, as he journeyed, came where he was ... ." The lawyer must have wondered why in the world He was bringing up a Samaritan! Of all people on earth to bring into the story—but Jesus deliberately introduces the Samaritan.

The Jews hated the Samaritans. The Samaritans hated the Jews. Centuries of hate and scorn divided them. The Samaritans were a mongrel race. They worshiped in one place while the Jews worshiped in another. Do you remember the day when they had exhausted their vocabulary of depravity in speaking of Jesus and had called Him everything evil they could think of? They finally said, "Thou art a Samaritan, and hast a devil" (John 8:48). They couldn't think anything worse to call Him—"Thou art a Samaritan!"

In some of my studies I have learned that some of the Jews would, upon approaching a Samaritan village, move at right angles around it. They wouldn't go through a Samaritan village. One of the laws of the Pharisees was that if a wall fell on a man on the Sabbath day, the only thing you could be allowed to do was take off enough of that wall to see if he were a Jew or a Samaritan. If he were a Jew, you could uncover him. If he were a Samaritan, let him stay. They hated one another! However, it was on this lonely stretch of road that "a certain Samaritan, as he journeyed, came where he was." What did he do? The scripture says he gets off that beast of burden, binds up the man's wounds, pours in acceptable remedies, and revives the spark of life.

I want to ask you, "Why didn't HE say, 'The robbers may still be near by.' Why didn't HE say, 'They might accuse me of this', after all he is a Jew. 'I am of a hated race. I surely will be accused of this.'" Why didn't HE do that? You see the difference—one of them was orthodox, but cold; the other scorned, but compassionate. Here was a man who had a gift to give, and that gift was compassion. The greatest gift that any man can ever possibly give is the gift of compassion. He got down to help. You know, there are times one needs a lecture, and we have all had them. But there are some times you don't need a lecture. The Samaritan doesn't lecture this poor man. He doesn't need a lecture: he needs to live. He is a human. He needs something. The good Samaritan translates the word "religion" into the word "life." That's what it is about. "He had compassion on him." What's his philosophy? His philosophy simply is—what is mine is thine. And that's a strange philosophy in the time in which we live. He is saying, "I will use what I have for others." That's God's man!

I was reading some years ago that when William Booth, the founder of the Salvation Army—which is neither salvation nor army—was very ill and his people were leaving for a convention of the movement that he had founded. Some of his people—some of his close associates—came to him and said,

"General Booth, do you have some message for the people?" The man by this time was so weak all he could do was take a pencil and scrawl one word upon the paper. It was the word "others." This was his philosophy of life. "Others, Lord, yes others. Let this my motto be," the old familiar song goes.

The Application

The Samaritan binds up the injured man's wounds and then says, "Why don't some of the other brethren do something sometime?" No, he didn't say that! He binds up his wounds, pours in oil and wine, puts him on his beast, takes him to an inn, spends the night cooling a fevered brow, and the next morning, of all things, takes out money and pays the host. Then he says, "Take care of him; and whatsoever thou spendest more, when I come again, I will repay thee." In our day we call this about tenth-mile religion. That is what the Lord called second-mile religion. What do we see in this man? We see a tender heart. We hear an assuring voice. We see an open purse. We see a willing hand. This is God's man!

This lawyer is standing there and now the Lord turns back to him and says, "Which ... was neighbour unto him that fell among the thieves?" What can the poor man answer? It just comes out, "He that shewed mercy on him." I have often thought that he must have gone home that day and wondered, "Why in the world did I answer like that?" But there wasn't anything else to answer. "He that shewed mercy on him."

When He says, "Which ... was neighbour," our Lord is teaching that love has its own measure. It's like the sun. The sun does not arise in the eastern gate in the morning and say, "On whom shall I shine today?" The sun just comes up and shines, and it shines on everything and everybody except those who will willfully hide themselves from its rays. And I will assure you there will be some who will hide from the rays of your love. But that's not your problem.

When I was a little child, I remember the pastor of our church had a problem: he was leaving after having been there for some time. He seemed like a pretty nice fellow to me. He had done a lot of visiting and a lot of talking. I remember the speech he made that night. He said, "Brethren, I have loved you, but," he paused, "some of you wouldn't let me love you." I was so young that I really didn't understand, but I understand tonight. I will tell you this: when you find that you just simply love, there will be some who won't let you love them—but that's not your problem. They are like a plant that is willfully placed down in the cellar. It matters not how brightly the sun may shine, it's not the sun's fault that the plant doesn't receive any of its benefits. The plant is simply in the wrong place. And so, tonight, our Lord is saying that we need to learn the lesson of love. I will tell you this: we have an alternative. Our Lord is saying to us tonight that we either learn to love—or be lost. That's the alternative. We must not say that in the church, in this congregation or in any other congregation, "I am going to love these people, but I am not going to love those. I am going to love this individual, but I am not going to love that individual." It won't work. That's not what He is saying.

Strange would be the person who could study this parable and not feel some sense of guilt as we look back down the road. "He that shewed mercy on him." May I mention before we quit—my title tonight is not anti-scriptural, but it is UN-scriptural. In the strictest sense, when you look at Luke 10, you won't find this word "good." It's not in there. I can still remember the day that dawned on me. It would be extremely difficult to announce that we shall study The Parable of the SAMARITAN. I open my Bible, and I notice on the top line that whoever put those titles there—it wasn't the apostles—said here is The Parable of the GOOD Samaritan. I don't ever remember reading anything about this story that did not call him the "GOOD Samaritan." And I think the point is well taken. That man was so good that, though the word is not there, we universally call him "good." Ought it not to be so with your life tonight? Shouldn't you live in such a way from day to day that people simply call you a good person. Like Barnabas—I have always thought that one of the greatest eulogies of Barnabas was simply the scriptures saying, "He was a good man" (Acts 11:22-24). A beautiful, beautiful thing.

Our Lord has struck at the great gulf that exists between what we know to do and what we do. I want you to think what would happen in Wichita, Kansas, tonight, if everybody began to do what he knew to do. This city would soon know about the Lord. There may be some here tonight who know they ought to be Christians. They know they should believe the gospel I think we know that we can't be a member of the Lord's church and be saved unless we are willing to repent of our sins, and this is what Jesus states in Luke 13:3. We know we ought to confess our faith in the Messiah. We know we ought to be immersed in His precious name for the remission of our sins because He said, "Go ye into all the world, and preach the gospel to every creature. He that believeth and is baptized shall be saved" (Mark 16:15-16).

Think what would happen in this city if everyone began to do what he knows to do. I just wonder if in this audience, tonight, you are here and you know what the Lord wants you to do. If you are not a Christian, that's what He wants you to do. Would you not do that? If you are in this audience and you are a Christian; but you have wondered back into sin, and you have not been faithful to the Lord, you know what the Lord wants you to do. I don't have to tell you that. He wants you to repent, doesn't He? He wants you to confess those things, He wants you to have the prayers of God's people and make it right—not with the people but make it right with God. He wants you to do that. There are those who have moved far away from God's eternal truth, from the age old truths of the Bible, who have gone out so far away from His pattern. They would come back if they did what they know they ought to do.

Tonight, do you have the ability? You have an opportunity. Do you have a responsibility? You have the ability to believe; you have the ability to repent; you have the ability to confess Christ; you have the ability to return to the Shepherd and Bishop of your soul. You have, for sure, an opportunity. Which are you tonight? Are you a priest? Are you a Levite? Are you a Samaritan? What's the question? Eternal life! As one of the old time preachers said, "The seas that we navigate are those which wash the shores of eternity." And, brother, that is right! It is no little thing we are doing here tonight. Would you think about all these things? Eternal life! "THIS DO and thou shalt live," while we stand and while we sing.

Sermon Three

*The
Parables
of
Jesus*

"And He spake many things
unto them in parables"

Matthew 25:1-13

"Then shall the kingdom of heaven be likened unto ten virgins, which took their lamps, and went forth to meet the bridegroom. And five of them were wise, and five were foolish. They that were foolish took their lamps, and took no oil with them: but the wise took oil in their vessels with their lamps. While the bridegroom tarried, they all slumbered and slept. And at midnight there was a cry made. Behold, the bridegroom cometh; go ye out to meet him. Then all those virgins arose, and trimmed their lamps. And the foolish said unto the wise, Give us of your oil; for our lamps are gone out. But the wise answered, saying, Not so; lest there be not enough for us and you: but go ye rather to them that sell, and buy for yourselves. And while they went to buy, the bridegroom came; and they that were ready went in with him to the marriage: and the door was shut. Afterward came also the other virgins, saying, Lord, Lord, open to us. But he answered and said, Verily I say unto you, I know you not. Watch therefore, for ye know neither the day nor the hour wherein the Son of man cometh."

3. The Ten Virgins

Once again we are privileged to study the Lord's Word together, and we appreciate your coming to study with us. We believe the Lord is in this place. Unlike a man so long ago who said, "The Lord is in this place; and I knew it not" (Genesis 28:16), I trust that we are aware that the Lord is here and that we will become increasingly aware of this fact.

The Bible teaches that when we gather by the authority of Jesus, He is in our midst. We do not believe there is some magic in the name of Jesus in that we can simply speak His name and automatically all things are well; but we do believe that when we gather by the authority of Jesus Christ, He is in our presence, making what would seem to some to be an otherwise-drab situation become something that is meaningful and viable. We speak to souls who will never die, and we have in our presence no less than the King of all kings. This should demand the best that we have to give, especially as we come to study one of the sermons that is His.

We are grateful that we have before us a divine record of the parables of Jesus Christ. I think we should be reminded, this evening, that as we come to Jesus' parables, we are not studying fables, we are not studying proverbs, and we are not studying allegories. The parables of Jesus are those things that are within the spiritual world, and yet they never transgress the natural order of things. These parables are like the cloudy and fiery pillars of so long ago. They led the Israelites to the places God would have them go, but it was total darkness and confusion to the Egyptians. It must be something similar to that as we come to consider the parables of our Lord.

It's not by accident that the Lord uses parables to draw so many analogies in the Word about the relationship between Christ and His church and the husband and his wife. We also have lessons about the new birth based on the idea of the natural birth and that He is called a King and He refers to it as a Kingdom. These are words and concepts that we mortals understand. So, as long as a person lives in this natural world, he should never be without reproof or rebuke because this whole world with its kings and its subjects, with its living and its dying, with its sun and its moon, with its sleeping and its waking, with its light and its darkness—the whole thing is one gigantic comparison that may be made. It was upon these things that the Lord capitalizes and says this is the way it is with the Kingdom of God.

You cannot walk into a jewelry store, pick up a beautiful diamond, take one look at it, and say that you can thus appreciate the beauty of that gem. It is only when you turn it about, view its many sides, and look into the depths of its brilliance from many ways, that perhaps then you begin to see the beauty of that stone. That is exactly what the Lord is doing. He is saying that you cannot take just one look at His Kingdom and see all of its beauties and all of its glories. So, tonight, we are privileged to listen as the Lord says, "The kingdom of heaven is like unto ... ." And, tonight, we are listening to one of these lessons that He gave so long ago.

The occasion of this lesson is found in Matthew 24. Here our Lord is answering the question of the disciples: "When shall these things be? and what shall be the sign of thy coming, and of the end of the world?" The Lord at this time begins to describe some of those things for them in this parable. In fact, He has a series of parables that grow out of this question. The Parable of the Fig Tree, The Parable of the Master of the House, and The Parable of the Talents. Now when He talks about the second coming, the Lord begins to discuss faithful and wise servants, evil servants, punishment, and salvation. He is discussing future events or something that will occur in the great out yonder, and it is thus we come to a most significant word in the opening part when He says, "THEN." He isn't saying simply, "The kingdom of heaven is likened unto ... ." He is saying, "THEN shall the kingdom of heaven be likened unto ... ." So He moves it to an event far into the future, and yet it has an impact on the lives that we live here this very night. And thus He gives to us The Parable of the Ten Virgins.

The Jewish Wedding

Our Lord says, "Then shall the kingdom of heaven be likened unto ten virgins, which took their lamps, and went forth to meet the bridegroom." It's interesting that the Lord takes something that is so simple and something that is so every day to those people and proceeds to teach a tremendous lesson. The structure here is a Jewish wedding. I must confess to you that I do not know much about Jewish weddings except what I read. I have gone back to try to learn about them, not only now but in the time in which Jesus spoke this parable. A Jewish wedding was a happy occasion. It was a time when people got together. And it was a time of the joining of lives that were dear and precious to them. There was an engagement. There was a betrothal. And there was some form of ceremony. I have no way of knowing what it was, but I do know that when they were engaged, or when they were betrothed, it was a binding thing. I will assure you of this, among the Jews you were not engaged to a certain young man or young lady this week and next week to somebody else or next month or next year to somebody else. It was extremely binding. If we had time this evening, we would discuss this fact in view of Deuteronomy 22 and Matthew 1:19. If for some reason this marriage or betrothal was not to be pursued, they had to make an issue out of it and agree to drop it. You remember the case of Joseph and Mary when he had found that she was with child.

After the engagement and the betrothal, several months or even a year would intervene. At a certain time the bridegroom with his company would go to receive his bride. Now in this case the bridegroom seems to be coming from afar, and they do not know at what time the bridegroom is going to come. In fact, I understand that even sometimes if it were a close home situation, they did not know; and so they would wait.

Ten virgins constituted a company, or we might just simply say, an escort. When the bridegroom decided the time had come to take his bride, some would run before him saying, "Behold, the bridegroom cometh." After receiving his bride, the entire procession would proceed toward his home. It is at this time that the ten virgins would join the procession. Upon arriving at their new home, the feasting would begin.

Now I think this is interesting. When the Lord says, "Then shall the kingdom of heaven be likened unto ten virgins," He wants us to understand that here are the central figures in this entire parable. And what's really amazing is that the bride is not the central figure. One would think, as you read the rest of the Bible, that the bride would be the central figure; but that's not true. It's the ten virgins! This realization gives you the thrust and the point of this parable. Notice the Bible says they "took their lamps," indicating that this procession would take place at night, and they "went forth to meet the bridegroom."

When we look at the word "virgin," we go back to the Hebrew word "ALMAH." This expression is used in Isaiah 7:14, as he speaks of the Messiah and the virgin birth of Jesus Christ. "Behold a virgin shall conceive ... ." This was a situation for which there was no precedent. It had never occurred before—nor since. The writer uses the term "ALMAH" to signify a young maiden of marriageable age. Some want to translate the word virgin "a young maiden of marriageable age," but will you please ever bear in mind that it also means one who is sexually and morally pure. And of that we must never lose sight when we use this expression. The Greeks used the term "PARTHENOS." If anybody ought to know, they ought to know. You recall they built a great temple, the ruins of which still stand at this very moment, and they dedicated it to the "PARTHENOS" or to the virgins—the temple of the virgins.

Thus, we have the basis of what the Lord is teaching; but when we lay aside the drapery of the parable, we want to know whom the Lord is talking about when he discusses virgins. I am persuaded He is simply speaking about us—about the professed followers of Jesus Christ, the Lamb of God. He is talking about those in whom there is the profession of a pure faith. He is discussing those in whom there is the absence of spiritual fornication—individuals who are Christians; and I would say that we are simply to take a look at ourselves, the children of God.

The Wise and the Unwise Virgins

Please notice that in this group we have both the wise and the unwise, even among those called virgins. So He will bring the discussion down to a fine line as to why some are wise and some unwise. Notice that Jesus gives many similarities in the parable. He immediately divides them and speaks about five and five. I do not think the number is necessarily important, but I think the division is extremely important. He wants us to understand that five are wise and five are foolish; and although there are some differences, I want you to think first about the similarities. First of all, the scripture states that they all went out to meet the bridegroom; they all had the necessary equipment. They all had an invitation. They all had a lamp. They all had oil, and they all slumbered and slept.

When I first began studying this parable, I thought, "There's the problem! They slumbered and slept—that is what made five of them foolish." But that's not it! The scripture clearly states, "they ALL slumbered and slept." So that fact really has nothing to do with the lesson the Lord is teaching.

The Lord just wants us to understand five of them are wise and five are foolish. Notice He does not divide them into the good and the bad. He will do that in Matthew 25 when He contemplates the end of time, and they are standing before the Lord as the Shepherd divides the sheep from the goats. He calls them the good and the bad, the saved and the lost. But here the distinction is between the wise and the unwise. So there is some good here—they are not all hypocrites. He simply says some are wise and some are not.

He comes on down in His sermon and says the "foolish took their lamps," but they "took no oil with them." Here is the pivotal point of the parable. I am persuaded that everything hinges upon understanding what "having oil" or "not having oil" is when He says the "foolish took their lamps." So does everybody! The foolish took their lamps, but "they took no oil with them." This point just leaps out and says, "Here is the problem! Here is the reason they are called foolish!"

The Lamp and the Oil

When we look at the lamp, we have at least two things involved: a lamp and oil. The lamp seems to indicate an outward profession of faith. It's something quite tangible, always very much seen, something that is always out there. The oil is something within the lamp—not seen but vital. In fact, it is so vital that without it He says one becomes a foolish individual. When I read that, I immediately think of James, who says, "the body without the spirit is dead" (James 2:26). You see it takes both. If, tonight, you are going to live, it requires both the body and the spirit. I think you might project that idea as you think about works and you think about faith.

The Lord is saying it takes both of these things to constitute what the Lord really wants. The Lord does not wish us simply to say, "What a beautiful lamp I have. What a great profession of faith!" I must say this: there is nothing wrong with a lamp. Every once in a while I meet someone who tells me that if you are really spiritual, you don't need the lamp—you don't need a means of worshiping God. I will promise you there are some people in Wichita, Kansas, tonight, who will tell you that if you are really spiritually minded, you don't need to gather in little church houses and, to quote one of them, "sing little songs to God" because God knows the spiritually minded. You don't need forms of worship! You don't need the lamp! But I disagree. For some reason the Apostle Paul says, "Not forsaking the assembling of ourselves together, as the manner of some is" (Hebrews 10:25). He not only lays down the fact of an assembly but also the rules and regulations for that assembly. He has actually structured the assembly and tells us the way we are to worship God.

We must never discount the lamp and our need for it. Our Lord says we do need it, but we need more. What would you say His purpose is? He wants to impress upon us the need for constant vigilance. He warns us to maintain good works. The erection of a building does not allow for its maintenance. Our Lord came into this world and erected a great thing called Christianity. But His erecting it does not make you a Christian. Simply to believe in Jesus Christ, does not make you a Christian. He has built a house and says, "Occupy till I come."

"Occupy" means more than just stay there. He says we must exercise constant vigilance; we must constantly draw upon the great supply of the Holy Spirit. As Paul says in Galatians 6:9, "Let us not be weary in well doing: for in due season we shall reap." He is saying that it is not enough to say, "Lord, Lord." It is not enough to have the outward, but we must from the heart be doing the will of our Father who is in Heaven.

When He talks about the oil, He is discussing our inward spiritual state. He wants us to know we must be people who are genuine—sincere. If we are not sincere to the core, I don't understand why we are here. We must be the most sincere people who walk this earth. We must be the BEST people who walk the earth. That isn't arrogance—that's Christianity. He expects that of us. Probably the greatest standard I have ever heard is, "Be ye holy; for I am holy" (1 Peter 1:16). That's the greatest standard we could possibly have.

In Colossians 3:1-5, the Apostle Paul says, "If ye then be risen with Christ, seek those things which are above, where Christ sitteth on the right hand of God." He says:

> Set your affections on things above, not on things on the earth. For ye are dead, and your life is hid with Christ in God. When Christ, who is our life, shall appear, then shall ye also appear with him in glory. Mortify therefore your members that are upon the earth; fornication, uncleanness, inordinate affection, evil concupiscence, and covetousness, which is idolatry.

He goes on in that third chapter to lay down the principles that should guide those who are risen with Christ. And I would suppose this evening that, in the main, I am speaking to people who are risen with Christ. He expects you to do what he says, "put ye on the Lord Jesus Christ" (Romans 13:14). He does not say just put off the old man with his deeds, but he says put on something—not simply the lamp, but also the oil.

Well, our Lord is saying to us, "And five were" ... what? ... "foolish." He doesn't say five were hypocrites. He doesn't say five were immoral. He doesn't say five were people of false pretense. He just says "And five were foolish." Who are these people? What are they? They are slothful in work and negligent in prayer. They are going through round after round of external duty but never amounting to anything for God. These are the husks and yet no kernel; these are those of whom he speaks in Galatians 4:19. This is a very descriptive, very beautiful passage. Paul says, "My little children, of whom I travail in birth again until Christ be formed in you." Do you realize what he is saying? Paul is saying that you have been formed in Christ, but, brethren, Christ has never really been formed in you. And he says, "I travail in birth again until Christ be formed in you." These are those in 2 Timothy 3:5 who had "a form of godliness," but they were ever "denying the power thereof." So here, indeed is a form, but where is the power? The real power comes when we draw upon God's Holy Spirit through the precious truths that He has laid down, which He declares to be the "sword of the Spirit."

The Time of Crisis

Did you notice? In the parable, these people have some oil. When they first start, they have some. In fact, it is burning. And you remember that when the cry comes, "Behold, the bridegroom cometh," they "arose, and trimmed their lamps" and they say, "Our lamps are going out." Can you imagine the frustration of standing there watching that flame on that wick get smaller and smaller—and they know what is happening. They KNOW what is happening! They say, "Give us of your oil; for our lamps are going out." I want you to think, for just a fleeting moment, how well this ties in with what our Lord has to say in the first parable we studied. He says these are they that "anon with joy receive the word ... and dureth for awhile," but by and by they begin to wither, they begin to die. He uses the expression over there, "they withered away." Here He is saying they "are going out." The flames are slowly receding because there is no supply on which they may draw.

So again we are talking about the temporary faith of people who are not rooted and grounded in the truth. I am persuaded that the only way some people are ever going to be saved is that they believe the Lord, repent of their sins, confess the holy Christ, and be immersed in His name, and then the Lord takes them immediately. They never seem to be able to stay. And, as on this occasion, their lamps are there but only for a fleeting moment; there just isn't enough oil to keep them going.

I am glad the Bible says, and they have always been around, "Five of them were wise." Who are these people? Jesus says these are they who settle down to live a Christian life. I hope, tonight, that I am speaking to people who have made up their minds and are here to stay. I want to tell you, if I understand my heart, I have made up my mind. This is it for me! I have come too many miles. I don't intend to do anything else. Do you? Do you ever intend to do anything else than live a Christian life? I mean, does it ever cross your mind that some day you might get into a situation that might cause you to give up being a Christian? I think this idea ought to be simply dismissed. I am here, and this is what I intend to do the rest of my days—just simply live a Christian life, settle down to patience, settle down to self denial as our Lord has already taught us in the other parables. A few warm, excited feelings just simply won't do it. It takes principles plus feelings for an individual to be what the Lord would have him to be.

One of my jobs when I was a child—and this puts me way back somewhere in the dark ages—was to keep the Aladdin lamp filled. I can still remember when we were sitting around at night reading, and that lamp began to go dim, I knew what was wrong. I also knew what else was coming because my father took a dim view of one not doing his job, however small it was. My job! And it didn't help a particle to suggest to my Dad that outside there was a great deal of kerosene in the barrel. He wanted it in the lamp, and he wanted a constant supply so that the lamp would not go out. And I am persuaded this is what our God wants. Through the Word, the Holy Spirit has made available to us an absolutely limitless supply.

They All Slumbered and Slept

Next He says, "While the bridegroom tarried ... ." Notice, the bridegroom comes when he gets ready. In this case the bride just waits until the bridegroom decides this is the time our wedding will occur, "While the bridegroom tarried, they all slumbered and they slept." First, I get the picture of their nodding, then gradually falling into a deep sleep. But as I told you before, I don't really see that as the main problem. We shouldn't make anything great out of the fact that they "slumbered and slept" because they ALL did it. The thing that we should see is that when he does come, they are not able to respond because they are not prepared. Notice, those five foolish individuals, who are headed toward outer darkness, sleep as soundly and as peacefully as those who are prepared. So, we should not let any sense of false security lull us and cause us to think the Lord is delaying His coming, so all is well. And we should remember this: just because we feel secure and we think everything is pretty good—that all is well. We can sleep pretty soundly and be headed for destruction. Our Lord says, "There is a way ... ." and that is one of the most frightening things in the Word of God to me. He says, "There is a way which seemeth right unto a man, but the end thereof are the ways of death" (Proverbs 14:12). I can think of no greater tragedy than to think about spending my life and come to the end of the journey and all has been in vain. We have but one life to live in THIS world. And if there is a way that "seemeth right," our Lord is immediately saying, of course, there is a way that IS right, and we must find that way.

Behold, the Bridegroom Cometh

These individuals are at ease, and yet they are headed for destruction. The scripture says, "And at midnight ... ." Notice the significance. At a time usually of deep sleep, at a time unanticipated, at a time unannounced, the cry rings through the street. Can you imagine these people sitting there and they're sleeping and everything is quiet and all of a sudden the cry rings out, "Behold, the bridegroom cometh," and they awaken. The scripture says, "Then ALL those virgins arose, and trimmed their lamps." They want to give their best right then. But, you see, you can't wait. Preparation may not be made at the time of examination. The very nature of preparation makes it something that must occur beforehand. And it is only at this time that the foolish discover they have no oil. Isn't it amazing that they did not inquire into the foundations of their faith, that they simply just assume that it is there. We must not just assume that everything is all right. The Apostle Paul is saying,

"Prove all things; hold fast that which is good" (1 Thessalonians 5:21). He is saying, "Study to shew thyself approved" (2 Timothy 2:15). He is saying, will you please inquire into the foundation of your faith over and over. Don't wait until it's too late. Now is the time to take a real look at this matter in your life.

Give Us of Your Oil

The time of reckoning had come and they said, "Give us of your oil." You know, that's bound to have been a despairing feeling. Sometime ago I was talking with a young man who had done his conscientious objector's work in a place where he had to deal with the insane. He said one of the most difficult things he ever dealt with, that was so hard to adjust to, was hearing the horrible cries and pleas for mercy from those deranged people when they thought that someone was beating them. In their demented state, they felt someone was beating them, and they cried for mercy. It must have been something like that when these individuals realized all of a sudden the despair of that moment, and they cry, "Give us of your oil!"

This situation reminds me of Luke 16 in yet another lesson when a man cries out across a gulf that cannot be spanned, saying, "Send Lazarus, that he may dip the tip of his finger in water, and cool my tongue; for I am tormented in this flame." Or to hear him ask that Lazarus be sent to warn his five brothers "lest they also come into this place of torment." Despair! Maybe you have been in a time when you felt a little bit of that. I have! Once or twice I have been in a situation where I felt absolute despair, and I perhaps felt what some of these individuals must have felt. They are indeed all of a sudden weighed in the balances and know that they are wanting, and they simply don't know anything to do but to cry out to those about them, "Give us of your oil!"

I want you to listen to the answer. Our Lord would have the other five say, "Not, so." That response seems pretty cold at first. How can I reconcile the idea of the five wise virgins, picturing Christians, giving this kind of answer to those who are now lost? But I am persuaded that what we are looking at here is not a put down, it's just simply dealing with the fact that you cannot borrow what must be bought. They could not borrow something they themselves had to buy. When you think about it, one must conclude that some things come only from God and not men. And if you are ever going to be supplied with it, it must come from Him. Every man must live by his own faith. We have passages like Galatians 6:5 where Paul says, "For every man shall bear his own burden." We have passages saying, "What must I do to be saved?" We have passages like, "work out YOUR OWN salvation with fear and trembling" (Philippians 2:12). You can help another person to a certain point. You can show one where the precious ore is buried, but you can't dig it for him. Every person must eventually deal with salvation on his own, as we say, on his own two feet.

I was in Salt Lake City some years ago, and I listened as one of the Mormon elders, as he styled himself, explained the doctrines of that particular church. He explained the proxy arrangements they have, which are many. In a certain place there, one could be baptized; and for certain considerations, one could be baptized for some loved one who had not been baptized—you could be baptized FOR them. But may I assure you, the Bible teaches no such thing. And I guess the best reason that no one can live for you, and no one can sin for you and no one can be baptized for you, is simply that nobody can die for you. There are no proxy arrangements. Our Lord is saying salvation is a personal thing. It's something YOU must take care of while in the body.

It is like character—you don't buy character. You don't loan out character. You don't bequeath character. How great it would be! I am sure there are many people who have lived who would like very much to make a will and bequeath to their sons and daughters their Christian character. But you don't buy it, you don't loan it, and you don't bequeath it.

This fact is also true with obedience. Paul says, "For we must all ... "—not some of us—"we must ALL appear before the judgment seat of Christ." To do what? To "receive the things done in his body" (2 Corinthians 5:10). It's like preparation. How do you share preparation? I think of something I read many years ago about one of the old time preachers. Brother

Wilson was a man who was extremely well versed in the Holy Scripture. I understand he was capable of presenting tremendous lessons from the Word of God, characterized by great depth, and did so with beautiful simplicity. One night he was preaching, as the story goes, and was doing a great job. After it was over, a sister came up to him and said, "Brother Wilson, I would give half of my life if I knew the scriptures like you know them!" The terse old fellow replied, "Sister, that's exactly what it cost me—half of my life!"

The virgins cried out, "Give us of your oil." What are we discussing? Salvation! Preparation! Planning! Getting ready! These things we cannot share. So we are not looking at something that we can just hand to one another. Now notice what they did. They said, "Go ye rather to them that sell, and buy for yourselves." This is not putting those people down. This is the counsel of love. The advice to those individuals was to go out to the dispensers of divine grace, go out into the markets of mercy. Find those who are laying out these great truths; find them and get your supply of this great oil. You have, as he puts it in Luke 16, "Moses and the prophets," remember? "Buy for yourselves."

The lesson would indicate that oil could be bought. But I will tell you what couldn't. Time couldn't! Mr. Shakespeare said that time and tide wait for no man; and that's right. Oil might be bought, but there was no time to buy it. I think the Lord is coming through strongly to us about a momentous thing—that precious commodity we sometimes refer to as "time."

The Door Was Shut

The scripture says, "And while they went to buy ... "—while they were out trying to repair the negligence of the past—"the bridegroom came; and they that were ready went in with him." If you want the whole sermon in a few words, there it is: "AND ... THEY ... THAT ... WERE ... READY!" There's what He is talking about. "They that were ready" went with him into the feast "and the door was shut." You talk about striking the note of finality, that's it! I can just simply feel it as He says, "and the door was shut." That is the note of finality! A closed door is for what? It's for benefit and it's for exclusion. It is for the joy and the benefit of those who are on the inside; but the same door is for the exclusion of those who are on the outside. I want to tell you what the tragedy of the closed door is—the individuals closed it themselves. Oh, I am sure they may have said, "They shut me out." No! They shut themselves out! They were not ready. The scripture says, "Afterward came also the other virgins, saying, Lord, Lord open to us." Here is that cry for mercy that I talked about a moment ago. Here are these individuals saying, "Lord." Notice, they claim an intimate relationship with him. They are saying, "Lord, open." How earnestly they seek, how much they would like for that door to open to them and just simply let them go inside.

You know what our Lord is saying? Our Lord is saying to us that lost opportunities cannot be recalled. I will guarantee you there is not a person sitting in this building tonight of any age at all who does not realize the tragedy of lost opportunities. There have been some opportunities we've had, and we let them go. We let them slip by, and there's no way we can recall those opportunities. But you have an opportunity now. The Lord is speaking not to the dead; He is speaking to the living. You still have an opportunity. You are still in the land of beginning again. We've had opportunities to believe the gospel; we have had opportunities to repent of our sins. We have had opportunities abundant to confess the holy Christ and to be immersed in His name for the remission of our sins, but we haven't. We've let them slip by.

Some time ago I heard my son use an illustration that I thought was pretty good, if I may say so. He told of one who went next door and knocked for entrance. He said he knocked and knocked because he knew someone was home—the shade moved. But still nobody opened the door. The person decided to leave and return the next day and try again. He returned to knock again and again and still nobody opened the door. Let me ask you—how many times, would you go back when you know they're home—you know they're there—they just simply won't open the door. But the real tragedy is some day you are going to knock and they're not going to be home. They will never be home. And that is what we are seeing in this particular lesson.

"Lord, open to us." What did Jesus reply? He says, "Verily I say unto you, I know you not." Do you hear what He is saying? Though they are saying, "Lord, Lord," He is saying, "I know you not." And that's the exact equivalent of saying you don't know Me. You have never known Me—in your faith. You have never known Me—in complete remission of your sins. You are not My child; you simply have not remained faithful. You were not concerned about your soul.

Finally, I think the thing that is most moving to me is that the Bible teaches that that exclusion is final. If there were only some way to open that door! But that door will never swing open. That door does not swing on purgatorial hinges—or any other kind. It will never swing outward. This is the failure of the foolish. That door is never going to open!

Watch Therefore

Our Lord concludes, "Watch therefore, for ye know neither the day nor the hour wherein the Son of man cometh." Almost two thousand years have rolled by, almost two thousand years since the day our Lord left and said He is coming back. You and I are living in that time tonight. If anybody in the world ought to be listening to Him say, "Watch therefore," it ought to be us. He says, "Ye know neither the day nor the hour," so you know the only sure way is to be ready. Our Lord is not saying that we are to be stargazers. When He says, "Watch therefore," He's not saying, as some people interpret this, that we need to dress ourselves in white robes and climb the nearest mountain and stand looking into the skies. He's not saying we should move off and form a commune until Jesus comes. What He is saying is, "Watch therefore." And the way we watch is by being ready every day.

The question we have tossed around through all the ages is, "When is the Lord coming?" If we were to put in the newspaper that we are going to preach on when the Lord is coming and we could convince the people that we think we know when He's coming, I think we would have an awful lot of people here. Of course, these would be the words of a fool—we don't know when. He says, "Ye know neither the day nor the hour." We toss around the question, "WHEN is He coming?" but we should be tossing around the question, "Are we READY for His coming?" It matters little tonight WHEN He is coming, what matters is—ARE YOU READY? Are you watching? Are you waiting? "Is your lamp trimmed and burning bright?"

I want you to think about this for a moment—that door is open tonight; and while it is open, repentant murderers and harlots may walk through it. But when that door is closed, the best moral man won't get in. And that ought to tell us something. So near! Where were they? Just outside the door, and yet they were lost. They weren't ten thousand miles from the wedding. They were just outside the door, but they were so lost. The door was shut. No penance, no amount of money, no prayers—nothing will open it! Think about it. That door, that ancient door if you will, which received Aaron after his idolatry, that door which received David after his adultery, that door which received Peter after his denial, that door is open now! Mercy's door is open now. It's open tonight.

If the cry were to ring out tonight, "The bridegroom cometh," would you be ready? I was in Tulsa two nights after a near tragedy that occurred among our young people there. A young man came down the aisle and said, "I want the people to pray for me, and I want to be forgiven of my sins." And he said to me, "I got to thinking, if I had been killed in that crash the other night, I would have been lost. I don't want to be lost!" How we need to stop and think what we are doing. We talk about when the "end of the world" is coming. Let me tell you, if you walk out those doors tonight and get killed out there on that highway, brother, that's the end of the world for you! You need to think about your condition, about the life that you live. "It is a fearful thing," Paul says, "to fall into the hands of the living God" (Hebrews 10:31). But have you ever thought what a fearful thing it would be to fall OUT of the hands of the living God? Either one is a real tragedy.

Are you here and you are not a Christian? Tonight won't you become a Christian?

Sermon Four

The
Parables
of
Jesus

"And He spake many things
unto them in parables"

Luke 12:13-34

"And one of the company said unto him, Master, speak to my brother, that he divide the inheritance with me. And he said unto him, Man, who made me a judge or a divider over you? And he said unto them, Take heed, and beware of covetousness: for a man's life consisteth not in the abundance of the things which he possesseth. And he spake a parable unto them, saying, The ground of a certain man brought forth plentifully: and he thought within himself, saying, What shall I do, because I have no room where to bestow my fruits? And he said, This will I do: I will pull down my barns, and build greater; and there will I bestow all my fruits and my goods. And I will say to my soul, Soul, thou hast much goods laid up for many years; take thine ease, eat, drink, and be merry. But God said unto him, Thou fool, this night thy soul shall be required of thee: then whose shall those things be, which thou hast provided? So is he that layeth up treasure for himself, and is not rich toward God. And he said unto his disciples, Therefore I say unto you, Take no thought for your life and what ye shall eat; neither for the body, what ye shall put on. The life is more than meat, and the body is more than raiment. Consider the ravens: for they neither sow nor reap; which neither have storehouse nor barn; and God feedeth them: how much more are ye better than the fowls? And which of you taking thought can add to his stature one cubit? If ye then be not able to do that thing which is least, why take ye thought for the rest? Consider the lilies how they grow they toil not, they spin not; and yet I say unto you that Solomon in all his glory was not arrayed like one of these If then God so clothe the grass, which is today in the field and tomorrow is cast into the oven; how much more will he clothe you, O ye of little faith? And seek not ye what ye shall eat, or what ye shall drink, neither be ye of doubtful mind. For all these things do the nations of the world seek after: and your Father knoweth that ye have need of these things. But rather seek ye the kingdom of God; and all these things shall be added unto you. Fear not, little flock; for it is your Father's good pleasure to give you the kingdom. Sell that ye have, and give alms; provide yourselves bags which wax not old, a treasure in the heavens that faileth not, where no thief approacheth, neither moth corrupteth. For where your treasure is, there will your heart be also."

4. The Rich Fool

We believe, this evening, that our Lord looks upon this assembly; and we believe He is pleased. He has so long taught us that we are to "gather the people together, men, and women, and children, and thy stranger that is within thy gates, that they may hear, and that they may learn, and fear the Lord your God ... and that their children, which have not known anything, may hear, and learn" (Deuteronomy 31:12-13). We believe the Lord is pleased when people come together to listen to His will and certainly when those people are willing to praise His name and to learn more of Him.

As we come to this particular lesson, we are continuing the parables of our Lord; and we have come to one tonight that is exceedingly valuable. I believe that if we may say The Parable of the Good Samaritan was extremely practical, we could say that this one is next to it in practicality when we consider the lives we live day by day as the sons of God. We have a valuable lesson, and one that is ever timely.

We would like to think that some of these lessons, somewhere in our growth through all the centuries of time, would be no longer applicable. We would like to think that we've outgrown these things and that we no longer need admonition like this, but I know this just is not true. I know these things are as current as today's headlines or perhaps even more current than that. If the Lord had written these words to us tonight, in this generation, they couldn't be more applicable or more needed.

You remember that on this occasion our Lord is preaching some of His greatest sermons. He is speaking to the people about Heaven and Hell. He is discussing the deity of Christ Himself as the Son of God. He is discussing no less than blasphemy against the Holy Spirit, and yet in the midst of this discussion, there is a man who is not listening to one word He is saying.

Often times a preacher wonders just how much the people sitting in the audience are getting out of what he is saying. Sometimes when I look over an audience, I see people who are talking or reading—it's amazing what you can see from up here! When you see this going on, you often wonder just how much those people are getting out of what is being said. The reason I am saying this tonight is that two thousand years ago Jesus dealt with the same thing. I can understand why someone is not too interested in what I am saying, but I fail to see how one could sit in the audience of no less than the King of all kings and the Master Teacher, the greatest Teacher who ever walked the earth, while HE is explaining the subject of blasphemy against the Holy Spirit, and not have his mind on what He is saying.

But on this occasion, this is the case as our Lord is preaching. All of a sudden, this man just blurts out, "Master, speak to my brother, that he divide the inheritance with me." Now that doesn't have a thing in the world to do with what Jesus is talking about; and it seems that in the midst of hearing all these great things, he is sitting there thinking about an inheritance. Evidently his father is now dead, and he must have been the younger son in that ancient arrangement of Deuteronomy 21 where it states that the eldest son was to receive about two thirds, and the rest was to be divided among the others. He came that day and for some reason decided to listen to or at least be in the presence of the great Teacher, but he is so obsessed by material things and by the fact that he just might not get what's coming to him that he simply cannot listen. So he blurts out, "Speak to my brother, that he divide the inheritance with me." I suppose that as he listened, he decided that Jesus is a pretty intelligent person, and it would appear that here is a Man who knows something about people. It just may be that He's the Man who can rectify some of these ancient arrangements and get something done.

I think it is worthy of note that our Lord dispatches this matter quickly. He quickly asks, "Man, who made me a judge or a divider over you?" Now, I don't think our Lord is saying there is anything wrong with material things. I don't think He is saying there is anything wrong with there being judges or arbitrators who may rightfully look over this kind of thing and make judgments. But He is saying that that's not the reason He came into the world. He came to save the souls of men, and He wants us to understand there are bigger and better and higher things than money. And so we find Him putting it down. He knows, as He speaks to that individual, that not only is it true with this man, but it seems to be ever true with us. We need the lesson that He then proceeds to give. There is not one of us here in this room, not one, but what we need to listen to this ancient lesson that our Lord teaches.

As we talk about the enemies that the church has faced, it is my observation, through the study of this Book and the study of history—both sacred and profane—that the church has always had enemies. And this fact should never come as a surprise to us. Since we are soldiers of the cross, I guess one of the first things we ought to recognize is that there are enemies.

There has always been radicalism, and there has always been liberalism; but I will tell you, as great and as formidable as those foes may be, I still believe that one of the greatest foes that the church of our Lord has ever faced is materialism. And so on this occasion, our Lord wants to speak to us one more time about the real, vital issues of life, And He chooses to do so in the framework of this particular lesson. Every child in this room of any age at all knows the story. But there's not an adult here who has ever learned the lesson as we ought to learn it. So let's listen to our Lord as He tells us about The Rich Fool.

A Rich Man

"The ground of a certain rich man brought forth plentifully." Our Lord introduces us to a man who evidently is well off financially. He is a farmer or at least he owns quite a lot of land. He did not gain what he has by stealing or by extortion. The Bible does not indicate that he is a spoiler in any sense of the word. But he is a man who simply works and reaps the blessings of God. I guess if there is anything that gets as close to honesty as one can get, it is when he lays open the earth and puts the seed inside and waits to reap the blessings of God. And this is what this man does.

We are not looking upon a man who caused others to lose by his gain. We are simply seeing a man who is industrious. I would suppose that if we passed by his house early in the morning, we would see this man out. He is already up. And he is out working in his field. And if we passed by late at night, the light is burning because he is working on his records; and we say—there's nothing wrong with that: he is industrious, and that's good.

One day this man wakes up to the fact that his fields are ready to harvest. The golden grain is waving in the winds out on those many fields, and he is confronted with the fact that his barns are filled, and he doesn't have any place to put this great harvest. What our Lord is doing, I am persuaded, is letting us look inside an individual.

Have you ever wondered what goes on in the heart of another person? I have. And sometimes I have looked at you and wondered why you do what you do. And I look at you and wonder why don't you do some of the things you should be doing. And I am sure you look at me and wonder why I act as I do. Our Lord is drawing back the curtain of a worldling's heart and saying that He wants us to see what really goes on inside his heart.

The thing that scares me in this lesson is that when the Lord pulls back the curtain from that man's heart and lets me see inside, it seems so akin to my own. That's the thing that bothers me, but I think that's the point. He wants us to see the similarities. He wants us to understand these things. We look at this individual, and his blunders are immediately manifested. He is doing what Paul said not to do—that is, to make "provision for the flesh, to fulfill the lust thereof." Paul says, don't do that (Romans 13:14). And this is exactly what this person is doing

Sometimes a sudden shift in circumstances is the best revealer of our true character. Now everything is going along pretty well for this fellow. Year by year he is planting and reaping, and he is putting into his barns, and he is enjoying it. But he has a real problem today. It's harvest time, and there is no place to put it. And so he begins to wrestle with this new problem in his life. This sudden shift in circumstance is a real revealer; and sometimes we find that situation within our own hearts and within our own lives.

In this study, the thing that is readily apparent is that here's a man who lives in an awful little world, and he takes up ALL the room in that world. I want you to notice the prolific use of the words "I" and "my." He begins to think, "What shall I do because I have no room where to bestow MY fruits ... MY barns ... MY goods ... MY soul." Over and over we get these pronouns. Six times he uses the word "I" and five times he uses the word "my," and he has no concept of stewardship whatsoever. He is simply saying I did it, MY fruits, MY goods, MY barns, MY soul, many years are MINE. All of these things are MINE.

This man is blind to the source of his blessings. He does not realize that God is the One who is giving these things to him. I remember being out on a brother's farm, in an area where we were conducting a meeting in Missouri; he had some hogs. The hogs were eating under an old acorn tree. While they were eating the acorns that fell from that tree, never one time did they look up to see from whence they came. But we expect that of hogs. But the Lord is saying He doesn't expect that out of those who are made in His own image. He expects people to look up and see from whence their blessings come.

The rich fool wrestled with this problem and said, "I have no room where to bestow my fruits"; my barns are filled. But that really wasn't true. He had barns aplenty. Ambrose, an ancient writer, said, "Yes, he had barns aplenty, and saw not one." Brother, he had the mouths of orphans and he had the houses of widows and he had the homes of the poor and he had people working for him, but those barns he could not see. All he could see was his barn, and that barn was full. Other barns he never recognized. You might say, "What does the Lord want him to do? I mean, after all, he's produced these things and his barn is full. All he wants to do is expand. He wants some capital improvements. Does God want him to lose it?" No!

I think what God wants him to do is to put it in a place where he will never lose it. He wants him to see places that he can put material things so as never to lose them so long as he shall live and on into the great eternity.

Is it not an amazing thing that man's wisdom is saying, "Keep it," while God is saying, "Give it"? And again, the problem we have is getting caught up in that same kind of reasoning. We are realistically seeing our own hearts in some of these things, and we are seeing the times in which we live.

Solomon said in Proverbs 1:32, "The prosperity of fools shall destroy them." He also said in Ecclesiastes 5:10, "He that loveth silver shall not be satisfied with silver; nor he that loveth abundance with increase." You remember that thing you wanted and just had to have and you thought you just couldn't live without? If you could ever get that, if you could ever obtain that, you would be satisfied! You got it, and you aren't.

"Things," this is what Jesus is talking about—and that is the reason I am so deliberate with the reading—"things." "Things!" He repeatedly uses the word "things." Ah, if I could only have this or that! What we learn is that these things that glitter so brightly today, tomorrow are somewhere in the secondhand shop, and the time after that they are in the junk shop or they are on the heap. "Things!" Our Lord wants us to get them in proper perspective, and He does it with this particular lesson.

Let's look at our man. Here he is. He has all of that harvest out there. I mean, the pressure is on! I know enough about farming that, brother, when the fields are white unto harvest, you harvest or you lose it. When the golden grain is ready, you reap it or it's all over. I watch this man as he wrestles with his problem. He wrestles with this matter until eventually he comes upon an answer. Here is his tower of wealth and his tower of strength. Listen to him, "This will I do: I will pull down my barns, and build greater." This is the thing to do. I will expand! I will broaden my vision. I will build my empire. I will build some great things.

You know what we'd say about this man? What would the world say about him, tonight? We would say he is a successful businessman. We would say he is "sitting pretty." We would say he has security, he has future, he has so many grand things, and we look at them and say what a wonderful thing this really is! And he sits back and says, "I will say to my soul" ... listen to him! ... "Soul, thou has much goods laid up for many years; take thine ease, eat, drink, and be merry."

The Bible teaches us that we are not even to say that we are going to do thus and so tomorrow. James teaches in James 4:13-15, "Go to now, ye that say ... ." That's an old English expression that means what shall we say to those that say, " ... Today or tomorrow we will go into such a city, and continue there a year, and buy and sell, and get gain." James says, "For that ye ought to say, If the Lord will, we shall live, and do this or that." Two things. Two very vital things—if we live and if it's the Lord's will, we'll "do this, or that." But what we are looking at is a man who does not boast himself of tomorrow; he rather boasts of many years—I have "much goods laid up for many years." What an amazing thing it is!

Here he is with all these things and sitting back and feeling grand about this situation; and God says, "Thou, fool, this night thy soul shall be required of thee." How different it really is. His soul was required, it was demanded. Here is a man who must leave! He must leave all of his earthly possessions and be jerked out by the very roots from the only solace he has ever known, and that's this world and his goods that surround him. That's his only solace, and the Lord is saying that tonight he would be leaving all this.

Have We Been Fools

As we think upon this parable that Jesus delivered so long ago, the question must be this—Have we been fools? Have I been a fool? Now, I don't think there is a person in this room who would like to think that he is a fool. I don't like to think of myself as a fool; I don't think anyone does, and yet we must face the fact that, even though we read this story and though we know what He is saying is absolute truth, yet many times we go blindly on seeking after the things of the world as if indeed eternity did not exist. We just simply pass over these great statements.

We must determine that we will always include God in our plans. Anytime you find yourself making a plan or plans in which God is not included, please don't pursue them. If you can't put God into your plans, whatever they are, just simply drop them—don't make those plans.

In business we often read about one of those arrangements in which there is a silent partner and an active partner; and every once in a while the active partner decides, "Well, he is never here. All he has done is invest in this business, and he is living somewhere else and never helps. I do all the work. I get together all these things, I keep the books and I send him a check every month." Every once in a while that individual decides the other party doesn't have the right to have all that. And so he doesn't send him all that he should. They call that embezzlement. They call him an embezzler, and they put such in the penitentiary. But I want you to think about this tonight.

Sometimes we decide that God is not right here and He is not walking by our very side, so He won't know, He won't miss all that's coming to Him. We just simply don't give to Him of our time and talent and ability and means. People, it is here that we must be so careful. Put God in your plans! This is the kind of thing we were discussing the other evening, and I have discussed all over this country.

I think it is marvelous when you have a job advancement; but, brother, wherever you are planning to move, if the church isn't there, if it's a place where there is no Christian fellowship or fellowship for your children, I want to tell you, you are planning a dangerous thing. Please include God in your plans; and if God is not there and His house is not—His assembly is not there—and there is no Christian fellowship for you, drop those plans because you and God will make it where you are. You won't likely make it in that kind of situation.

The best reason I know that we always ought to include God in our plans is simply this—WE are in the plan of God. I believe that tonight! I believe that every person sitting in this room and outside this room has a place in God's great plan. There is a pew in His plan for you. We are all in His plan. We need to stop and think—and I'm a fool tonight, if I don't—I need to think, "Why was I born?" I get so caught up sometimes in this material world. Every morning I wake up in a material world. I go to work at a material job. I deal with material things. I get so caught up in such things that sometimes I really lose my spiritual equilibrium, and I forget what I am doing here. Why was I born into this world? Where am I headed? What is this all about? What should have priority? Is this now what our Lord is saying? What is "life?" We use this word and the Bible uses this word. It labels the time from the moment one is born until the time that he dies as "life." Life is a proving ground. Every once in a while, passing through certain parts of this country, we come across one of the great proving grounds of one of the automotive companies. They put their cars there and run them through rigorous tests to determine if they can really stand the test. I want to tell you that life is a proving ground, and we should see it as that. One thing we should see that life is not—life is not to attain fame or fortune: that's not its purpose. I think that we must, to be true to what the Lord is saying, remind both our young people and ourselves that that's not what it's for.

I know you are living in a world that is saying to you, "Get ahead." Brother, it is saying, "Climb the ladder of success and fame and fortune, it doesn't make any difference on whom you step. Simply make it up there; that's what you ought to do." But that's not what THIS Book says.

One of the interesting stories from history, and I am not sure that it's a totally historical fact, but they tell a story of Philip of Macedon and that little child of his that grew up with quite an ambition. He grew up with an ambition to conquer the world! Daniel, the prophet, had already prophesied about this event and said that that nation would bear rule over all the earth. And Alexander the Great, with his brazen-coated soldiers, conquered the entire world. The story is told, be it true or no, of his coming to the time and the place where he stood upon the very peak of the world insofar as conquering it and, having done so, went into his tent and wept bitterly because there were no more worlds to conquer. Evidently he thought that was what life was for.

Shortly before he died, Albert Einstein said, "If I had it all to do over ... ." I want you to think about this. The genius that he was, with all of his theories of relativity, said, "If I had it all to do over, I would rather be a barber, or a plumber or something like that." He also said, "This is not what life is about."

I have often thought about the man in this parable. Don't you think people wondered what happened to him? He's not been sick. I mean, there is no indication he had any problems. I don't know what they called it; I don't know what they wrote on the certificate, but I'll tell you this—he left that night. He left that night, and I am sure there was a great oration as it was with rich men in that day. There were great orations, and they would have some marvelous funerals. We read in Luke 16:22, "The rich man also died, and was buried"—and that meant in style. I don't know what they wrote on his stone, but I'll tell you this, the Lord does not see us as men see us, and I am persuaded that though it may have said some very flattering things, God wrote—HERE LIES A FOOL. Here lies a fool!

What Made Him a Fool

Now the question is this: "What made that man a fool?" If you are like me, you want to know because he's too much like us. I see too many similarities between him and me. So I want to know more about this man. Would you say that this man was a fool? And what would you say caused him to be a fool? The first thing is his money. We often hear people say, "Money is the root of all evil." But you know, that's not true. With all due respect, the Word doesn't say that. It does say, "The love of money is the root of all evil: which while some coveted after, they have erred from the faith, and pierced themselves through with many sorrows" (1 Timothy 6:10).

It is not just because of money that this man was called a fool. It is not because of moral weakness. The Bible does not suggest that he is of low character. It doesn't say he is lazy, it doesn't say he is a pleasure seeker; it doesn't say any of those things. So what's the problem if it wasn't money? I believe the reason God called that man a fool is simply because he left God out of his life. God had no part in his life. God made no difference to him. IT was MY fruits, MY goods, MY soul, and everything belongs to ME. God simply was not there.

And then our Lord says, "Whose shall those things be, which thou has provided?" And so the Lord concludes, "So is he" ... listen ... "So is he that layeth up treasure for himself, and is not rich toward God." Do you hear what He is saying? It is not merely the state of being rich. He is saying, "So is he that layeth up treasure." It is the ungodly greed in trying to attain those things. Covetousness is a deadly sin.

During the time that I have preached, I have seen drunkards repent; I have seen profane persons repent; I have heard so many different kinds of things that people have confessed and have wished to have forgiven, but I'll tell you this, in twenty-seven years I have heard only one person ever say he was a covetous man. That's all! Only one man who ever said he went to bed at night thinking about how to make money. He got up in the morning and the first thought that hit his mind was, "How do I make money; how do I think, how do I act in order to get rich?" He said he was that. But why is it that he is the only one in twenty-seven years?

Covetousness is a dangerous and a deadly thing! We may think we are a perfectly good member of the Lord's church and all is well with our soul, and yet we can be so afflicted with this thing that our Lord is discussing here.

Our Lord is saying that if the purpose of our existence is to enrich ourselves outwardly, we shall perish inwardly. All will be gone some day. You remember in Revelation 3:17, the congregation there said, "I am rich, and increased with goods, and have need of nothing." That's quite a situation when anybody thinks they are in that state. Jesus said they did not know they were "wretched, and miserable, and poor, and blind, and naked." How differently God looks upon our situations. I think we must, tonight, take a look at ourselves.

We will not take it with us. That's one expression we toss about that is so true. In 1 Timothy 6:7 Paul says, "For we brought nothing into this world." Please remember that the word "nothing" is composed of two. It just says—no thing. "We brought no thing into this world." And that's what He is discussing. "And it is certain we can carry no thing out"—not one!

When the late and great J.P. Morgan, the great industrialist, died, at his massive funeral someone in the audience leaned over to another and said, "How much did he leave?" Back came the sobering answer, "He left it all!" And that's the thing that I want to emphasize. He left it all! It doesn't make any difference what he has, brother, when one leaves this world, he leaves it all. So we must be concerned about not leaving God out of our lives.

I am not trying to make some great story out of this, but I have talked with people who were coming down to the last moments of life, and that is to me an awesome time. I mean, when you are sitting there talking, and in a few moments they are not talking anymore. In fact, they are not even there. The spirit has taken its flight. I want to tell you, that in those last moments of life, they're not concerned about, "How is it on the farm?" They're not concerned about, "How is it with my bank account?" or "How are my savings accumulating?" There is one thing that totally consumes the mind in that last few moments of life—HOW IS IT WITH MY SOUL? It is so important that we understand that and that we understand it now.

Solomon: A Man Who Had It All

Better than all these is an account of a man given to us in the Word of God; in fact, we read about him tonight. Jesus said, "Solomon in all his glory ... ." I'll tell you, when you go back and read the story of Solomon, brother, it was what He said, "Solomon in all his glory ... ." And I still like to go back and read what Solomon said one day. I want to read it to you tonight. I think the lesson would be incomplete without it. I am reading from Ecclesiastes 2:3-11. I want you to picture this great man in all of his glory. He said:

I sought in my heart to give myself unto wine, yet acquainting my heart with wisdom'; and to lay hold on folly, till I might see what was good for the sons of men, which they should do under the heaven all the days of their life. I made me great works; I builded me houses; I planted me vineyards: I made me gardens and orchards, and I planted trees in them of all kind of fruits: I made me pools of water, to water therewith the wood that bringeth forth trees: I got me servants and maidens, and had servants born in my house; also I had great possessions of great and small cattle above all that were in Jerusalem before me: I gathered me also silver and gold, and the peculiar treasure of kings and of the provinces: I gat me men singers and women singers, and the delights of the sons of men, as musical instruments, and that of all sorts. So I was great, and increased more than all that were before me in Jerusalem: also my wisdom remained with me. And whatsoever mine eyes desired I kept not from them, I withheld not mine heart from any joy; for my heart rejoiced in all my labour: and this was my portion of all my labour. Then I looked on all the works that my hands had wrought, and on the labour that I had laboured to do: and, behold, all was vanity and vexation of spirit, and there was no profit under the sun.

There's the testimony of a man who had it all.

Tonight, whatever it is, whatever desire is in your heart, you think if I can just get that, then I would really be living; that's what it's all about. Well, whatever it is that you want, here is a man who said he had it. Be it good or be it bad, whatever it was, he possessed it all! And I think it is so beautiful what he then states in chapter twelve as he comes down to the last statement that he makes in verse thirteen. He said, "Let us hear the conclusion of the whole matter: Fear God and keep his commandments; for this is the whole duty of man." He said this is all! "For God shall bring every work into judgment, with every secret thing, whether it be good, or whether it be evil."

I'm not trying to say this evening that a person should not make a living. I am not saying that. That isn't what Jesus is saying. Our Lord put us into this world, and He knew that we would have certain religious and secular responsibilities.

Someone observed that there are a few individuals in this world who are so heavenly minded that they are of no earthly good. Now there may be a few like that around, I don't know of too many, but there may be some. But what we are trying to say is this: while the Lord has said you not only may, you must engage yourself in some kind of gainful enterprise to support your loved ones and to have to give to those that are without, that same God also told us, "Upon the first day of the week," we are to gather with the Lord's people (Acts 20:7). He also teaches us, according to 1 Corinthians 16:1-2, that we are to lay by in store as He has prospered us. He also gives us many other religious responsibilities.

We sometimes—and I say WE as I speak of the Lord's people and things I have personally dealt with—we sometimes obligate ourselves for some of the luxuries of this old world, and we get ourselves so bound down that we can't live for God. We can't even carry out the commands that He laid down for us to observe each week. To be better off is not necessarily to be better. I think sometimes we equate the two. That's not what He is saying. They are two different things. One does not inventory his goods and then say he has inventoried his soul, because Jesus said "a man's life consisteth not in the abundance of the things which he possesseth" (Luke 12:15). Do you hear what He is saying? That a man's soul or a man's life is not the same as a man's possessions. They are two different things. And although man needs both, He is saying, please do not equate those things. And yet what do we do? I assure you that we are creatures who still tend to think that one who lives in a fine house and drives the biggest automobile and has the most land has it made. Remember: "A man's life consisteth not in the abundance of the things which he possesseth." There is a difference between the two.

Jesus says, "Man shall not live by bread alone" (Matthew 4:4). Now you think what He is saying. Think of yourself. Think of your family. Think of your children. "Man shall not live by bread alone, but by every word that proceedeth out of the mouth of God." I want to tell you, man shall not only "not live by bread alone," he can't even live by bread principally according to the scriptures. He isn't saying man shall not live by bread, He is just simply saying, "Man shall not live by bread alone."

What we are concerned with, tonight, is attitude. What was the rich man's attitude toward life? What did he equate with really living? "I will say to my soul, Soul, thou hast much goods laid up for many years; take thine ease, eat, drink and be merry." That's living! What does the world say, tonight? "Brother, you had better take care of number one, and you had better get together all you can. You get all the gusto you can get because you don't go this way but once." Isn't that what it's saying? Two thousand years ago this fool equated what he possessed with happiness. They are not the same. They are not the same at all. "Eat, drink and be merry!" This is the old Epicurean philosophy, and it's very much with us tonight.

Paul says in Philippians 1:21, "For me to live is Christ, and to die is gain." If you will pardon this personal word, one time I was privileged to take a few voice lessons from an old professor at Indiana University. I remember going up there at night for lessons after he had taught music all day long. That night he would take us in and would try to teach us music and voice. He just simply loved music. His world was music. He would teach and teach and work and would always go over the time allotted. And I want you to know, there were several occasions in which he followed us down the stairs and out onto the walk, and I remember sitting in the car and him standing beside the car door still talking music. He wouldn't have known a cow if he had seen one, but he knew music. For him to live was music! And I thought of Paul. If indeed, tonight, we could get some people this concerned about Christ. Paul said, "For me to live is Christ." If you live anything, what do you do? You think it, you talk it! As we sometimes say down in Texas, "You live and breathe it." When Paul says, "For me to live is Christ," he is saying, I think Christ, talk Christ, practice Christ. No wonder Paul says in Galatians 2:20, and it's one of my favorite passages of scripture, "I am crucified with Christ: nevertheless I live." Listen to him! Are you dead, Paul? No, he says, "I live!" "Nevertheless I live; yet not I, but Christ liveth in me: and the life which I now live in the flesh I live by the faith of the Son of God, who loved me, and gave himself for me." What a beautiful, beautiful thing. Listen to him! "The life which I now live." We are so concerned sometimes about the life we HAVE lived. What He wants to know is: What are you doing TONIGHT? Where are you going TONIGHT? How are you going to live TONIGHT—from now on? "The life which I NOW live." This is the thing with which you should be so concerned tonight. What is life going to mean to me from this time on? For me to live is what?

Remember: "He died for all, that they which live should not henceforth live unto themselves, but unto him" (2 Corinthians 5:15). He loved us, and He gave Himself for us. How beautiful that passage really is. I am a fool if I do not recognize the brevity of life. I am! People, I must recognize the fact that this life is short, as Job said so long ago, "Man that is born of woman is of few days" (Job 14:1). Did you ever notice that passage? You might say to Job, "Who is not born of a woman?" That is not what he is talking about. He said, "Man that is born of woman is of few days." He is discussing mortality. Mortal man, he insists, is simply of few days.

The rich man stood there that morning, after he had solved his problem, and said, "Many years"—when in actuality, he was leaving that night. What a difference! "Many years," but God said, "This night thy soul shall be required of thee." You see, death is not coming for YOURS. Death is coming for YOU. If indeed, tonight, death were coming for yours, you could say, "Death, here; I will give you half of all I have. Take it and be gone." But death is not coming for YOURS—for your THINGS—it's coming for YOU.

And so our Lord is saying we must get this matter in proper perspective before death comes. When I think about this fact, I think about a thing that really made an impression on me. I was down in South Texas preaching, and I visited in a home and met a young man in whom I saw possibilities of a preacher of the gospel. I am sure you do not know that young man; not many people did. But he had possibilities. As I talked with him and as he became a Christian, he began to work in the congregation, I began to write him and show him how to give lessons, to teach, to sing; he was one of our most promising prospects for leadership in that congregation. He could preach the gospel for Christ.

Later, I went back to that place, and he wasn't there. He had gotten a job in a town quite some distance from there, making more money than he'd ever made. I can understand why that was a temptation to him. I really do. The next time I saw him, he had more things than he ever had in his life. But he was out of duty, with the wrong group, with the wrong strata of society, feeling that to stay in that position, it would require these things of him; these were things he simply couldn't turn down. But I thought, we'll regain him. We'll get him back. I want you to know, one of the most difficult things I ever did was to preach that young man's funeral. A young man—gone! Lost! It was so sad! He couldn't get this matter in perspective. The lure of tearing down barns and building greater barns was just simply so great he couldn't get it all together. "It is appointed unto men once to die," the scripture states, "but after this the judgment" (Hebrews 9:27). We've got to face up to these things. We simply must.

Tonight, do you realize that the Lord wants you to die so that you can live. He wants you to become "dead to sins" that you might "live unto righteousness" (1 Peter 2:24). Are you here, tonight, and you are not a Christian? We would implore you to become a Christian, to believe the Gospel of Jesus Christ, to repent of your sins as our Lord states in so many places. He wants you, tonight, before people, before witnesses, to confess His lovely name. He wants YOU, tonight. He wants YOU to be immersed in His name for the remission of your sins. He wants you to become a Christian now. He wants you to die to sin that you may truly live unto God.

I wonder, tonight, if we realize that we ought not to be dying to live like the world, but we ought to be living to die. I am reminded of something I read some years ago. A preacher said he was knocking on doors out in California, and he came up to a house and saw an elderly lady rocking on the front porch. He said, "Ma'am, how are you today?" And she said, "Fine. I am living to die." What a new approach in a world that is dying to live. Friend, if you can make this world think that they can eat and drink and be merry and if you can make them think that they can take their ease, you can make a million. What was wrong with her that she said, "I'm living to die"? She was a Christian. That's a different perspective. And this is exactly what we ought to be. If you're not prepared to die, our Lord is saying in this parable that you are not prepared to live. If you are not ready to die, you are not really ready to live.

What if God were to say to you, "This night thy soul shall be required of thee." Oh, but you don't think He will; and I am just that much of a human, too. I really don't plan to leave this world tonight. I'll tell you frankly, I just am that human. But I at least ought to understand the possibility.

What if God said to us, "Tonight!"—while we are saying, "I have a lot of things planned for tomorrow and the next day and next year and I have some goals set for many years from now." But that may not be what God has in mind. He may be planning for you to leave tonight. Is God in your plans? You're in His, and He wants you to come with Him. Think about all this while we stand and sing.

Sermon Five

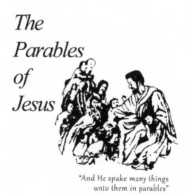

The Parables of Jesus

"And He spake many things
unto them in parables"

Matthew 13:1-3 and verses 24-30

"The same day went Jesus out of the house, and sat by the sea side. And great multitudes were gathered together unto him, so that he went into a ship, and sat; and the whole multitude stood on the shore. And he spake many things unto them in parables, saying ... The kingdom of heaven is likened unto a man which sowed good seed in his field. But while men slept, his enemy came and sowed tares among the wheat, and went his way. But when the blade was sprung up, and brought forth fruit, then appeared the tares also. So the servants of the householder came and said unto him, Sir, didst not thou sow good see in thy field? From whence then hath it tares? He said unto them, An enemy hath done this. The servants said unto him, Wilt thou then that we go and gather them up? But he said, Nay; lest while ye gather up the tares, ye root up also the wheat with them. Let both grow together until the harvest; and in the time of harvest I will say to the reapers, Gather ye together first the tares, and bind them in bundles to burn them: but gather the wheat into my barn."

5. The Problem of Evil

Jesus says, "I, if I be lifted up from the earth, will draw all men unto me." We believe the world, to a large measure, is still waiting for the sun to rise. Malachi said that unto them that fear Him "shall the Sun of righteousness arise with healing in his wings." Jesus is saying to us, "I, if I be lifted up from the earth, will draw all men unto me." We are grateful tonight for the privilege that is ours to have a small part in attempting to lift up the Lord; and we are doing so not only by speaking of Him and by singing as we have done this evening and by our praying, but we shall attempt to do it by reiterating, or by calling to mind, one of the sermons He preached a long, long time ago.

We come tonight to sit at the feet of the Master Teacher. I have long felt that if a person wants to learn how to preach the gospel, one of the best things he could ever do is to sit at the feet of the greatest Teacher who ever lived and that's the Lord Jesus Christ. We learned last evening, as our Lord stated, that there is one "greater than Solomon." Our Lord is more than all and greater than all. And we have the privilege of sitting at His feet and listening to His divine Word.

So many times our Lord used various word pictures. He used parables. He used many things to try to reach into the hearts of His people and to make them see the many-sided duties and glories of His great Kingdom. As someone has so well said, the Lord made it all come down in the reach of humble doers. It's not something that was for the elite or for the select few here and there but something for the common masses. And one thing I appreciate about the sayings and the teachings in the parables of Jesus is that He says it just as it is. And if we will just put it out as He says it, I think we will see that. For instance, the Lord never did say that we should beware of ostentatiousness in religion. What He did say was, Don't blow your horn when you are doing your giving. And I think this point comes through extremely well to us tonight.

Often times the Lord laid truth along side truth. He said, on the basis of some things you already understand, I want you to understand these great spiritual truths. I think it is evident that if our Lord had not done so with many of these things, we never would have understood some truths.

What I like about the parables of Jesus, as I have been saying night after night, is that the Lord starts to relate a story, and it's something that they know is true because it is a part of their every day living. And all of a sudden, in the midst of that story, even unsuspecting to them, the truth just leaps out; and they know that it applies to them. Even though they weren't expecting it, that truth was very much there.

This evening we invite your attention to this particular parable. And I simply would choose to call it, if we would want to call it anything other than The Parable of the Tares or The Parable of the Wheat and the Tares, The Problem of Evil. There is not one in this building who is not confronted with the problem of evil. There is not one outside this building who is not confronted with the problem of evil. Men have always wrestled with this problem. And you are looking at one tonight who wrestles with the problem. I think it is so appropriate that we sit and listen to One explain it to us. He gives the solution. He gives the answer to the problem of evil.

Why Does God Let it Happen?

Some years ago it was my task, as it has been on several occasions, to take a tragic story to a lady, to a family. And I shall not forget that day. It was not a pleasant thing at all. Two loved ones had been lost, and it was my task to talk to the family. When I related that message as kindly as I knew how, almost as if it were a spontaneous thing, out came the words, "Why does God let it happen?" Well, I think we are not looking at questions of doubt. What we are looking at are questions of faith. I want us to see that it's exactly that. The same was true on this occasion as these men come to this householder and say, "Sir, didst not thou sow good seed in thy field? from whence then hath it tares?"

We sometimes sing the song, "This is our Father's world, I rest me in the thought," and we go on with those beautiful words while all the time we know there are occasions on which we raise the question—Is this really the Father's world? Have any tares ever escaped the hands of God? Is it just possible that somewhere back there a tare escaped the hands of God, and that that thing has grown and grown until it has filled the entire world? If it is not true, then why all this violence and lust and disease and wretchedness and folly and toil and anguish? Everywhere you go, the world is filled with that kind of thing. And if this is the Father's world, why do these things exist?

Well, I'll tell you tonight, there is no easy answer. In fact, I would propose to you that the only answer is given to us by our Lord and by this Book; and the best way I have ever found to explain it is through this particular lesson that we have before us.

Our Lord proceeds as He has every time. He simply says I want to talk to you; I want to give you a true story. And it was something that was a part of their everyday living. He tells about a Galilean farmer who has secured a field and has fenced it, to use an Old Testament expression. He has fenced and he has plowed and he has thrown out the stones and he now has his place ready for the seed.

One day he finally has everything prepared; and as we learned in the lesson the first night, that is so necessary. Everything is now prepared. One day he goes out and commits the seed to the ground; and if there is ever a time when one must feel akin to God or at least in business with God, it is bound to be when he lays the seed inside the furrow and covers it over with soil, realizing he has done all that he can do and that it is only through God's great plan of things that that tiny seed would ever spring up.

He tells about a man who plants the seed and goes home that night as Solomon said to sleep the sleep that is sweet—"the sleep of a labouring man." And one thinks what a beautiful story. A man plants, he sows, he goes home, and he sleeps and this is good. But there is something that is not good. Our Lord says that that night somebody didn't sleep. That night someone, under cover of darkness, went out into that man's field and took some noxious seed, the weed seed or tares, and he just simply broadcast them throughout all that prepared field.

I was reading just recently, trying to get a little more information on these things, that this situation still occurs in some of the oriental countries. Now hopefully it does not occur in this country. Personally, I would think, coming from an agrarian background, that's about one of the worst things you could ever do to a farmer—to sow that field full of tares.

We have already learned in The Parable of the Sower, and we have learned by human experience, that you don't just go out and say, "Well, you know it will all come up and all I have to do is plow it down and we'll start over." That's not true. You will wrestle with the result of that seed for many years. Some of it will stay there through all kinds of weather, and eventually it will be coming up.

Our Lord is telling us that we are discussing the Kingdom. We are not just talking about a field. We are not just simply discussing sowing seed in somebody's field. He says I want you to know we are discussing the great Kingdom of God; the fact that He uses the word kingdom shows us that He is accommodating divine language to the human. We understand the framework of a king, of a kingdom, of territory and subjects, of law and all of that.

I want you to notice that our Lord gives us an authentic interpretation. I am glad He did. On The Parable of the Sower, and on this particular parable, our Lord does not leave the interpretation to us. He says I want to tell you what I am talking about; and when we deal with the problem of evil, I think it is so vital to adhere strictly to what He says the interpretation is.

The Sower

First of all, He says, "He that soweth the good seed is the Son of man." I want you to listen to that expression. He tells us that the one who sows is the Son of man. I want you to think about this. Here is a favorite expression of the Lord. While He was here in His earthly ministry, Jesus used this expression when referring to Himself more than any other expression.

He said this is who I am. I am the Son of man. So He is saying, I want to identify with YOU in this great sowing of the seed and in this great Kingdom, He said I am the Son of man, I am the Sower. When we get involved in this situation, we are in some very fine company because Jesus said He is that individual. In Acts 7:56, Stephen, as he looked up into the heavens, saw "the Son of man standing on the right hand of God." Indeed it was our Lord's favorite expression.

One of the greatest thoughts one could have is that God the Son one time came to live among men. One of the greatest compliments that was ever paid to this human race is that at one time God came to live among men in the person of His Son, Jesus Christ. "In the beginning," John said—and this is bound to be one of the most beautiful passages in the Bible— "In the beginning was the Word, and the Word was with God, and the Word was God ... And the Word became flesh, and dwelt among us." As the only begotten of the Father, Jesus came to this world. He lived on earth. But let me tell you something greater, if there is something greater: it is the fact that there is at this moment a man in Heaven. And the reason I know is that in 1 Timothy 2:5, Paul says, "For there is one God, and one mediator between God and men, the MAN Christ Jesus." There is one in Heaven, and our whole salvation rests upon the fact that there is a man in Heaven tonight. Not just a man, but He is the Son of man. He wants us to understand—that here is the only perfect flower that ever unfolded out of the stalk of humanity. Not one of us is willing to ask what Jesus did. He just threw out the question, "Which of you convinceth me of sin?" I promise you, you won't hear that from any of us. But Jesus not only could put it out, He did, and no man could answer. He was the Son of God, yet He called Himself the Son of man.

The Seed

Let us go on. Our Lord wants us to understand that the seed—and I think this bears some careful thinking—are the children of the Righteous One. Now if you remember, last Monday evening we began with The Parable of the Sower. What did He say the seed was? The seed was the Word of God. So why does He switch in this parable? This evening He is saying to us the seed are the children of the Righteous One. I don't think we have a contradiction. I think we have an extension. We have the outgrowth of the seed in the lives of men. And our Lord is saying to us that people ought not to be able to think of us separate and apart from the Word of God. So it's growing and it's living within us, the Lord's people. There is no disagreement in that particular thing. James 1:18 reads, "Of his own will begat he us with the word of truth." In 1 Peter 1:22-23, "Seeing ye have purified your souls in obeying the truth: see that ye love one another with a pure heart fervently. Being born again not of corruptible seed, but of incorruptible by the word of God, which liveth and abideth forever."

The Field

The Lord says next that this man's field, in which the seed has been sown, is the world. "THE ... FIELD ... IS ... THE ... WORLD." Major religious divisions have ensued over the meanings of those five words. It seems pretty unseemly to me that that's the case; but if history be true, it's a fact. Some say the field is the church, or the church is the world and all kind of things, but Jesus just says, "The field is the world." And that's the only thing that will fit because you will run into some real problems before you get through with the parable if you try anything else. "The field is the world."

Do you remember what Jesus states in Matthew 28:18-19? He says, "All power is given unto me in heaven and in earth. Go ye therefore, and teach all nations." Mark 16:15-16 reads, "Go ye into all the world, and preach the gospel to every creature. He that believeth and is baptized shall be saved; but he that believeth not shall be damned." In Luke 14:46-47, he gives the account of the Great Commission, "Thus it behooved Christ to suffer, and to rise from the dead the third day; and that repentance and remission of sins should be preached in his name among all nations." What's He saying? "The field is the world." What did He say in The Parable of the Sower? He said the field is the heart of men. But there is no problem there. This is what He is saying. You go teach the gospel, You sow the seed in the field. The field is the hearts of men. Where are men? Throughout the world.

I have often thought about this world that our Lord is here discussing. The field is soil, and we are dealing with the world. Sometimes we become disturbed about the fact that we have not been into ALL the world, and we ought to be disturbed. I am not putting down anybody going anywhere, but there's a lot of world right here. There is an awful lot of world in Wichita, Kansas. There is an awful lot of world right around us because every place you find a human heart you have found a field, you have found the world. If you never move out of Wichita, Kansas, in your life, there is an awful lot of field— there are many people—right here We should be dropping the seed of the Kingdom, the Word of God, in the hearts of those individuals.

The Enemy

Our Lord next tells us that the servants came back into the house. I try to visualize this scene. One day they were out there working among the plants—and I guess these men were pretty experienced—and they looked at this field and realized something was wrong. There was a problem. Something didn't look right.

They came back in to the master of the house and said, "Sir, didst not thou sow good seed in thy field? from whence then hath it tares?" Please notice, the fact that he states there are good seed immediately implies there are such things as bad seed. Also note, if good seed is sown, the tares are not to be expected. They do not go together. Immediately the Lord says, "An enemy hath done this."

I like the way Jesus puts it—the Bible just puts it as it is. What does He say? "An enemy hath done this." He does not say this is a product of somebody's unfortunate environmental circumstance. He doesn't say these poor fellows are suffering from some kind of a temporary stumbling in the upward progress of men. What does He say? "An enemy hath done this." And He calls him "the devil."

The Bible acknowledges the presence of an evil personality in the world, and there is no way you can get away from that. The Bible insists there is one who is set for our destruction. In Ephesians 2:2, Paul calls him "the prince of the power of the air, the spirit that now worketh in the children of disobedience." Now he is here. Two thousand years ago Jesus said, "An enemy hath done this."

Please notice his sphere of activity. The devil works in a field that is not his. You see, he wasn't off in some remote corner of the world. He wasn't working where no one had done anything. He was working where somebody had secured and worked and toiled and prepared. It is there the devil works. You see, he already has the rest and so he wants to deceive, if possible, the very elect of God. This is what he is concerned with. When you think about this individual or this evil personality who is out there working and planting seed, he is planting, of course, the noxious seed or as one translation puts it—just a weed. And that's what it really is. Though it appears to be just like the wheat, it really isn't. Satan, of course, is operating a counterfeit system.

I am persuaded in a careful study of what our Lord is saying and what we now see in the world, that there is a Mastermind, and the Bible calls him that—a Mastermind who is so well schooled in the art of human nature that he can present whatever you want. And if indeed it is not here, he will get it for you. His plan is opposition, by imitation. That's the way he works. He does not come with some radically different idea. I mean he doesn't come out and sow something that immediately appears to be no good. It is not until these things begin to move toward fruition that they even become aware there's a problem.

So what is He saying to us? He is saying that this field has been sown with that which is not good. And He wants us to understand that when we look at seed, we may not necessarily know this is good or this is bad. We must do as He said in 1 John 4, "Beloved believe not every spirit, but try the spirits whether they are of God: because many false prophets are gone out into the world." Jesus says there are those who will say, "Lord, Lord," but they "do not the things which I say."

Now notice this, too, that the field is not of itself bad. Whatever came up in the field came up as a result of sowing in that field. What I'm saying, tonight, is this: that men are not inherently evil. That field was clean. And it produced only what was sown IN that field. If you sow good seed, you reap good things. If you sow bad seed, He insists, you reap bad things.

Jesus is so emphatic about the enemy. Let's notice some things that He calls him. He says, "An enemy hath done this," and He calls him "THE ... WICKED ... ONE." We must see Satan for what he is. I rest you assured that we do not see him out here in this world as he really is. The Bible calls him a serpent. The Bible calls him a devil. The Bible calls him a slanderer of God, and we should see him as he is. He is REAL tonight. I don't know really how to put that so that it lives to us. But Satan is very real. He is very much present. An enemy—active hostility toward God and everything that is good. The more that is done, the more he is going to be revealed.

You will notice he doesn't do much in this patch until somebody else begins to do something. Until somebody begins to sow the seed of the Kingdom, he has no problem anyway. So unless we are sowing the seed of the Kingdom in various parts of the world, Satan won't worry about it. We must not assume that just because there is some part of the world over there where there happens to be some people, the Lord will take care of them somehow. We have to sow seed. The point is, our Lord is saying that when we get busy, Satan gets busy.

Let me promise you tonight, that if you decide as an individual that you are going to really do something for God—you would like to be a Christian, you would like to begin to serve the Lord—I will promise you that you are going to get some opposition. If indeed this congregation decides that it wants to really do something for God and you are going to really function for Him, let me promise you—you are going to have some problems. And it shouldn't come as any shock to you. Satan labors in a field that is not his. Let me put it this way, as the sunshine gets brighter, I promise you the shadows are going to get deeper. And this is what He is saying—Satan begins to operate when we begin to work.

What are we looking at? We are looking at a struggle, we are looking at a battle between right and wrong, between our God and Satan, between all good and no good, between light and darkness. And you know what is great? You and I are in the middle of it. We are privileged to be in this great drama of human kind. And we are in a position just exactly as man was so long ago in the Garden of Eden. We have the capabilities of serving God. We have the capabilities of sinning, but there is no reason that we should do so. God has eliminated the reasons that we should sin or that we should be under the captive power of sin. So we have some marvelous things going for us tonight. The victory will be a moral triumph.

Now notice, He says that after the enemy had sowed the seed, the enemy "went his way." I have often thought about that expression. How innocent Satan seems. He goes out and sows the noxious seed and walks off. The job's done. He doesn't need to do any more until it comes up. His work's the same way, you see. And the scripture says, "When the blade was sprung up, and it brought forth fruit, THEN appeared the tares also." Please notice, He does not say when the little blade came up, they knew it was a tare. No! And when the stalk began to grow, they still didn't know it was a tare; but when it began to bear fruit, then they understood. Our Lord says, "By their fruits you shall know them." Our Lord does not say we are known by the way we look. He doesn't say "by the leaf," "by the branch," but "by their FRUITS you shall know them." It is true with evil, also. I think the main thing our Lord is saying is that the beginning of evil is just barely discernible.

James says in James 1:15, "When lust hath conceived, it bringeth forth sin." When this child is conceived, then the child of sin is born and "when ... it ... is ... finished." Please notice, sin is a progressive thing. I will amplify this in another lesson later. Sin is progressive. It's like Paul says in 2

Thessalonians 2:7, "The mystery of iniquity doth already work." As leaven, it is working. And so he is saying, "When lust hath conceived" ... not before ... but "when lust hath conceived, it bringeth forth sin; and sin, when it is finished, bringeth forth death."

One of the greatest needs is simply to have men within our congregations and men who are teachers of His Word, who can discern evil before it's full grown. So many times we are simply reacting to situations. We are not acting; we are reacting. Our Lord is saying that evil is not bad looking when it is little.

You know, I think a baby ANYTHING looks pretty good. Now my wife doesn't agree with that, but I'll tell you, a baby frog is not bad looking ... just any little tiny thing looks pretty good. In fact, I suppose some of us looked pretty good when we were very small, but things have a way of changing as we grow and as we get older. And the Bible is saying that sin is born; and he says when it is little, it doesn't look too bad. That's the reason we so often hear, "I don't see any problem with that." We need somebody who can see the end result of that thing. We need to be able to say—this is the way it will look ten years from now, fifteen years from now, twenty years from now. We need to ask how is that thing going to look?

So our Lord is saying, "When the blade was sprung up, and brought forth fruit, then appeared the tares also." So it's a lesson in contrast. Our Lord is saying that in this field we have wheat and we have tares. And He is saying all of us are one or the other. Now I know we are living in times where even sometimes our own brethren are talking about potential Christians. We talk about half-Christians. We talk about good Christians. But Jesus said two thousand years ago that all men are either wheat or they are tares. And as we occupy this room tonight and as I occupy this place, at this moment we are either wheat or we are tares—one or the other. Please let us remember that in all of our dealings with the Holy Scriptures. It is so vital that we do so.

Rooting Out the Tares

Now the servants of this householder came to the man and said, "Sir, didst not thou sow good seed in thy field?" What happened in this situation? Now I want you to notice what they proposed. Remember the servants said, "Wilt thou then that we go and gather them up?" Now they had a solution—Sir, we know what to do; we'll go out in that field, and we'll put these things out. We'll get rid of these tares for you, and we are going to produce a harvest because we are your servants and we want to take care of this. What are they proposing? They are proposing violence. We're going to jerk them out! And we are going to get rid of them. But immediately the Lord said, "No!"

The spirit of these individuals so reminds us of the times in which we live. Today we may look at this and we say, "They ought to have known better than that!" But I'll tell you, there are times when we are tempted to root out the tares even today. I still see some situations, and you still see some things, that are repulsive. There are some things that are repugnant. The Bible calls them abominable situations, and we think those things need to go from the world in which we live.

It reminds me of Luke 9. You remember the time when our Lord had spent the day teaching. He was simply worn out, and it was time to rest. James and John went down into a village of the Samaritans; it was probably a problem for them, but they went. It wasn't long though until they came stomping back—no wonder He called them the sons of thunder—they came back out of that village and said, "Lord, wilt thou that we command fire to come down from heaven, and consume them?" That's an amazing thing! You know why? The Samaritans didn't want Jesus to spend the night down there, and James and John didn't appreciate it a little bit. They said the thing to do with tares like that, Lord, is to root them out. Let's simply annihilate them. But Jesus "rebuked them, and said, Ye know not what manner of spirit ye are of." He said, "The Son of man is not come to destroy men's lives, but to save them." I still feel a little of the spirit of James and John when I sometimes see some of the situations that exist in the world in which we live. When I see parents—and I've seen this all over the country—when I see parents who have worked to teach their kids and have tried to educate them and have tried to teach them to be honest and to be decent and to be good, and then down the way someone is waiting to push across a polished bar a drink to that young man or young lady—caring less about his soul, but simply about what he can get out of him. Or when you see the person standing over on the periphery of the school ground pushing his dope to our young people; or you read about children being forced into prostitution; or the times in which we live in which we vote on whether we will accept homosexuality or not. These are strange days. These are times in which we, like these people of old say, Lord, there are some things that need to be gathered out. Why, if indeed this is your world, Father, why are things like these going on?

It's not just in the realm of morals that that occurs either. People are teaching some things that are amazing. I sat in a class of sixty young men some years ago—sixty young men who were going out to become the preachers of a leading denomination. I was sitting there to receive what benefit I could from what was being said. But I couldn't believe that man who stood there and said the Red Sea was not a Sea. This was not in some far out college somewhere. This was in what was supposedly a southern orthodox institution. The Red Sea is not a Sea—indeed the walls did not pile up on either side, and they didn't go through on dry ground, and they weren't "baptized unto Moses in the cloud and in the sea"! It was just a marshy place, and they just walked over. He didn't bother to explain how the Egyptians were drowned in that place! But these are the things these people were being taught. The walls of Jericho—never were! That reminds me of a painting I saw some time ago by Bruegel. Some of you may have seen it. He shows the picture of some poor French peasants who were walking along looking straight ahead through unseeing eyes— they were blind. They were following a man—and this is what makes it so pathetic—the man they were following was blind, too ... and they were all headed for a ditch. He was illustrating what Jesus says, "if the blind lead the blind, both shall fall into the ditch." We are living in the times of the blind leading the blind. And our Lord wants us to understand these things.

Talk about something current, not long ago—in fact, during the month of May—the issue came up again as to whether horse racing and pari-mutuel betting would be accepted in the state of Texas. They never stop trying. An individual came on television—on national television, and I couldn't believe this—he stood there, he was a preacher from Lexington, Kentucky. He said the Bible sustains horse racing. And I thought, what in the world would the Bible say about horse racing? I listened. He said, "The Bible says, 'Let us run with patience the race that is set before us.'" I couldn't believe that! These are the times in which we live. Blind leaders of the blind! And I can understand why these individuals so long ago would simply say, "Lord, wilt thou then that we gather them out." But now the amazing thing is this. He just puts it all down with one statement. "Let both grow together until the harvest,"

What is our Lord saying? Our Lord is saying that we will not use force. If we ever gain a victory in the realm of religion, it will be a moral victory. It will not be a matter of force. I think the most unholy things I've ever heard about were the Holy Crusades. I remember in school when I was first introduced to the Holy Crusades, I used to wonder, "What's holy about the crusades?" Nothing! You hear about the Christians fighting so and so—it wasn't the Christians I promise you.

We cannot use force. Let me put it this way: you can destroy the seed, but once it becomes a tare, He said let it alone. He is saying you can destroy the germ; but once an individual contracts the germ, you can't destroy the person to get rid of the germ. And so our Lord is saying that here is an individual, let him alone. The law of the Master, "Let both grow together until the harvest."

Let me give you another reason—our own unworthiness. If we were to proceed to root out all the tares, where would we start? Ah! I know where to start! Somewhere across the ocean. There are still people who walk down to the Ganges River and throw their first born to the crocodiles to appease the anger of an idol god, and we say that kind of thing has to be stopped. That just can't go on! And let us start with Buddhism and Shintoism and the Islamics. Let's start with all such. But you don't have to go over there. If we want to talk about simply rooting out all tares, we don't have to walk out the door tonight. You see, if we are going to do away with all of it, and all the Jonah's shall be cast overboard, we can start here tonight and cast the first stone. But I think one of the best reasons is this—tares can become wheat. Now biologically that isn't possible, so you say you have a flaw in this matter. No! That's not true out there in the world, but in here tonight, that's true. Why? Because we are not trying to reform men, we are not just trying to put people in a good environment—that alone doesn't change people. We are talking, tonight, about rebirth—being born again! So tares can become wheat.

If I had been living in the days of the early church, I could have gotten some of the brethren together and said, "Look, brethren, we need to root out some tares. We have got some poor situations here. I'll tell you who we are going to start with. We need to dispense with Saul of Tarsus. Get rid of Saul of Tarsus." But what a mistake that would have been! That tare became wheat! He became THE apostle. He became one of the greatest preachers who ever walked the face of the earth. What a mistake it would have been! Who knows when an individual has crossed the line and cannot be recalled: only the Master knows. And we are the servants, so He is saying please stay out of my field. In fact, He gives His reason. He says, "Lest while ye gather up the tares, ye root up also the wheat." You may destroy some of the existing wheat.

Let Both Grow Together Until the Harvest

The Lord has a real concern for His people. I think at least we ought to get that point tonight. He is saying He doesn't want his people destroyed. He doesn't want his people pulled up; He doesn't want his people torn up with storms of doubt. He who notes the fall of the sparrow is so much concerned about us. He loves you, and He says—Please don't walk over my people; please don't pull my people up. Leave them alone; I want them to grow. The Lord is not saying we are not going to pluck them. But He is saying that we are dealing with a time factor. We are going to let them both grow together, not forever, but we are going to "let both grow together UNTIL THE HARVEST." I want to propose to you that that is one of the greatest statements in all the Bible. I want you to listen to it. The law of the Master, "Let both" ... please notice how many there are ... "Let both grow together until the harvest." That is a statement of tremendous importance! Our Lord is saying that evil and good will exist, not in the church, but in the world: "The field is the world." He says, "Let both grow together."

There is going to be a constant unfolding of good, a constant unfolding of evil. There is a time when a plant first comes into this world, and that little plant is struggling to live. It feeds off of itself until it can put down roots, and it lives; and for a long time it's struggling to put out first the blade and then the stalk. But when it comes toward fruition, something occurs within that plant as designed and programmed by the infinite mind of God. It begins to throw all of its strength toward the seed. Everything is moving to strengthen the seed. Do you hear what He is saying? He is saying that this world is going to get better and better, and worse and worse. And that's not a contradiction. He is simply saying that until the end, there will be righteousness; and He said that righteousness is going to grow, and it's going to unfold until it comes to fruition. When our Lord comes, "Will he find faith on earth"? Yes, He will! But He also says that evil is going to be here and, brother, it's going to grow, and it's going to unfold, and it's going to move toward fruition. Good and evil are going to stand face to face until one is ripe for salvation, and the other is ripe for destruction.

I would like to tell you that things are going to get better and better—and they are in that sense. But I am here to tell you that we need not expect the world and evil to get any better. I am telling you, tonight, Jesus is saying it's going to get worse. And it is going to get progressively worse until the harvest. Now we don't have to be a prophet to understand that.

Regardless of what else you want to know about the great Revelation story or what Daniel had to say about some things, I can tell you, it won't contradict what He is saying here. We said in the first lesson that we would be proceeding from the simple to the complex and that truth always harmonizes with truth.

Our world will get better and better and worse and worse. I am not saying they are going to get more and more. I am not saying, this evening, that some day we can go out there and say, "What a tremendous wheat field," and well look in there and find a few tares. I am not saying there will be more and more Christians. It may well be a great field of tares, and you have to look for some wheat; but I'll tell you they are there, and they are going to be there.

We are going to have to get stronger; we are going to have to get better. We are going to have to expect more than we have ever expected of ourselves as the Lord's people. We've got to bring the best that we have to give. We have got to bring up the best talents that we can muster—better than we have ever known. He said THIS is what's going to occur.

Some have used this passage to prove that the church can have no discipline because they both grow together. No! Not in the church! He says, "The field is the world." This does not negate 1 Corinthians 5 and other passages where the Bible teaches the church to deal with problems in its midst; it does not offset the fact that the reputation and the strength and the power of the church and its integrity should be maintained. He is simply saying—in the world these things will be.

Then the Lord says, as we mentioned earlier, it's just a matter of time: "In the time of harvest I" ... I like that. He is still on the throne tonight! Daniel said a long time ago that the great Ancient of Days "removeth kings, and setteth up kings" and that He rules in the kingdoms of men. I still believe that. He's still in control! "In the time of the harvest, I will say to the reapers" ... the reapers, of course, are the angels. The separation is inevitable. Acts 17:31 says, "Because he hath appointed A DAY, in which he will judge the world in righteousness by that man whom he hath ordained; whereof he hath given assurance unto all men, in that he hath raised him from the dead." In Matthew 25, Jesus says, "When the Son of man shall come in his glory ... then shall HE set upon the throne of his glory: and before HIM shall be gathered all nations: and HE shall separate them one from another, as a shepherd divideth his sheep from the goats." The separation is inevitable. The tares must be separated from the wheat.

Burning the Tares

Then the Lord commands, "Gather ye together first the tares, and bind them in bundles to burn them." Notice there is no room here for discussing two separate resurrections and discussing a thousand years reign and all the kind of things we sometimes hear. He is simply saying we come to the end—it's harvest time. And what does He say? "Gather ye together first the tares." And do what? "Burn them."

Seeds can undergo some extremely adverse conditions and still live, still maintain their germinating powers. But once a seed is burned, it's all over! And so Jesus is saying that when we come to this time, "death and hell shall be cast into the lake of fire," and in all these expressions, He simply is saying that there is coming a day in which all the evil shall be removed, but it will be the harvest time—it will be the end of the world, and then He says you will "gather out of my kingdom all things that offend."—those things that entangle others and those things that cause men to fall.

If you will notice in the marginal reading of your Bible, He is going to gather out all the "scandals" and the scoundrels. So He evidently has some, and He is saying He is going to "gather out" all these, too. And He says they shall be "burned in the fire." Terrible doom; terrible destruction.

My people, this is the Bible's constant picture, parable or no; this is the thing He uses all the way to indicate the finality of judgment. Burned in a "furnace of fire," call it what you want to call it; but it is so fearful, as pictured in the Holy Scripture, that it took Jesus Christ, no less than Jesus Christ, coming to this world and giving His life on the cross to make it possible that you might miss that place that's called Hell. And He goes on to say in this lesson that in this place is a "furnace of fire" where "there shall be wailing." That ought to say something to us. "Wailing" and "gnashing of teeth" indicate intolerable pain and unutterable woe.

Years ago I remember reading a little poem that I came across one night. One of the old time preachers, and I mean old time, way back yonder, was trying to describe for the people this very scene and this very thing. He went on to say something like this:

> Descending down into caves of hopeless depth, I saw most miserable beings walk, burning continually yet unconsumed, forever wasting yet enduring still. Some wandered lone in the desert flame and some encounter fiercely met with curses loud and blasphemies that made the cheek of darkness pale. And to their everlasting anguish still, the thunders from above, respondingly spoke these words which through the caverns of perdition forlornly echoing fell on every ear, 'You knew your duty, but you did it not.'

I'll never forget those words. He was describing intolerable pain and unutterable loss and unutterable woe.

Then Shall the Righteous Shine Forth

I like what He says next: "Then" ... after we have dispatched the evil that exists in the world ... . "Then shall the righteous shine forth." The light so long struggling finally, eventually will come to fullness. Here are the people of God! The Lord's people have been put down, they have been maligned, they have been nobodies for ages and ages, but He is telling them someday it's not going to be that way. Some day the righteous shall "shine forth" or as Malachi says when the Lord "makes up His jewels."

As fire is the element of Hell, so light will be the element of Heaven. And one more time we shall see, as He said so long ago, "the morning stars sang together, and all the sons of God shouted for joy." The sons of God will shine forth— redemption, eternal redemption. We will sing the song of Moses and the Lamb in the fullest sense that you can ever even think about.

I want to ask you tonight, are YOU in the Kingdom? What are we discussing? We are discussing the Kingdom of Heaven. The Lord's Kingdom. He says it is like this: it's like sowing seed, and it's like opening up your heart and letting it come inside. It's like believing the gospel; it's repenting of your sins;

it's confessing Christ; it's being immersed in His precious name for the remission of sins. It means obeying the Lord, letting Him add you to His church or adding you to His Kingdom. The question tonight: Are you in the Kingdom? Are you ready?

You know evil is here. I don't have to tell you that. And, people, if evil is here, sin is here. And if sin is here, transgression of law is here. And if transgression of law is here, law is here; and if that's here, God is here. The fact that evil exists in the world tonight must logically be moved all the way back to the fact, GOD IS—He lives tonight—and there is also Satan. There is an evil power. Are you a Christian? Surely we ought not listen to one of the great sermons of Jesus and then just dismiss these truths and walk out and forget them.

Our Lord taught these so that we would understand, so that we could be free from the things we have discussed. How are you classified tonight? Are you wheat or are you a tare? That's not pleasant, but it's a fact. And if you know, or if you even remotely think you are anything but wheat, a child of God, you ought to make that right with Him while we stand and while we sing.

Sermon Six

*The
Parables
of
Jesus*

"And He spake many things
unto them in parables"

Matthew 22:1-14

"And Jesus answered and spake unto them again by parables, and said, The kingdom of heaven is like unto a certain king, which made a marriage for his son, and sent forth his servants to call them that were bidden to the wedding: and they would not come. Again, he sent forth other servants, saying, Tell them which are bidden, Behold, I have prepared my dinner: my oxen and my fatlings are killed, and all things are ready: come unto the marriage. But they made light of it, and went their ways, one to his farm, another to his merchandise: and the remnant took his servants, and entreated them spitefully, and slew them. But when the king heard thereof, he was wroth: and he sent forth his armies, and destroyed those murderers, and burned up their city. Then saith he to his servants, The wedding is ready, but they which were bidden were not worthy. Go ye therefore into the highways, and as many as ye shall find, bid to the marriage. So those servants went out into the highways, and gathered together all as many as they found, both bad and good: and the wedding was furnished with guests. And when the king came in to see the guests, he saw there a man which had not on a wedding garment: and he saith unto him, Friend, how camest thou in hither not having a wedding garment? And he was speechless. Then said the king to the servants, Bind him hand and foot, and take him away, and cast him into outer darkness; there shall be weeping and gnashing of teeth. For many are called, but few are chosen."

6. Marriage of the King's Son

We welcome you to the assembly this evening and to another study of the Lord's Word. We believe we should come to this place determined that we will strip our souls of any semblance of pride or arrogance or selfishness—determined that we shall "be conformed," as Paul would say, "to the image of His Son" (Romans 8:29). Tonight we surely are people who realize that we live in a world where there are great problems. What we need in our world is not more problems: we need some answers. We believe there are many answers in this room if we understand what the Lord would have us to do and to be. So I hope we came here determined that we will prepare ourselves, that we will deny ourselves, that we will simply cast ourselves on the altar of service and sacrifice, determined that we are going to be what the Lord would have us to be.

This evening, as we come to this study on Matthew chapter twenty-two and to this another sermon of Jesus Christ, we are looking at the closing portion of the His earthly ministry—and this fact is of particular significance as we come to study the parables of Jesus. It is for this reason that you should expect to find in the teaching of our Lord—and especially in the things being said tonight—some things that are a little different; different, for instance, from what you would find in Luke 14, as He speaks another parable that is akin to this one. On this occasion our Lord is confronted by every enemy, every organized group that confronted Him while He lived in this world. I have gone through Matthew 21 and Matthew 22 and circled some of the passages that refer to the various individuals who are dealing with the Lord on this occasion. Some of those are the chief priests, the Pharisees, the

Herodians, the Sadducees, a lawyer, and so on. You will find all of them there. They're coming down to the last moments of His life, and they are determined they will dispense with Him.

It isn't often that one speaks to an audience composed entirely of those who are plotting to kill him. Now, I've spoken to a lot of audiences in my time. I've spoken to audiences that were large, and audiences that were small. There were audiences rural; there were audiences urban. I've spoken to audiences in which there was no one in the audience who agreed with me— not one soul—except my wife. And as I often jokingly say to her, I'm not sure before it was over whether she agreed or not. As I have spoken to those various groups, I never recall having spoken to an audience that was composed only of those determined to get rid of me. These people, on this occasion, were determined to drive the Christ all the way to the cross; and they were bringing everything they had to bear against Him. But even in the face of this situation, our Lord does not curse them. He does not even suggest that He can live without them, but He rather issues one last appeal to these individuals who are giving Him such a difficult time. That appeal is couched in these three things—He wants them to come, He wants them to see, and He wants them to live. And He sets forth a plan whereby this, of course, would be possible.

As we come to a study of the parables of our Lord—as I've repeatedly said throughout the course of this week—the Lord is taking one thing that we understand, at least to some degree, and putting along side it something that otherwise we would not understand. I think it's something like a parent experiences as his little child comes to him and says, "Daddy, what about this?" and he finds himself pretty hard pressed to explain. He takes this little lad upon his lap, begins to explain to him, and finds it extremely difficult to adapt the things that he knows to the language that the child understands. Now I'm sure there isn't anything difficult for God; but if there were, it was when He was trying to adapt the language of the Kingdom to people like you and me. That is what He is doing. One more time our Lord is saying, "The kingdom of heaven is like unto ... ." On this occasion, He wants us to understand that the Kingdom is like the marriage of a king's son; and I find this comparison extremely interesting and profitable.

The Kingdom Is Like a Wedding

I want you to notice that as He sets forth the main theme—the fullness of the mercy of God extended to man—He states that it's like a wedding. At least eight times—not in parables—but at least eight times in the Holy Scripture, the Lord refers to a wedding. And I like this comparison. He is not saying the Kingdom of Heaven is like a funeral; He doesn't say it is like a monastery. He says the Kingdom of Heaven is like a joyous, happy, bright occasion.

Sometimes we sing the song, "There is Joy, A Real Joy in Serving Jesus." I want to tell you tonight, if there is no real joy—if times like these are drudgery to us—there is something radically wrong! It ought to be a beautiful thing when we come together and privileged to sing and to pray and to study the Master's Word. Our Lord is saying we're considering something that's a time of joy, a time of feasting, a time of fellowship, a time of warmth.

Notice that it's like a king who "made a marriage for his son." I like the way He puts that. He "MADE A MARRIAGE for his son." And he sent out his servants at suppertime to say to those who were bidden, "Come; for ALL THINGS are now ready." Our Lord wants us to understand that not SOME things, but EVERYTHING is ready And, of course, we understand that "when the fullness of the time was come, God sent forth his Son, made of a woman, made under the law" (Galatians 4:4). At the perfect time in the history of humanity, our Lord came and made for the world a Great Feast.

Please notice that the "oxen" (not one, but the "oxen") and the "fatlings" (plural) have been made ready. This point tells me that God does things on a grand scale. Any time the Lord does anything, He does it on a grand scale. I think that we must not limit our God. He is saying that these things are here for our good. And as Paul would so often say, "My God is able!" He is exactly that! He's able, He's powerful, and He's saying that He has an infinite wealth to share and He wants to share it with you—with His people. He has everything ready, and He wants you to come. It's rich, it's full, it's satisfying. The Lord is saying, "Come!"

The Invitation

I want you to notice the invitation: "Come; for all things are now ready," and notice to WHOM. First of all, it isn't sent to everybody. First he said—and I'm putting Luke 14 with this passage—he said go out to "them that were bidden." I understand it was the oriental custom that one would be invited to a wedding or to a feast on a particular day; they did not specify the hour. Then a servant would be sent on that day at that hour, saying, "Come; for all things are now ready."

There were many through the years who should have known about the Great Feast. When you want to look forward to the coming of the Lord Jesus Christ, you think about the Law. "The law and the prophets were until John: since that time the kingdom of God is preached" (Luke 16:16). Here He is telling us there are people who should have known because the Jewish people had the prophets who were telling the story that someday Messiah would come: some day the Great Feast would be made known. He is saying, "Go say to them that WERE Bidden." So you see they knew about it. "Say to them that were bidden, Come; for all things are NOW READY."

Please notice that eventually he sends them "out into the highways and hedges," to "the poor, and the maimed, and the halt, and the blind." He eventually extends the invitation to everyone—that's mercy and that's grace. If you don't think it's a great thing, let me ask you this: How many suppers have you made lately, how many feasts have you made lately, and invited your enemies over? I must admit to you, I don't really remember any time that I made any suppers and invited my enemies over. Maybe that's what I ought to be doing, but I haven't done that! Have you? We like to invite people that we love, people that we like. We like to have these individuals in our presence. But here is the graciousness of our God: He extends the invitation to all human kind. Please remember that our Lord was standing preaching to people who were His avowed enemies; yet He was saying come, and see, and live.

Let's look farther. Let's take a look at the other side of God's mercy. The king sends out the invitation. He's generous, he's kind, he's gracious, he's hospitable. He does something that he didn't have to do; and he sends out the invitation. But may I point out that although he is all of the things we mentioned, he is also a king. And this doesn't happen to be just anybody's wedding. This just happens to be the wedding of HIS SON. And that makes it pretty important. He's not comparing the Kingdom of Heaven to MY wedding or YOUR wedding, however good they may have been. He wants us to know that He is discussing the wedding of a KING'S SON, and so the invitation that went out was not just an invitation like yours or mine: it was a real challenge. One doesn't treat lightly the invitation of the king when his son is being married.

You remember that the servants go out. I like to think about them as they left that day with the charge to go out and invite the people. They go out "into the streets and lanes of the city," and they're knocking on the doors, and they're out looking and talking to this one and that one, saying "Come in to the Great Feast." You know, they found some amazing things! They were treated violently in some places. There were some places where they were evilly entreated and were killed. Now some of them weren't—some of the people just simply made light of the invitation. You remember, they came back and explained that they had told these people, but they hadn't all come.

May I point out a difference between this parable and the one in Luke 14? It is the one we usually hear, probably more than this one. In Luke 14, you remember, they went out and one said, "I have bought a piece of ground, and I must needs go and see it: I pray thee have me excused." Yet another said, "I have bought five yoke of oxen, and I go to prove them: I pray thee have me excused." Yet another said, "I have married a wife, and therefore I cannot come." At least two of them in Luke 14 asked to be excused; but in this parable (Matthew 22) they don't ask to be excused. And this is why I'm saying we're looking at a great difference between what occurred in the early ministry of Jesus and what's occurring now in the later part. They, by this time, have come to hate Him. They have built to a fever pitch. By this time they have exhausted their catalog of depravity, and they don't even ask to be excused; those in Luke 14 did. It is not the same parable.

An Angry King

But notice, as they come back and the king hears about this, "he was wroth." He's angry; he doesn't like it because they have not accepted all that he has done for them. The servants didn't come back and say that these individuals COULD NOT come. They said they had extended the invitation, and they WOULD NOT come. I want to tell you, there is a difference when people "cannot come" and when people "will not come." Here is the determined will of man saying, "We don't want to come, and we aren't coming!" They don't say, "I pray thee have me excused." They just simply say they are not coming.

How would you feel if you made a feast, the kind of feast that even WE talk about? You've cooked a big supper, shall we say, you've invited some people over, and you've made plans for a great evening. You've really put everything together, and they just don't come. They just don't show up! It isn't a matter of saying, "Look, we couldn't make it." That's one thing. But it's another thing when one lets you know, "Look, we aren't ... we're just not coming. We don't want to come." That's a different story. And this is exactly what is being taught in this particular lesson. They would not come.

The king "was wroth" and sent forth his men to take care of those wicked ones; in this parable, He wants us to understand that the same love that can save is the same love that can punish. Every parent in this building ought to understand that one does so because he loves his child. Now, that may be a little hard for our young to understand—I can remember a time when it was difficult for me—but I want to tell you, I understand it now. They were doing those things because they genuinely loved me, and they were determined to shape, to mold, to correct, and to do some good things for me.

In Luke 8:18, Jesus says, "Take heed therefore HOW ye hear." Do you hear what He is saying? Our Lord does not say just take heed and hear. He says, "Take heed HOW ye hear." I think that admonition is particularly good for this generation. We hear so much in our generation, "Well, church is church." We hear, "Preaching is preaching." What we're really saying is that it really doesn't make much difference so long as we're hearing something; that's good enough. Jesus says, "Take heed therefore HOW ye hear." Now, what's He saying? Let me relate this to 1 Corinthians 11:29. Here, as Paul discusses the Lord's Supper, he says, "He that eateth and drinketh UNWORTHILY, eateth and drinketh damnation to himself, not discerning" ... or not seeing or not recalling ... "the Lord's body." You see, the same love that sets the table for us says that if we fail to observe it correctly, we eat and drink damnation to our soul. The same love that can save is the same love that can punish. The love that sent out the invitation is the same love that sent out to punish.

I don't know how long I have to read something before the point really dawns on me, but I've learned that I can read some things a number of times before I see the point. The sixth chapter of Revelation, verse 16, is a passage that I have read a lot of times, but its truth had never really dawned on me before. He discusses the time when the rocks and the mountains will be moved out of their places, and people will cry to be hidden from the "wrath of the Lamb." Do you hear what he is saying? The "WRATH of the LAMB"! I know about the wrath of a lion. I know about the wrath of a bear. But the wrath of a LAMB? He wants us to understand that though He is the Lamb of God, though He surrendered Himself on the cross, He is also "the Lion of the tribe of Judah" (Revelation 5:5). He is not just the Lamb.

Our attitude toward God sometimes is best revealed when we're confronted by His mercy. I guess those people were getting along pretty well, as far as they were concerned, until all of a sudden somebody knocked at the door and said, "Sir, you're invited to sit in the banquet room of the king." Well, it is different now. They're confronted by his goodness. They're confronted by his mercy, and they have an opportunity now to tell him what they think about the king; in doing so they evilly entreat his servants.

This story reminds me of something that occurred some time ago. One of our ambassadors to South America was killed; and so far as I could determine from what they were saying, it was not because of anything in particular against him. But it was their way of showing the United States: "We ... don't ...

want ... you ... here! We resent your interference in our affairs." I think this is the reason some of these poor souls were evilly entreated and even killed. After all, it's pretty easy to be evilly entreated when you're armed only with an invitation. And that's what you have tonight. If you sometimes feel evilly entreated as you go out and invite people to come to the Great Feast, it's not just you. I want you to know, they are having something to say about the One who sent you. In this way the Lord reminds us that the servant is not above his Lord; and if the day ever comes that we rise to the place that we are above our Lord, we have reached a sad day.

They Made Light of the Invitation

As we ponder the sermon and as we look at these who were evilly entreated, we are aware that most of them weren't so treated. Most who were invited simply "made light" of the invitation. They just wouldn't go, and they could care less about such things. You know, there are some expressions in the King James Version—and this is not a "put down" of it, by any means—but some expressions are the Old English that we don't use today. For instance, I don't use the word "vaunt," as in "Love vaunteth not itself" (1 Corinthians 13:4). I don't talk about bearing John the Baptist's head on a "charger" (Matthew 14:8). I would say, "a platter." But here's a word that still means the same thing; we still use it the same way as when the scripture says, "They made light of it." Ever since I was a little boy, I've heard that word. And Jesus, two thousand years ago, used the word to indicate an attitude of heart and life.

What did they do? Did they mistreat them? No! Did they harm the messengers? Not so far as I can read. They didn't go to the palace grounds and set up a demonstration. They didn't run a picket line. What did they do? How did they "make light" of the invitation? They didn't do anything! That's exactly what the Lord is saying. You "make light" of the Lord's invitation by simply doing nothing ... by not accepting ... by not going. I guess that's the main idea—they just didn't go! And if we hear the Great Invitation tonight, and we just don't go, and we could care less about the Great Feast, we're "making light" of it. Our Lord is saying that in the long run, it is just as evil to "make light" of His way as it is to do violence to it.

Now remember, our Lord is preaching to those individuals who were plotting His destruction. But evidently He is saying that those who were there actively plotting His destruction were really no worse than those like Gallio who "cared for none of those things" (Acts 18:17). They just didn't care. They just couldn't be bothered. Between Jesus Christ mocked and Jesus Christ crucified is a very short step.

Now, isn't this true as we look at this particular lesson? I think it's so appropriate. I know it is, and I don't have to get out and look at someone else to determine if that's the case. I can just look at myself and know that it's so true. This is as current as if our Lord had said to me this morning—which He didn't—but if He had said to me this morning, "When you get to church, here is what I want preached tonight in Wichita, Kansas!" I want to tell you, it could not be more current than what He preached two thousand years ago.

What is He saying? He is saying there is an individual who said, "I have bought a piece of ground, and I must needs go and see it." What's wrong with that? Nothing! Except ... he's putting something BEFORE the invitation. Now there's nothing wrong with the purchase of land; it's perfectly compatible with the law of terrestrial things (Acts 6 and various other places) as far as I know. But our Lord is saying the problem with this individual is that he's in love. Every once in a while I find somebody who says that the trouble with our world is that we don't have any love. I don't agree with that. I don't think there's ever been a time in the history of humanity that there has been any more love than we have in the world tonight. But, people, what in the world are we loving? We love, and the world is filled with love, and this man was in love. That was his problem: he had a LOVE OF POSSESSIONS—it's mine, I simply must go walk over it; I must see it! Now, he had bought it—and as far as I know there is no problem in owning it—but since he had bought it and the transaction had been made, he could have gone to the feast. He just didn't want to go; so he uses this excuse.

Let's consider another; you know the story. Another man said, "I have bought five yoke of oxen." I'd like to point out that this man's in big business! He doesn't say he bought one yoke—he bought five! "I have bought five yoke of oxen, and I go prove them." Do you ever wonder what the difference is in those two excuses? Why does the Lord use two excuses that are so similar? Notice the differences. "I have bought five yoke of oxen, and I go to prove them." He has already bought them. They're not going to get away. He could have gone to the feast. The point is, here is a man who is so wrapped up with the AFFAIRS OF BUSINESS that he couldn't make it. He had something else to do, and it must come first!

Another man said, "I have married a wife." He doesn't even ask to be excused. He supposes that this is wholly incompatible with the feast. I think our Lord is telling us that this man, because of his SOCIAL TIES, just couldn't make it. It would appear that the "havers" and the "getters," whether they have it or whether they're still trying to get it, all face the same temptations and the same problems. This is what our Lord would have us to understand. The love of possessions! The affairs of business! And I believe this, if you're not a CHRISTIAN—if you've never come to the Lord's great Kingdom, you've never obeyed the gospel and entered God's Kingdom, you've not come to His Great Feast—or if you have come to the Feast but you're doing nothing for God ... . I want to tell you, the reason is right here! Now, it may be in one of these or it may be a combination of them. It's either because of the LOVE OF POSSESSIONS ... or it's because of the AFFAIRS OF BUSINESS ... or it's because of our SOCIAL ENTANGLEMENTS! In one of these or in a combination of these, we find the reason.

As I go from place to place, I sometimes feel the press of the people as they say, "Tell me what sin is!" They want me to spell it out—tell me this is sin, this is sin, this is sin. There are many specific sins mentioned—at least seventy or eighty of them—but you can't just always give a list and say that is the end of the matter. Paul gave us a list and then said, "and such like" (Galatians 5:21). These are sins, but he says there are some things that are cousins to these sins; they are like them. I think it is evident what our Lord is doing. He is telling us that anything—whatever it is, good or bad—that is keeping you out of the Kingdom of God, whatever it is that keeps you from being the person you ought to be, and whatever is keeping you from sitting at the Great Feast, whatever it is … it's wrong! Isn't that what He is saying? Be it good or bad, whatever is keeping you away from that Great Feast is wrong!

In this lesson, I think He wants us to understand that we are studying the MISUSE of some things. I think of what an old time preacher once said, and he said it so well. He said, "In the day of judgment there shall be more people lost over the misuse of things that are perfectly good than over the use of things that are perfectly wrong." And there may be a tremendous amount of truth in that statement. I'm speaking to people who don't have any particular problem with using the thing that's wrong. But I'll tell you this, one of the problems we face is the misuse of things that are perfectly right. And our Lord is saying it can keep us out of His great Kingdom.

Would You Have Gone?

I look back at this sermon, and I watch these servants as they go out and invite the people. Some say they're not coming and then evilly entreat some of the servants; others simply stand there and make light of the whole situation. You would think nobody was going. But, some went! There have always been some to go. God has never been left without a witness. He has never been left without someone. Let me ask you, "Would you have gone?" A better question might be, "Would I have gone?" To answer this question properly, I really think what we ought to do is see where we are TONIGHT. Where are you tonight? Are you in God's great Kingdom functioning, working, doing the things the Lord would have you to do? If you're not, it may well be that long ago, had you been there and they came out and invited you, you would have said, "Look, I know I really ought to go, but I have something here I must see about." Or … "I've got something I must take care of." Or … "I have some social appointments, and I can't possibly break them right now; soon I'll take care of this situation." I would like to think that had I been there, I would not have had this attitude.

I don't know where I would have been—whether I would have been one of those in the city or out on the highways or out in the hedges of the country. But somewhere someone would have knocked on my door, or somewhere someone would have stopped my plow and said, "You are invited to the feast, to the banquet room of the king." I think that would have been overwhelming. And I think I can appreciate why the Lord states in Luke 14 that these individuals would feel so unworthy; however, he said go out and "COMPEL them to come in." Some would not feel worthy to sit in such a place.

The Banquet Room

You know, the only time—and I've tried to visualize this situation—the only time that we've ever even seen the king's palace is when we walked past and looked inside at those great, beautiful grounds. We walked up to those massive gates and looked through at the place where, of course, we would never get to go; that was the king's palace and was so far removed from our little life. But now we hold an invitation to sit at the king's table. The day of the feast finally arrives. We walk up this time, not to look through the bars, but this time those great doors swing open wide. Servants bow low, and one leads us down the way and somewhere he says, "Here." He gives us a beautiful garment, and we slip that garment on. It's the most beautiful thing—we've never had anything like this. The banquet room of the king! He opens the door to that room; it's a place of light; it's the most beautiful place we've ever seen. And inside there is fellowship and there is warmth. We go into a place of dazzling light; and as we make our way to a table, we look around at those present. One thing that really strikes us is seeing some there who are lame. And we see some groping around because they're blind. You remember, he said, "Go out ... and bring in hither the poor, and the maimed, and the halt, and the blind." They're trying to find a place to sit. We look around and wonder, "Where are the doctors of the Law? Where are the scribes and where are the Pharisees? Where are those professionals of Old Testament Law?" We must remember they're not here because they're too busy. They are occupied with other things. We continue to look around at this diverse group and wonder, "What are all these people doing here?" They are so different, and yet everyone seems happy and joyful. We soon decide that about the only thing all these people have in common is—they came. And that seems to be what is so important to the king. They came! It doesn't matter who you are or what your status is outside the Kingdom of God, that really doesn't make much difference. What matters is—He wants you IN. He wants people to come.

The thing that occurs next really impresses us: suddenly someone announces that the king is at the door, and the king and his son and all his royal party enter. We don't have to be told to stand when the king comes in. Everybody stands as the royal party enters, and the king has them seated. We think, "What a beautiful, auspicious occasion this is. Nothing can mar the beauty of such an occasion."

The Man Without a Wedding Garment

We watch as the king is about to be seated, but all of a sudden he looks over the audience, and his gaze settles upon one individual; we wonder, "What is he doing?" We have noticed this individual; we couldn't help but notice him. The man is sitting there without the proper wedding garment. But surely, surely he isn't going to let one man mar the beauty and the joy of this occasion. Surely he'll let this matter go and just forget it. But he doesn't! He stands there before that audience of people and demands an explanation. He said, "Friend, how camest thou in hither not having a wedding garment?"

The king is insulted. You see, the king provided a wedding garment for every guest. The king provided one for him, too; he just simply did not choose to wear it. He'll do his own thing. He will do it his way! After all, what matters, you know, is that you're there. It doesn't make any difference what you do. You're there. After all, a feast is a feast—to use some of the ideas of our modern time. The king is insulted.

The Bible teaches that not only are we invited to a feast, not only are we invited to be in Christ and to sit at His great table and to come to all that the word feast suggests; but I'll tell you something else to which we are invited—we are invited to just plain obedience. And there is nothing so important to the God that we serve tonight. He wants people to obey Him, and it doesn't make any difference if we have a house full of people, and everything seems lovely and beautiful—it isn't lovely so long as we have those who just simply don't care and are not going to obey Him. Our Lord wants us to understand that it's just as bad for one to come and be in disobedience as it is for him to stay away.

Notice, the king demands an answer. Can you imagine how that man felt? The Bible says, "He was speechless." What is he going to say? This is no joke anymore! Shame covers that man like a garment. The nearest thing to this scene that I can think about is when we were children in elementary school and we were doing things we shouldn't be doing. And, all of a sudden, the teacher stopped everything and demanded to know, "What ... are ... you ... doing?" Shame? We just wanted to melt to the floor! On this occasion the king said, "How camest thou in hither ... ? And the man was speechless." That reminds me of what Isaiah said in chapter six, verse five. He said, "Woe is me! for I am undone ... mine eyes have seen the King." What a difference it makes when you see the king.

The man had rejected the garment; other people had made light of it. They, however, stayed home and made light of it while he had the audacity to come and sit at the man's table and make light of it. It's one thing when someone stays away from the supper you have prepared and makes light of it; it's another thing for him to come to your table and make light of it. Now, our Lord is saying that if we come into His great Kingdom, He expects us to conduct ourselves around HIS table in full obedience and true service. He wants us to conduct ourselves as befits those who are sitting at the King's table.

I would like to point out that he went unchallenged until the king came. It would be a little difficult for me to believe that he sat there and no one said anything to him before it started. Surely, someone is bound to have noticed and said, "What are you doing here? Don't you see everyone else has on a wedding garment? Can't you see everyone else has conformed to the king's wishes and to the king's will? What are you doing here?" I don't know what he told them, but he seemed to feel that simply because he was there he could do it his way and he would do exactly as he pleased. He went unchallenged until the king came.

There are many things going on in this world that ought not to go on. Things are occurring that should never occur. But please be reminded that the King is coining; and if you do go unchallenged, if you get by with some of these things for a while, rest assured that when the King comes, it's going to be a different story. He is going to demand an answer.

Who is this man without a wedding garment? He is a man of unpardonable rudeness—a man with no sense of propriety. He is a man who doesn't believe the Lord when he says repent or perish (Luke 13:2-5). He is like the prodigal son who wanted to live in the far country of sin yet at the same time have all the privileges of home. One of the great dangers we face as the Lord's people is pointed out to us. We have come to the Feast. Many of us in this audience have come to the Feast, but we're taking some of it too lightly. We're still trying to wear our own filthy rags instead of the lovely garments the Lord provides. Sometimes, in spite of all He has done, in spite of the fact He has died for us, we still are not putting on the Lord Jesus Christ. We're still going our own ways.

You remember when the prodigal son went into the far country, he lost not only the father's goods, but also he lost all the signs of sonship. There were no shoes on his feet. There was no ring on his hand; there was no good clothing for his back. He was still a son, but he had lost the signs of sonship. But when he got back home, the first thing the father said was, "Bring forth the best robe, and put it on him; put a ring on his hand, and shoes on his feet ... . For this MY SON was dead, and is alive again; he was lost, and is found" (Luke 15:22-24). You see, if you're in the Father's house, He expects you to look like Him; you belong to Him. He expects you to act like His and wear the signs of sonship.

One of the problems—constant reoccurring problems—that we face as members of the Lord's church is that we are not taking it seriously. There are times when the Lord's people assemble and when the Lord's work is being done, many of us just aren't there. And some of us could care less. Let's face it as it is. Some of us could care less about the things of God, and we're not taking seriously that which is so serious to God. Let me tell you this: you start talking to me about something that would cause the death of just ONE of MY sons, and it is serious business. Anything that concerns His Son or the death of His Son on the cross, is serious business to Him. We're talking about His Son and His church. If the church is not a serious matter to you, you're in a dangerous place. If we're not the most sincere people on earth, I don't understand what we're about. We must be the best people on earth; that's not ego, that's scripture. The best people who walk the earth tonight should be God's people. These are they who take seriously this great institution that is called the church of the living God. It is so important: it cost His Son.

Through the years I've learned there are some people who hate the church. You might say, "That's terrible to say that!" But that's true. There are some people who hate the church! But most people don't hate it—most people just love the world better. And I think that's the big problem of our generation. They take it lightly; they love the world better.

Cast Him into Outer Darkness

Notice what he does. Does he rebuke the individual and say, "Friend, how camest thou in hither not having a wedding garment?" and let it pass? No! He called some servants, right there in the middle of all of this, and said, "Bind him hand and foot ... and cast him into outer darkness"—just like that! It was serious business with him. This teaches me that God is going to deal with us as individuals. After all of these years of dealing with the Lord's people, I still believe they are the best people on the face of God's earth. I know we have problems; I know we have sins, and we have troubles; but in spite of all that, I still think the best people on the face of the earth are His people. But I don't expect in the day of judgment to be able to say to the Lord, "Lord, I have lived among some good people in this world; I've functioned among the best. I've worked among YOUR people, Lord; and since we are one great people, why don't you just let me be in the middle of these people, Lord, and let us all move on into Heaven?" No! He is going to deal with us as individuals. It doesn't make any difference how big the audience may be, if our life is not right, He is going to pick us out as He did on this occasion. He dealt with an individual. No one can conceal his sin.

We ought to preach salvation's story. I have preached it all over the country under the heading, "What Must I Do To Be Saved?" We need to be preaching it. And we need to teach on those beautiful examples in Acts 8, 9, 10, 16 and 18 to answer the question, "What must I do to be saved?" But I think another sermon that we ought to be preaching sometimes is, "What Must I Do To Be Lost?" And I want to tell you this— number one point by priority and place ought to be ... "NOTHING!" You don't have to do one thing to be lost. You can die and go to Hell in a most respectable fashion. You can be known as a fine outstanding citizen and still be lost by just doing what this man did ... NOTHING!

I've always heard about Niagara Falls, and for years I have used an illustration drawn from it. Three or four years ago, on my way to Michigan to hold a meeting, I went by and saw the great Falls. I was impressed! To stand there and feel the earth moving beneath my feet and to see the water pouring over into that great chasm and to watch it dashing into a million diamonds out there in the sky was impressive! But what really impressed me most was the actuality of the illustration that I had used for years. There is a point on up the river where you can put in your boat and get out. And there is a place a little farther down where you can put in your boat and get out, but there IS a place that you put in your boat and you are not getting out! There is a point of no return!

Tonight we would do well to stop and ask ourselves, "How do we know where WE stand?" Why do we say, "I can still get out; there will be another day. There will be another time for me to come to the Great Feast. After all, He's out knocking on my door inviting me to the Great Feast. I can go any time I want." People, the Feast won't always last! Someday there will be no invitation. There is a point of no return!

We sing the old song by Tillit S. Teddlie, titled, "What Will Your Answer Be?"

"Some day you'll stand at the bar on high,
Some day your record you'll see;
Some day you'll answer the question of life,
What will your answer be?"

I'll tell you this, I won't be able to stand up there and say, "God, you never did anything for me, and that's the reason I didn't come to the Great Feast." And I won't be able to stand there and say, "Lord, you never did anything for me" because He gave His life for me (Romans 5:8). I can't say to the Holy Spirit, "I've never had a guide, I've never had a record" because He gave me a "perfect law of liberty" (James 1:25). I guarantee you that when I stand in the great day of judgment, I'll not be able to say, as I have heard some say, "Well, I would be a Christian, but my brethren didn't treat me right." Let me tell you, I can never say that. Some of the best people I know are my brethren. I wonder where I would be, and more than that, I wonder where my children would be if it were not for my brethren. So I won't be able to say anything. I won't have an answer. I am going to be like this man; I will be standing there "speechless."

So you know the only reason you are not a Christian—the only reason you have never believed the gospel (Mark 16:16), and repented of your sins (Acts 2:38) and confessed the holy Christ (Acts 8:37), the only reason you have never been immersed in His precious name for the remission of your sins (Acts 2:38)—is that you have not really decided that's what you should do? When you decide what you are going to do, there are not enough powers in Hell itself to keep you from doing it because Jesus died on that cross to make it possible.

Is it a matter that you cannot obey? If you can say, with all truthfulness, I can't—I can't believe the gospel; I can't repent of my sins; I can't confess Christ; I can't be immersed in His name; I can't come back to the fold; I can't come back to the church—if it's a matter of cannot, that's different. But I think everybody here tonight will admit that's not the case. The basic problem is "will not." Jesus says, "Ye will not come to me, that ye might have life" (John 5:40). Is there one here tonight who will quit saying, "I can't," and just say, "Lord, I will"? Let me remind you, friend, the King is coming. I don't know when He is coming, but I will guarantee you one thing—HE IS COMING. And what a difference it will make when the King arrives.

Sermon Seven

*The
Parables
of
Jesus*

"And He spake many things
unto them in parables"

Luke 15:1-2 and 11-24

"Then drew near unto him all the publicans and sinners for to hear him. And the Pharisees and scribes murmured, saying, This man receiveth sinners, and eateth with them ... And he said, A certain man had two sons: And the younger of them said to his father. Father, give me the portion of goods that falleth to me. And he divided unto them his living. And not many days after the younger son gathered all together, and took his journey into a far country, and there wasted his substance with riotous living. And when he had spent all, there arose a mighty famine in that land; and he began to be in want. And he went and joined himself to a citizen of that country; and he sent him into his fields to feed swine. And he would fain have filled his belly with the husks that the swine did eat: and no man gave unto him. And when he came to himself, he said, How many hired servants of my father's have bread enough and to spare, and I perish with hunger! I will arise and go to my father, and will say unto him, Father, I have sinned against heaven, and before thee, And am no more worthy to be called thy son; make me as one of thy hired servants. And he arose, and came to his father. But when he was yet a great way off, his father saw him, and had compassion, and ran, and fell on his neck, and kissed him. And the son said unto him, Father, I have sinned against heaven, and in thy sight, and am no more worthy to be called thy son. But the father said to his servants, Bring forth the best robe, and put it on him; and put a ring on his hand, and shoes on his feet: And bring hither the fatted calf, and kill it; and let us eat, and be merry: For this my son was dead, and is alive again; he was lost, and is found. And they began to be merry."

7. Parable of a Prodigal

We welcome you to the morning assembly of this congregation, to worship the Lord. We welcome you to a time of reverence and a time of respect. The Bible states in Hebrews 12:28 that we should have "reverence and godly fear," that we may serve Him acceptably, and we sincerely believe that that is the desire of the people assembled in this room.

We must serve Him acceptably if, indeed, we plan to serve Him at all. I remember reading in the Old Testament that before Israel could come to Mt. Sinai to be in the presence of God, there were several things that were necessary. One, they had to purify themselves. Two, they had to wash their garments. Three, they had to abstain from various secular and everyday duties. In short, they could carry nothing to the foot of the mountain that would be unworthy of being in the presence of the Eternal One. I would think today that since we serve under a better age, that we "are come unto Mount Zion, and unto the city of the living God, the heavenly Jerusalem ... to the general assembly and church of the firstborn" (Hebrews 12:22-23), that surely we ought to come to this place today determined that we will worship our Lord and that we will bring nothing that will be unworthy of such a time as this.

We have been discussing, as you well know, the parables of Jesus. I've chosen this sermon this morning because of the particular occasion and because I would consider this to be the pearl of all the parables of Jesus. I think we are looking at a sermon that has touched more hearts and more lives than any parable that Jesus ever spoke. We come to something that touches our very being; it touches the fabric of civilization itself. You remember the occasion of the parable. Our Lord chooses, because of that occasion, to preach this particular lesson. He chooses to speak of a lost coin, and of a lost sheep, and then eventually of a lost son. I think there is a progression in these three stories.

The Occasion of the Parable

Notice the occasion of this parable. The publicans and sinners have drawn near "for to hear Jesus." I would remind you, today, that many of those who came to hear Jesus on this occasion were considered the scum of the earth, so far as the Jews were concerned. They were the outcasts, they were the nobody's. They were the people about whom they could care less. When the publicans and the sinners drew near to hear Jesus, you will notice that the Pharisees and the scribes began to murmur and complain. They said, "This man receiveth sinners, and eateth with them." They simply could not tolerate the fact that He, though He be the Great Physician, and though He would have, indeed, a super abounding power to cure the ills of these individuals, they could not accept the fact that Jesus would have anything to do with these people. And so our Lord proceeds to give us these lessons about proud and penitent sinners. We must realize that they're all sinners, and our Lord will amplify that difference in this lesson.

There are two things I'd like you to look for as we go through the study this morning. First of all, I'd like for you to look for the great guilt of man; yet at the same time, I want you to look for the sovereign grace of God. If you miss these two things, you've missed the full import of the Lord's sermon: our guilt and His grace. And this, of course, is what we've been considering over and over, night after night, throughout this meeting, but you'll see it so much in this sermon.

The Two Sons

Now the story is as usual. It is a simple everyday thing, and I don't guess you could get anything that's more everyday than the fact that He says, "A certain man ... "—and this man, of course, we are looking upon as our God—"A certain man had two sons." He wants us to understand that here is a home in which everything is proceeding as normal as possible. He wants us to know that this man has two sons, and he calls one of them the "younger son" and the other he simply refers to as the "elder son."

The younger son is a picture of penitent sinners. The other individual is a picture of those who were proud sinners. And if we had time today, I would like to preach two sermons. One about a prodigal who wandered so far from home, and one about a prodigal who never set foot out of the house. Both of them were prodigals, and both of them were so wrong. Our Lord is giving us a picture of the Pharisees who are saying, "This man receiveth sinners, and eateth with them." On the other hand, we see an individual who will be made to realize, I am simply a sinner.

Everything in the household is going along pretty well until we detect some dissatisfaction. The younger son is getting tired of home's rules and home's ways. He's tired of the same old thing day after day and decides, "There are better things for me; I'm going to make my way over yonder somewhere and live as I please—I shall do what I want to do."

According to the law in Deuteronomy 21, the younger son could not receive nearly so much as the elder son. In that day it really paid to be born first in a household because as such he would receive about two-thirds of his father's goods. You will remember in Deuteronomy 21, the reason for that is situation: the first son was, he says, of his father's strength. It was a custom among those people, and this young man realizes that though all of it is not his and he doesn't receive what the older brother receives, a certain portion of it belongs to him. Day by day the dissatisfaction grows and grows until eventually he says, "Father, give me the portion of goods that falleth to me."

In the first place, his portion was not to be given to him until later. But that's, of course, the prerogative of the father to give it to him when he pleases to give it to him. So here's a situation that's a departure from what we would expect. We see the father, even prior to his death or his last days, because of the demands of this young son, giving him what is his.

I'd like to say, as we begin this study today, that this parable is so elaborate and is so far reaching that I do not know how to give you first the parable and then the application. We're going to do both as we go along. I think the lessons just simply leap out at us. They are so abundant, and they are so apparent.

He wants us to understand that, in this case, here is home; and everything was going along pretty well when all of a sudden, because of dissatisfaction, things seem to fall apart. And I'll assure you it doesn't make any difference what age you are, you can identify with that. If, indeed, you haven't reached that age, some day you may. And those of you who've already passed it can look back upon the time you decided that the best thing in the world would be if you could just get out of this place; there's bound to be something better and greater over yonder than there is around here.

Sometimes we become dissatisfied with the church—we get tired of church Sunday morning, Sunday night, Wednesday night. We get tired of study. We get tired of visiting the sick. We get tired of so many things; we decide there's bound to be something better. We become so dissatisfied that we, like this young man, decide to leave. You know what the problem is, of course, with this young man: it's so evident. He wants to live in the far country, and yet at the same time he wants to have everything that is coming to him. He says, "Father, give me the portion of goods that falleth to me." I want all of the benefits of home, but I want to live in the far country.

Sometimes in the church, I see this very thing. Sometimes we become dissatisfied. We want to be known as a Christian. We want to have the benefits of a Christian. We want to be able to die in the Lord. And yet, at the same time, we want to live in the far country of sin. But there's one thing for sure: we must decide today whether we will stay at home or whether we are going to live in the far country because we can't live in both at the same time. We're either in one or moving toward the other, as is evident by what Jesus says.

We watch as the father looks at this situation and as this young son day after day says, "I'm tired and I'm dissatisfied; I want to get out of this place, and I want what's coming to me." You may wonder why the father would grant the inheritance, but I suppose he decides it will do no good to retain this young man against his will. His heart has already left. And so the scripture says, "he divided unto him his living."

When a person gets tired of living a Christian life, and he's determined to quit living it, I really don't know much to do about it. Now we may talk to the person. If, indeed, I get tired of living for the Lord and doing what I'm doing, and I decide, "People, I'm walking out; I'm through," I hope somebody will talk to me. I hope somebody will try to remind me. That is what the Book says that you ought to do. But it might not do much good, as is evidenced in the lives of other individuals.

Man is a free moral agent. We're not into something we cannot get out of. I wonder sometimes if people don't look at certain ones in the church and wonder, "Why do they stay? Are they into something or have they learned something that they can't get away from? Is there something that constrains them and forces them to stay?" No! Anyone may leave home any time he will. Certainly we are a free moral agent—we can go or we can stay. And, of course, the Lord wants us compelled by love.

You remember the apostle said, "the love of Christ constraineth us" (2 Corinthians 5:14). This is one time I like the New English version. It says, "The love of Christ leaves us no choice." And I really believe when you get down to it, the love of Christ leaves us no choice, if you really face it just as it is. Sometimes we ignore the love that is there; and we decide, "I'm going to make my way!"

The Journey Away From Home

The scripture says, "Not many days after the younger son gathered ... "—I want you to notice—"the younger son gathered all together." Please notice he did not leave immediately, but he waited until he could get everything together and then took his journey.

Now, our Lord wants us to understand that an apostasy of heart always precedes an apostasy of life. Every once in a while, I meet someone who says, "You know, now my heart's not really like this. I mean, I know I'm not living for the Lord as I ought to be living, but my heart's not really this way." Friend, that's a little hard to believe because Jesus is saying that an apostasy of heart always precedes an apostasy of life. And if, today, you find your heart growing a little cold, and you find that times like these don't thrill your soul and that this is not meaningful for you, you'd better take serious inventory; your heart may be leaving or may have left. And it won't be long, according to Jesus, that you'll go to join it. So this young man does exactly that. He goes to be with his heart. He "took his journey into a far country." And he goes to be what he wants to be and to do what he wants to do.

Please notice this fact: he was not born in that far country. Infants are not born in sin; they're born in a place that's good. But I think the significant point is that the Lord calls this a "journey." That's exactly what sin is. The Lord is saying that sin is not a static thing. It's not something that just lands, just happens, and there it is, never to move again. This idea of saying that we are "holding our own," I seriously doubt. You're either moving closer to God and submission to His will, or you are gradually slipping away from God. It's a "journey," according to Him.

I was out in Los Angeles some years ago; and after services one night a brother asked, "Would you like to go down and see part of this big city?" I said it's okay. So we drove and walked through what is called Skid Row in Los Angeles. And I want to tell you, I saw sights there that I shall never forget. People were weaving down the street drunk, barely able to walk. People were sitting on the sidewalk, holding their drunken heads as they vomited into the streets. And we saw all those derelicts who just had hit the bottom. But I thought as I looked at those individuals, "They weren't born this way." There was a time when a mother held that individual, a little child as pure as Heaven itself. She had great dreams and great aspirations for that little one. But, brother, somewhere along life's way they took a journey. Jesus calls sin a "journey." And it's always moving out and away and down from God.

The psalmist says, "Blessed is the man that walketh not in the counsel of the ungodly, nor standeth in the way of sinners, nor sitteth in the seat of the scornful" (Psalm 1:1). Please notice the progression, moving from one to the other. He walks, he stands, and eventually he just simply sits down with them. So sin is a progressive thing. "When lust hath conceived, it bringeth forth sin: and sin, WHEN IT IS FINISHED, bringeth forth death" (James 1:15). So, it's a moving, growing thing. And it always is, as our Lord states, a "journey."

As the young man makes his way into that far country, his steps are so familiar to us, aren't they? And as he makes his way into that place, there are the "fair weather" friends. You know, if you have money, you have some kind of friend. At least they call them that. And the scripture declares he "WASTED his substance with riotous living." I want you to look at this word. I don't think it's by accident that our Lord puts in that word. He "wasted" ... "wasted his substance with riotous living." People, sin is a thing that will waste you. It will waste your name, it will waste your reputation, it will waste your character, it will waste all that you are. And you know that! You are aware that this is the case.

And then the scripture declares that after living this way, he wakes up one morning and the money's gone. And when the money's gone, the friends are gone. What is He saying? Jesus says, "There arose a mighty famine in that land." What a beautiful picture. What's happening to him? The inevitable law is in operation: "Be not deceived; God is not mocked: for whatsoever a man soweth, that shall he also reap. For he that soweth to his flesh shall of the flesh reap corruption" (Galatians 6:7). That law's inevitable. He insists that's the way it is going to be. "God is not mocked." He is painting a picture of the downward progress of sin. Not only is it a journey, not only is it a waste, but He is saying you're going to find that the fields of sin are ever swept by the howling storms of destitution. There's not anything out there! Sin promises so much: it delivers so little.

I think of what Jeremiah said as he was speaking to Israel (chapter two) of their two evils. He said you have left the "fountain of living waters, and hewed you out cisterns, broken cisterns, that can hold no water." I want you to think of that contrast. Think about a living, flowing fountain in contrast with, not only something that does not produce, but is just simply what? A cistern, a clay jug in the earth, and besides that, it's a broken cistern; it can hold no water. This is exactly what you're seeing in the life of this individual. He's left it all; he has left a place where there was everything he could desire. And he wakes up one morning ... and there is nothing. Not one thing is there for him! And then our Lord says, "And he began to be in WANT." I want to propose to you, he woke up in a new sensation. That's something he had never felt before. Never before had he felt the sensation of want, need. And you know, this should have been the first divine summons, "Young man, go home; because at home there is no need. At home all is full and satisfying, even servants have all that they want." And here is the divine summons, but would he go home? No! His heart is still too proud. He's still too set on his own ways. He still is determined to go it alone.

Next the scripture says that he "JOINED ... "—I want you to look at this word, I think they're all so significant—he "joined himself to a citizen of that county." Our Lord is painting a picture of a fall within a fall. He is painting a picture of a plunge within a plunge. We have watched the decline; but when he comes to the place that he joins himself to a citizen of that far country, we're seeing a new fall.

I want you to look at the distinction between these two: a citizen of a far country and a young son from his father's house, with all his guilt. There's not anybody but who will say he's guilty. He's wrong. But with all of his guilt, he is still not a citizen of that far country. And with all of his pride, he's still not satisfied over there. But those people who are there are satisfied.

Do you know what our Lord is saying to us? He wants us to understand that out there that world is pretty happy. They're satisfied. They have what they want, and they seem to be satisfied. But, why is it then that when we leave the Cause of Jesus Christ and we go back into sin, we're not really satisfied? Oh, we tell ourselves we are, and we feel like things are pretty good; but really we're not. Do you know what the difference is? We know better! What a difference it makes when you know better! That old citizen didn't know any better. That was his world. That was his element. But this young man was miserable in that element because he knew better. I want to propose to you today that you'll never be able to walk out of the Lord's house and truthfully say, "I'm going to be happy out there," unless you keep moving to the point that you become reprobate or void of judgment and sear your conscience. You'll never be happy with that situation because you know better. What a difference it makes when you were reared in a home in which you were taught properly and you know better.

Feeding Swine

Well, we look at the new job situation. Jesus says he didn't give him a lofty position. He didn't give him a good job. What did he do? He sent him into the field to do what? "He sent him into his fields to feed swine." I want to tell you this, for a Jewish young man, any Jew, he hit the bottom! To be sent out into the field to feed hogs, the unclean beast, was as low a job on earth as you could get.

I think this is what the Lord is saying—that you can just keep going until you eventually just hit the bottom. And this young man—this person who would not live with his father in that beautiful situation—now finds himself joined to a foreign taskmaster, and what a change in his life. You know, when you go into another country and you exchange currency—you give them your money, they give you theirs—you learn the rate of exchange. I want you to know that spiritually there's a certain rate of exchange, and you can see the rate of exchange in this situation.

When we change countries, and we walk out of the Lord's country into the far country of sin, the world is saying, "Look, here's what I'll do for you!" Oh, there's an allurement out there in the world that looks great. It looks grand! And we think, "Ah, there are some great things over there; what a great time I'll really have." But I'll tell you this: here's a young man who could tell you that it isn't that way.

Judas Iscariot could also tell you. Judas found out what the rate of exchange was. Remember when he covenanted with those individuals to betray the Lord? And he did exactly that! I want to tell you, when those people stood there with the howling mob, and they were casting, as the scripture says, "the same in his teeth," and they were crying out against the Lord, "If thou be the Son of God, come down from the cross" (Matthew 27:40), there was one man who wasn't there that day crying, "Come down from the cross." He was making his way back over to the Temple. The Bible paints that beautiful picture of a man who walks into the Temple and throws those coins down before those individuals, and says, "I have betrayed THE innocent blood" (Matthew 27:4). Oh, I think that is beautiful! He doesn't say I have betrayed "innocent blood." He says, "I have betrayed THE innocent blood." Do you want to see the rate of exchange? Do you remember what they told him? They didn't say, "Judas, come on in. You've done a good job. We'll take care of you. I mean, after all, we covenanted about this matter. We decided what we would do. Come on Judas, we'll take care of you." Do you remember what they said? I think they are some of the coldest words I've ever read in this Book. They said, "See thou to that. What is that to us? See thou to that" (Matthew 27:4). He had done his job. There is the rate of exchange. And that is exactly the rate of exchange that is still offered to us today.

Our Lord said that young man was so hungry that "he would fain have filled his belly with the husks that the swine did eat." He was starving to death! He'd never known need. He'd never known hunger. He'd never known want. What has he done? He's exchanged a father for this foreign man. He's exchanged home for a hog's field. He's exchanged good food for "the husks that the swine did eat." He exchanged his brother for the hogs. That is where he was. Do you know what Jesus is doing? He is drawing for us the face of sin. It tears you, just sweeps you away, farther out. Every step takes you farther down the ladder until eventually Satan will take you all the way. Our Lord is saying that shame and contempt and distress are wed to sin, and you'll never divorce those things. We try in our day. We try to gloss it over and say, "Well, you know, it's not too bad. It's nothing more than a temporary stumbling block in the upward progress of mankind." No, no! He is saying it's shame and it's distress and it's contempt. They're married, and you are not going to divorce them.

He says, "he would fain have filled his belly with the husks that the swine did eat." He wasn't satisfied. Those husks wouldn't satisfy, but maybe they'd fill. There are many things that we try that may fill temporarily; but they really don't satisfy, do they? How many times have I seen people leave the Cause of Jesus Christ having decided, "Brother, we're going to live like we want to live. I mean, it's not the Lord's Day anymore. It's OUR day. We're going to live it up. We're off to the mountains, we're off to the lake, we're off to wherever. It's our day, and we'll do what we very well please."

I think about a couple down in Texas who many years ago came to that place. It's an amazing thing to me! For some reason they got dissatisfied, they gathered all together, and they took their journey; and they tried to tell us, "Look, we're having a great time!" But not long after that, they came back to the fold and confessed, "We were absolutely and totally miserable. We tried and failed." The allurement was there, the infatuation was there, but it never did satisfy. "He would fain have filled his belly with the husks that the swine did eat."

He Came to Himself

I like what Jesus said: "He came to himself." Did you ever notice that? Those two words "came to" would suggest that here was a young man who had been deceived. He was infatuated. He was beside himself. He wasn't really in love with the world. He wasn't really in love with that situation, but he had been so deceived.

No wonder Paul said in Hebrews 3:13 that we should "exhort one another daily, while it is called To day; lest any of you be hardened through the deceitfulness of sin." There's not a person in this building who cannot be hardened by sin. We can be moved. We can be taken away from the Cause of Jesus Christ. Paul says, "Exhort one another," and never put yourself in a position where that can occur.

"He came to himself," and do you know what he thought about? That's a beautiful thing to me. He's not at home. He's still out feeding hogs, and he wakes up. And what was the first thing he thought about? The servants. The "servants of my father's have bread enough and to spare, and I perish with hunger." What a ridiculous situation! It's an amazing thing that in the father's house they have all they want to eat, and he's dying out here in this miserable, wretched place. The old animals are happy, they don't know any better. The old citizen is happy; everybody is happy ... except him, and he alone is miserable. He knows better!

You know, this tells me something that wasn't readily apparent at first, but it's a grand lesson. My people, home is indispensable. He was not indispensable to home. When he moved, when he walked out, home didn't fall apart. And I just know this today, that if I were to quit the church, just totally forget it, quit it, the church isn't going to fall apart. It was getting along very well before I arrived in this world, and I just know that should I leave today, the church will get along very well. It will go right on. This tells me forcibly that I am not indispensable to the church. But the church is absolutely indispensable to me. And so it is with home. Home didn't fall apart. He's the one who fell apart, and his only hope was that home was still there. And I'll tell you this, we ought to be grateful, when we've left the fold of God and we haven't been what we ought to be, that there is somebody still keeping the home fires burning so that when we do come to our senses and come back to the fold, it's still there. We will not destroy the church of the living God.

What we need to do is what he did. He just "came to." He stopped; he really looked at the situation. And you know, this is the job of the church today. The job of the church is not to pet people. The job of the church is to uphold the truth and make men see, as David said in Psalms 9:17, "The wicked shall be turned into hell, and all the nations that forget God." He wants us to understand that we either repent or we perish (Luke 13:2-5). This is exactly what we are seeing here. We either change our mind and change our course of action, or perish. And we CAN change, and we can go home.

Do you know what he said? Listen to him talking to himself. Brother, sometimes you need to sit down and talk to yourself. He is saying I will go back—that's what I am going to do. "I WILL!" Listen to that determination. "I will arise." "I will ...

go to my father." Now, think about what he is saying. There is a young man who believes that home is still there. And it is. He believes that his father is still his father because he said, "I will ... say unto him, Father ... ." He still is that. And please notice that although he believes he can go home, although he is penitent, where is he? He is still standing in a hog's pen. It is not enough to say, "Lord, I believe," and "Lord, I repent." You've got to do what He said. "I will arise." You must DO something. Believe, repent, and then do something. And notice what he is saying: "Father, I have sinned against heaven, and before thee." I want you to notice he puts it into perspective for us.

You know, by our sins, we may cause a lot of heartaches. We do! We cause a lot of heartaches, we cause a lot of tears to freely flow, we hurt others. But when it comes right down to it, sin is against God. "I have sinned against heaven, and BEFORE thee." And that is a beautiful statement. A beautiful perspective and a correct view.

What do you see? I see true repentance. I see that old cold heart beginning to thaw and the waters of repentance now are beginning to flow freely. "I will arise." And then I like what He said. "And he arose ... ." You see, he didn't just stand and say, "I can do it." He didn't just stand there and say, "I believe it; I repent." He DID something. "He arose." And the scripture says he "came to his father. But when he was yet a great way off, his father saw him, and had compassion, and ran, and fell on his neck, and kissed him." I do not possess the ability to tell that story as it ought to be told. I think this is one of the most beautiful pictures that one could ever possibly imagine. I suspect that the longer we live the more beautiful it will become to us.

The young man finally decides he is leaving that place. The scripture says, "He arose." He started out of that place. And he hadn't just gone next door. The scripture says he went "into a far country." It is a strange land and a strange place. The scripture declares that by now all the signs of sonship had been removed. He didn't have any shoes. His clothes are tattered. He is hungry. He is in a miserable state. He turns around; he begins to make his way back toward home.

On his way back, he passed through unfamiliar country. I don't guess that did much for him except to quicken his pace to get out of that place. But somewhere on down the road he came to scenes that were so familiar to him. I don't know how many times I've left home to go preach. I've long since lost count of that. I don't know how many times I've driven off that hill to go somewhere to preach the gospel, but I can tell you this: I have never yet driven back close to home without it being a meaningful thing to me. It is good to come back to places that are familiar to you, places where you played as a child—because it's home. There is always something that's good about home.

The Father's Welcome

Jesus continues to describe the homecoming. "When he was yet a great way off, his father saw him." By now the servants have forgotten him. They can live without him. There's an elder brother who hopes he will never come home. But there's someone who never, never gave up. He's still there. The scripture pictures the son with no shoes, tattered garments, and no ring; the world had taken them all. Even in that condition, while he was yet a great way off, there was somebody who recognized him.

You know, we sometimes sing the song, "There's Someone to Care." You may think that nobody cares about you, that no one really cares about your soul. That's not true. Now, there may be some elder brothers. I am not saying there aren't. There may be some servants who could care less about you; but I want to tell you, there is Someone to care. Your Father has never given up. Fathers don't give up.

His father is still looking. And when he sees this child coming, the scripture says he "ran" to meet him. You remember the son begins to go ahead and do exactly what he had planned. He said, "Father, I ... am no more worthy to be called thy son. Make me as one of thy hired servants." I think we ought to notice this. Brother, it's better to be a servant in the house of the Lord than to dwell in the tents of the wicked (Psalm 84:10). He learned that lesson. "Father, I have sinned ... and am no more worthy to be called thy son: make me as one of thy hired servants." His father, the voice of love, cuts the confession short and calls his servants and says, "Bring forth the best robe, and put it on him; and put a ring on his hand, and shoes on his feet ... . For this my son was dead, and is alive again; he was lost, and is found." The world has sheared from him all the signs of sonship, but the father knew him and restored every sign. And there was great rejoicing.

If you're not a child of God in the Father's house, think what you're missing. Think what you're missing in that you have never known the real joys of being a Christian. And there is, today, a real joy in serving the Lord. You can be a child in the Father's house. You become a child in the Father's house by being born into His house ... through faith (Hebrews 11:6), through repentance of sin (2 Peter 3:9), through confession of the Holy Christ (Matthew 10:32), through being baptized (Acts 2:38; Mark 16:16). You must be born into the family of God and you become His child, His son or His daughter in His great house. You can do that today.

I'm especially concerned at this moment about those of us who are in His house. We know what it means to be home. We have obeyed the gospel. We have been placed there; but if for any reason, you're not serving the Lord, if you're not really faithful to Him, if you have left Him, you know what happened. I don't know how it happened, but in some way, Jesus says, you became dissatisfied about something.

I don't know what it was, whether it was the allurement of things in the world, the promise of great things, or what. But something happened, and you became dissatisfied; so you gathered things together and took a journey. You've been on a journey, and you've learned that in that far country there's waste, and you've learned that there's famine. You've learned that there are trials. You felt a want and a need out there that you had never known before, something different; and you joined yourself to this and that. You've tried all those different things.

The world didn't give you much in exchange did it? In fact, you learned that the world loves its own, but it doesn't have much love or respect for those who say, "I know what it means to be a Christian, but I'm not living it." It could care less about you. You've tried various things. I don't know what all you've tried, but you tried to fill your heart, you tried to fill the void, the emptiness, the ache that was there.

Won't you today, through this great sermon Jesus preached, "come to." Won't you wake up today and realize what's happening to you, and say, "Father, I've sinned"? Come now, the Father is waiting for you, today. Won't you just say, "Father, I have sinned against heaven, and before thee; I want to come home?" This is what the Lord wants you to do.

Sermon Eight

The Parables of Jesus

"And He spake many things unto them in parables"

140

Luke 18:9-14

"And he spake this parable unto certain which trusted in themselves that they were righteous, and despised others. Two men went up into the temple to pray; the one a Pharisee, and the other a publican. The Pharisee stood and prayed thus with himself, God, I thank thee, that I am not as other men are, extortioners, unjust, adulterers, or even as this publican. I fast twice in the week, I give tithes of all that I possess. And the publican, standing afar off, would not lift up so much as his eyes unto heaven, but smote upon his breast, saying, God be merciful to me a sinner. I tell you, this man went down to his house justified rather than the other: for every one that exalteth himself shall be abased; and he that humbleth himself shall be exalted."

8. The Pharisee and the Publican

We are grateful this evening for the privilege of being here and joining in the singing and the prayer. Should I at this moment turn around and go home, I could say that my time has been so well spent. To join in songs such as we have sung and to praise our Lord is always uplifting to me. I can assure you that sometimes I can come feeling not quite as encouraged as I should or maybe I am not quite as thrilled as I ought to be and a few songs such as we have sung tonight simply put me where I need to be.

This evening we are listening to one of the sermons of the Lord Jesus Christ. I have long felt it is quite an awesome thing to stand before any group of people anywhere, and especially before my Lord, and propose to teach His sermon. I suppose it should always give us that kind of feeling since we are standing before all of Heaven and before Him who spoke the sermon. I hope to remind you of the sermon that He preached so long, long ago.

In Luke 18, we have two sermons; we have two lessons on prayer. And the preacher, of course, is Jesus. The thrust in the first is persistence in prayer, and the second concerns pretention in prayer. You will notice that the Lord addresses the one we are studying tonight to those who "trusted in themselves that they were righteous, and despised others."

To accomplish His purpose, our Lord brings into view a contrast—two individuals, two men. One of them is a Pharisee, and the other is a publican. One of them is at the top of the social ladder; the other is at the very bottom. One of them is respected and honored while the other is despised and rejected. What Jesus dares to do is to compare these two individuals and to draw some conclusions about them.

Profile of a Pharisee

First, let's look at the Pharisee—he was one who separated himself from others. I suppose, as we think about a Pharisee, that fact is one of the first things that comes to mind. He was a meticulous observer of the Law. He was a strict legalist. He was one who considered himself not only to be a protector of the Law, but one with whom it would either stand or fall.

To protect that Law, which the Pharisees felt had been committed into their care, they built great fences around it that Jesus called "tradition," thereby making void the principles of the Law itself. I guess one of the classic examples of that is found in Mark 7 where Jesus discusses the matter of eating bread with "unwashen hands." You remember, they came to Jesus and asked why the disciples "eat bread with unwashen hands?" They simply could not accept such.

I read that one group of the Pharisees had a rigid procedure. They would use at least one and one-half egg shells of water and wash their hands; then they would hold them up and let them drip even to the elbow so that they might effect further cleansing. They would then take that much more water and let it drip off the tips of their fingers. They were extremely meticulous about this whole matter, and they condemned those who did not do so.

This is one of the men whom Jesus is discussing on this occasion, and we see the Pharisee as he goes to worship. I get a pretty vivid picture. I don't know what comes to your mind tonight; but when I think of this man going up to the Temple to pray, I get a vivid picture of a man who is supremely religious. He is one who comes into the Temple at the precise hour. He is not one who can be deterred by a crippled or impotent man at the Beautiful Gate as some others might be. He will be at the Temple at the precise moment. I watch him as he sweeps up the steps with robes flowing; and he makes broad his "phylacteries," little pouches of scripture. This appearance, of course, would make him look more pious than any other. He enters the court of Israel, and it is there that he begins to pray.

Honor to Whom Honor

But before we consider his prayer, I would like to remind you that everything wasn't bad about Pharisees. I suppose we tend to think because some things weren't so good, that nothing was good. But I think there are several things about Pharisees that commend themselves to us. In fact, Jesus on one occasion taught that "whatsoever they bid you observe, that observe and do; but do not ye after their works: for they say, and do not" (Matthew 23:3). They knew the law; these were men who could quote the Word, and I don't think anybody is ready to condemn a man because he knows the scriptures. I must admire anyone who takes the time and the effort to learn the Holy Scripture. And this man, I am sure, was one of those people. He was a man who spoke the truth, and I understand you could depend upon these individuals to speak truth to you when it came to what the Book had to say.

His prayer begins with, "God, I thank thee ... ." At least, he acknowledges God. You see, he believes in God, he worships God, and he acknowledges that God has had something to do with his life. Although we don't hear a great deal more about it, he does acknowledge the fact that He is there. Furthermore, as the man prays, he makes known that all is not negative. He said, "I fast twice in the week."

Custom required them to fast on the Day of Atonement, but here is a man who is going to go it a lot better than that. He is going to fast according to the ways of some of his people; he is going to fast every Monday and Thursday—the traditional days that Moses went upon the Mount and came down from the Mount. And I don't think there is anybody waiting to discount him because of that. If, indeed, he chooses to fast twice a week, I am not going to argue with that at all.

Furthermore, he said, "I give tithes of all that I possess." Like Jacob of old (Genesis 28:22), he said I will give tithes of it all. Here is a man who was willing to count the very dill seed of the garden. He is willing to say, "Nine for me and one for God; nine for me and one for God." He was the kind of man who was willing to do that. He was willing, at least, to lower his standard of living as far as the world is concerned to give to God the tenth that belonged to Him. God was, at least, as real to that man as the money in his pocket. I'm not always sure that God is that real to people in our day. So there were some good things about that man who was going up to the Temple. He was so respected that the publican stood "afar off" from him in the Temple.

The Publican

But let's take a look at the publican. The publican was a tax collector. This man was despised and rejected. The decent and honorable absolutely abhored him. You remember that Rome simply contracted with the highest bidders, and Rome didn't care what more you collected. There was no board of examiners breathing down their necks. They set up their tables on the road, and you didn't go anywhere without dealing with the publicans. They had you by the neck and extortion was the name of the game.

You weren't going anywhere without passing by their tables, and they were going to take from you all that was coming to the Roman government plus whatever they pleased to take for themselves. Whatever the traffic would stand was what they extracted. And, consequently, the only friends they had were the rough, the immoral, and the loose; they were abhored by almost all people.

I found it interesting to learn that Tacitus, the Roman historian, wrote about a town in which there was an honest tax collector. They actually erected a monument to the man because he was the only one they had ever heard of.

Well, this is the publican. And if we had been there, we probably would have felt a little more comfortable with him because, you see, he was a religious man. He was not of the despicable crowd, and we probably would have gone his way.

Standing in the Presence of God

Jesus said these two men "went up into the Temple to pray." And that is exactly where they ought to be, and there is nothing wrong with that. You remember, there were certain hours of devotion when they went into the Temple. Peter and John (Acts 3) were going up at the time of prayer, and they were intercepted by the man at the Beautiful Gate. It was the time of prayer, and these two were where they ought to have been. At least, they were not out on the golf course, or they were not fishing, or they were not doing ten thousand other things that a person might be doing on the day they were supposed to be in the Temple.

They did not subscribe to this modern "walk in the park" theology that says when you really grow up spiritually, you don't need to come together in little church houses and sing little songs to God. What you, rather, need to do is to take a walk through the park and adore God's great creation and imbibe the spirit of the great Jehovah. Well, they didn't believe that. They were exactly where they should have been.

I think what our Lord wants us to do as He preaches this sermon is to step back a little into the shadows of Solomon's porch and take a close look. Look at these two men. Look at what is occurring in the lives of two men who were as different as they could be. First of all, we find that, "the Pharisee stood and prayed thus with himself." Now, there is no problem with "standing" and "praying" because the man who goes down to his house justified does the same thing. You might begin to suspect a bit of a problem when the scripture says, he "stood and prayed thus with HIMSELF." He excluded himself from the other people. By his very actions, I am sure others really thought, they shouldn't be where he was.

Pretentious Prayer

It isn't until we hear this man start to pray that we get suspicious. We hear him saying, "God, I thank thee, that I am not as other men are, extortioners, unjust, adulterers, or even as this publican." It is indicated to us from what Jesus says that the Pharisee is standing with uplifted hands—and according to

1 Timothy 2, there is no problem with men thus praying. He is standing, and he is praying. Evidently he is looking up, praying about his situation ... "extortioners, unjust, adulterers"—and his eye lands upon that hapless publican— "or even as this publican, Lord." And then he proceeds to say, "I fast twice in the week, I give tithes of ALL I possess."

The thing that bothers us about this man's prayer is that he sounds conceited, and there isn't anyone who likes that. A conceited person is someone who is always putting others down and trying to raise himself at the expense of others. And we don't like his prayer! We would like to get him off and talk with him about it and say, "Look, you can't pray like that! You can't stand in the presence of God and tell Him how great you are."

You know, I think we have never really realized what it means to stand in the presence of God. We become so accustomed to walking in God's world and breathing His air and eating His food and spending His money that we take it all for granted, and we forget even the little that we know about being in the presence of God.

Here is a man standing in the Temple, which was God's dwelling place at that time, and it doesn't seem to bother him at all to inform God of all of his virtues and all the great things that he has done. It would appear that the Pharisee thinks what matters on earth is bound to matter in Heaven. And if it matters among men, it's bound to be extremely meaningful to God. According to this Book, that's not always the case, as is evident from what Jesus has to say at this time.

Trusting in Self

Notice that he uses the personal pronoun five times in his prayer. Five times he is discussing himself and what he did and what he has accomplished and what he is not and all such. It is pride. Remember why Jesus is preaching the sermon, verse 9; He said He spoke this to those who "trusted in themselves that they were righteous, and despised others." And as He is preaching to those people, He wants to talk to them about pride–the condemnation of the devil.

Evidently the Pharisee feels that if he can put someone else down, it will make him stand a little taller. What kind of spiritual insanity is it that would cause us to feel that if we can put someone else down and stand upon their carcass, we stand a little higher in the courts of Heaven?

Notice what he does. He divides all humanity into two classes. He says, "God, I ... " HE is one of the classes. "God, I thank thee, that I am not as OTHER MEN are." Now, that's a pretty broad classification, isn't it? I am here, and every other man is bound to be somewhere over there, and he says he is glad that he is not like those individuals. By pointing out the sins of others, he feels better about himself. By stretching out the black backdrop of another's life and putting himself in front of it, he feels better in the sight of God.

As we stand in the shadows of the Temple and look and listen, we begin to detect a distinct odor. We are picking up an old and familiar smell. There are certain odors once smelled that we never get away from. Someone can mention the word formaldehyde and a lot of old associations in a science lab come to mind; I can still smell it.

There are certain places in this world that I have been, and you can mention the place, and I can still smell them. What we are smelling in this case in the Temple of God is the smell of grace gone sour. If you have ever caught the smell of grace gone sour, you will always recognize it.

The Pharisee WAS better—and he should have been better. Look at the man's background. He had a religious background. He had advantages. He had knowledge of the scriptures that the publican didn't have. He should have been a little better; but for some reason he decided that because he had those things, that made him better in the sight of God.

I can still remember revival meetings in the denomination that I was formerly in; there would be one night called "testimony night." It was always announced at the beginning of the revival that there would be one special night in which the preacher would tell the story of his life. And it always seemed a little strange to me that on the night the preacher told the story of his life, there was always a better crowd than the other nights. And I still remember the testimonies. I always stood amazed at how devils became angels. For some reason we seemed to feel that if we could parade these vices, they would become virtues!

I think of those times when I come across this passage. One thing I know is that self-righteousness expresses itself in self advertisement. Any time you hear someone greatly advertising himself and his virtues, you may rest assured there is somewhere a degree of self-righteousness.

Every once in a while, as I go over the country, I meet some people who are humble. How do I know? They tell me they are! There are certain people who insist they are humble, they INSIST they are; and I think about this man. What's he saying? He is standing there saying, "Lord, now we are both involved in this. Lord, you've done a great job, but you had a great person to work with. What a great vessel you've made, Lord. But look what a fine piece of clay you had to work with." That's what he is saying. He is saying that he is a cut above everybody else. He is saying, "Thank you, Lord, that I'm not like my ignorant brethren. Thank you, Lord, I know the book of Revelation, and they don't. Thank you, Lord, I have never fallen into some of the sins and the errors that I have seen other people fall into." Any time you hear that somewhere, you are seeing self-advertisement, and back of it there must be something similar to what we are looking at right here. The Pharisee had a good eye on himself. He had a bad eye on the publican. And he had no eye at all on God. God doesn't figure into his plan in any way.

The tax collector stood "afar off." Seemingly an humble man, he realizes his position. And yet, one might think, "Well, he ought to be!" Have you ever met those who seemed to be contrite and humble, and you think, "Well, brother, they have a lot to be humble about." And as you look at this man, he ought to be humble! After all, extortion was the name of his game; he's had people by the throat—he has some pretty filthy hands. I think you could look at it like that. Humility ought to come easy for him. I guess there are people who think that ought to be true with some of us because of the lives we live.

He could have said—and I keep listening for it but it never comes—"God, I thank you that I am not a Pharisee." He could have said, "God, I thank you that I am not a hypocrite. I don't wear long robes, Lord. And I don't have any phylacteries, and I don't pray long prayers, but I'm honest about it. I'm a terrible person; I have done terrible things, but I'm no hypocrite."

The Greatest Sin

Do you know what I have decided? With all due respect to the blasphemy against the Holy Spirit, do you know what the worst sin in the world is? When you go out and begin to talk with others, it appears that hypocrisy is the worst sin on earth. When you talk with someone who's left the church and he's decided to go back into his sins, or when you talk with someone who knows he ought to be a member of the church but he has just never gotten around to it, the worst sin on earth must be hypocrisy because that's the first thing people bring up. I have listened to more people explain about the hypocrites in the church; and they insist, "I am just as good as they are." I have never yet figured out what that proves. What advantage is it to be just as good as a hypocrite?

This man stands there and prays, "God, I thank thee, that I am not ... as this publican." That doesn't help him any. He is still just where he was, but it would appear that for some reason—and I have been trying to figure out what's back of it—for some reason we feel that if we can unwrap the running sores of our lives and parade these horrible sores of sin and say, "Look, there they are, and I'm not trying to be a hypocrite about it," that makes it all right. They are still sores, it matters not how much we make of them. One does not parade vice and cause it to become a virtue.

That reminds me of a story I heard some time ago about two robbers who had been charged and were now arraigned before the judge. One of them said, "Your Honor, before you pass sentence, consider my plea. It is true that I was there. It is true that I helped rob the bank. It is true that I walked in with my friend; but I want you to know that when I went in there, I didn't wear a mask—he did. I just walked in there without a mask." I don't think that impressed the judge very much, do you? What difference does it make to the judge whether he wore a mask or not? He walked in, and he did rob the bank. And I think we are trying to say to God, "Lord, you know, things have not been very good with my life, but I have not been a hypocrite about it." You see, the Judge must still deal with us on the basis of what we DID, not our circumstances.

But we look upon the scene, and the publican stands there and doesn't say any of those things. The scripture says he "smote upon his breast," which was an outward sign of inward anguish. You remember that when Jesus was crucified, the people came by and saw that terrible scene and "smote their breasts" and went their way (Luke 23:48). It was an expression of terrible anguish. It was customary among these people to do that. "The publican ... smote upon his breast, saying, God be merciful to ME a sinner." You know what he realized? That man realized he was in the presence of God. That's what made the difference in those two individuals.

In His Presence

In the presence of God, he saw his sin. He wasn't there to discuss his successes: he was there to discuss his needs. That's one of the values of private prayer. Of course, it should be true with any prayer. But who wants to go before the God of Heaven, Who knows our hearts and our thoughts and our motives, and discuss his successes? You rather discuss your needs! You're not there to say, "Lord, look how far I've come." You're there to say, "Lord, look how far I have to go." You're not there to say, "Lord, I want to discuss my virtues." Can you imagine anyone in private prayer wanting to discuss his virtues with God? We need to discuss our sins.

I find this situation to be true throughout the Bible. In the case of Job, you remember his miserable situation. He had lost his children. He had lost it all. His so-called friends sat about him, and finally just came out and said, Job, why don't you deal with this matter? Why don't you just say that the reason you are suffering superlatively is that you have sinned superlatively? Job denied that. In fact, God had said to Satan, "Hast thou considered my servant Job ... a perfect man" (Job 1:8). But, you know, when you come to the last portion of the book of Job, in which Job sees a vision of God, it is then that he said, "Mine eye seeth thee ... . I repent, in dust and ashes" (Job 42:5-6). What made the difference? All of a sudden, he realized the presence of God.

It was true with Isaiah. You go back and start reading the book of Isaiah and what do you find? Isaiah was the cream of the crop—a beautiful, wonderful young man. He was the best they had, and yet, one day he came into the Temple and saw a vision of God; he saw God "high and lifted up, and his train filled the temple" (Isaiah 6:1). Do you remember what he said? "Woe is me! for I am undone; because I am a man of unclean lips, and I dwell in the midst of a people of unclean lips: for mine eyes have seen the King" (Isaiah 6:5).

I find this situation to be true when you come to the New Testament. That night when everything seemed to be falling apart out there on the stormy sea, Jesus stepped on board and spoke to the elements that He had made; and those elements, which were a raging storm, fell into a mirrored calm. It was then that Peter said, "Depart from me; for I am a sinful man, O Lord" (Luke 5:8). All of a sudden, he realized he was in the presence of God, not just a man.

The Apostle Paul felt the same way. Over in 1 Timothy 1:15, he said, "I am the chief of sinners." I might point out to you, he doesn't say, I WAS. Do you mean, Paul, that after thirty years of preaching the Gospel of Jesus Christ throughout the Roman Empire, after establishing congregations that dot the whole Empire, after spending and being spent for the Cause of Christ, after leading thousands to the Lord Jesus Christ, you are still saying, "I AM the chief of sinners"?

Do you know why I think he said that? Right after that statement, he said, "Howbeit for this cause I obtained mercy, that in me first Jesus Christ might shew forth all longsuffering, for a pattern to them which should hereafter believe on him to life everlasting. Now unto the King eternal, immortal, invisible, the only wise God, be honour and glory for ever and ever. Amen." He knew the presence of Almighty God; and that makes a tremendous difference.

Paul became aware of his needs—he became aware of the need of the grace of God. Perhaps you sit in this assembly thinking, "These people don't understand my situation. These people have studied the Bible for years and are strong in the faith. These people don't really need the grace of God." Let me tell you something. There is no one here tonight, sitting or standing in this room, who does not have a tremendous need for the grace of God. There will never come a time when you can go it alone; I have learned that. And I continue to learn that. I need the grace of God tonight as much as any person who walks the street. "God be merciful to me a sinner."

Elements of True Prayer

I wonder if we've ever really learned to pray. It takes some terrible things to make us learn to pray, to really realize what we are doing, to realize we are in the presence of the Creator, the One who holds our breath in His hands; as Paul put it, the One "with whom we have to do" (Hebrews 4:13); the One who is my Judge for all eternity—we're in His presence and surely like this man, we say, "God be merciful to me a sinner."

Did you notice, when the Pharisee is praying, he uses the personal pronoun over and over and never one time—not one time in his prayer—is there a confession of sin. Not one time in his prayer does he express a need. Not one time does he open up a wound to the trusted eye of the Great Physician. If there is anything we ought to remember when we come to pray, it's to say, "Lord, forgive me of my sins." No one should mind baring the wound to the trusted physician. We do it all the time because that's the way we can be healed. No confession of sin—no expression of need—and yet he took thirty-four words to pray his prayer. The publican prayed his in seven. The man who was justified said it all in seven words.

Listen to the publican's prayer. He stood "afar off," not from God, but from the Pharisee. He just stands there with bowed head saying, "God be merciful to me a sinner." He has no book of directions that tells him how he is supposed to do it. No one handed him a program when he walked into the Temple, and said, "Look, here is the way you worship; here is the way you pray to God." Jesus says he "would not lift, up so much as his eyes unto heaven." He will not lift up to Heaven those hands that are so polluted and so sinful. He isn't going to look up into the face of the God of Heaven. He simply stands there with head bowed and says, "God be merciful to me." He feels that guilty distance between him and God.

Notice, he doesn't say, "God, be merciful to me, a reformed sinner." He doesn't say, "God, be merciful to me, a penitent sinner" or a "praying sinner." Neither does he say, "Lord, I want you to be easy with me because, you see, I have just been doing my duty. A man has to make a living, and I was just doing what they told me to do. I realize things haven't gone so well, but I have just been doing what everybody else has." He doesn't say any of that.

Do you know what he reminds me of? He reminds me of another sermon Jesus preached about a prodigal son who came back and said, "Father, I have sinned against heaven, and before thee" (Luke 15:18). Not one time did he discuss a brother who didn't want him back. Not one time did he say, "You never treated me right." Not one time did he say, "Home wasn't what it ought to be." You see, when you come face to face with your sin, there is only one thing that really matters, and that is saying, "Father, I have sinned against heaven ... ." —that's the proper perspective " ... and before thee." It reminds me of Psalms 51:10 where David said, "Create in me a clean heart, O God; and renew a right spirit within me."

The publican said, "God be merciful to me ... ." It's interesting to note that some translations put it—and I understand it's closer to the original—"God, be merciful to me, THE sinner." He felt as if he were THE sinner of the world. Notice, he pleads for mercy—it's mercy I need, Lord. And mercy, I am persuaded, from what Jesus said in the beatitudes, is a high compound of love plus forgiveness.

Just because you love somebody, doesn't mean you have had mercy on him. It is a compound of love plus forgiveness. He doesn't ask for justice. Can you imagine a person praying for justice? That, to me, is unthinkable. I can't imagine bowing before the Creator, the all-seeing and all-knowing One, and saying, "Lord, would you grant me justice?" Justice would fall on him—and he knew it—like a naked sword. And he didn't want that. He sought, and he found, love and forgiveness. His prayer ascended to the Lord like sweet incense while the prayer of the Pharisee blew back in his face like smoke. "God resisteth the proud, but giveth peace unto the humble" (James 4:6).

In the early 1800's, a preacher wrote a little poem about this story, and he did a good job, I think. He said:

> "Two went to pray? O, rather say,
>   One to brag, the other to pray;
> One stands up close and treads on high,
>   Where the other dares not send his eye;
> One near to God's altar trod,
>   The other to the altar's God."

He had a beautiful grasp of what our Lord is saying.

Settled in Heaven — Heart — Home

And then our Lord says, "I tell you"—listen to what He is saying—"I tell you, this man went down to his house justified." When you talk about justification, you are talking about an account that is settled in Heaven. He declares him acquitted. He insists the man is righteous; and if it is settled in Heaven, it is also settled in the heart. It's a transitive thing. Settled in Heaven ... settled in the heart. And I like, too, what Jesus says, "This man went down to his house justified."

I thought as I was studying this parable, how I would liked to have been in that house while he was still an unjustified publican. And THEN I would have liked to have been in the house that night when he came home. Something's happened to Papa! Things are different now!

I want to tell you, I wouldn't give a dime for a religion where everything's all right in the Temple while it's miserable in the house. Brother, if it's all right in the Temple, and it's been settled—the old account's been settled in Heaven—it ought to be settled at home. God forbid that we are one thing at church and something else at home.

He "went down to his house justified rather than the other." A change. Jesus says—and I think we ought to look at that— "Rather than the other." Our Lord is not suggesting one man is justified more than the other one is. You see, you are either justified or you are not! Not, one is justified MORE than the other. He is simply saying—one is justified completely and the other not at all.

One of them goes home with all of his virtues and all of his sins; one goes home justified and cleansed of sin. This teaches me there is grace to help in time of need. And I know that's true. We are all learning more and more that it is true. We sometimes sing the beautiful song titled, "When I Survey The Wondrous Cross," by Isaac Watts:

> "When I survey the wondrous cross
>   On which the Prince of glory died,
> My richest gain I count but loss,
>   And pour contempt on all my pride."

Then he so beautifully wrote the second stanza:

> "Forbid it, Lord, that I should boast,
>   Save in the death of Christ my Lord;
> All the vain things that charm me most,
>   I sacrifice them to His blood."

I wonder, tonight, if you, like this man, have been playing the old religious game. You have been going up to the Temple, you have been going up to the house of God, thinking about your virtues. You have been thinking how good the sermon has been for the person down the seat from you or across the aisle. You have been thinking about the good things you have accomplished through the years and how great it is. Have you been thinking about the hypocrites in the church, the great needs of your fellow man?

Surely, tonight, our Lord is saying to us we had better think about ourselves and realize we are sinners. I wonder if you are here, and you are not a Christian, would you become a Christian tonight? Would you just simply face it and say, "I have sinned, and I want to become a Christian; I want to believe the gospel. It doesn't matter what other people think or what they're doing. I'm here, and I am in God's presence. I want to believe, and I want to repent of my sins, and I want to confess Christ, and I want to be immersed in His precious name."

Are you here, tonight, as my brother or my sister and need so much to say, "God be merciful to me a sinner." How are you going home tonight? Are you going to walk out of here with whatever virtues you may possess and still, like that man, with all your sins? Are you going to go down to your house justified in God's sight? Rest assured, while we're singing, there is grace that is greater than all of our sins, and it's here tonight. "God be merciful to me a sinner."

Sermon Nine

The
Parables
of
Jesus

"And He spake many things
unto them in parables"

Luke 14:15-24

"And when one of them that sat at meat with him heard these things, he said unto him, Blessed is he that shall eat bread in the kingdom of God. Then said he unto them, A certain man made a great supper, and bade many: And sent his servant at supper time to say to them that were bidden, Come; for all things are now ready. And they all with one consent began to make excuse. The first said unto him, I have bought a piece of ground, and I must needs go and see it: I pray thee have me excused. And another said, I have bought five yoke of oxen and I go to prove them: I pray thee have me excused. And another said, I have married a wife, and therefore I cannot come. So that servant came, and shewed his lord these things. Then the master of the house being angry said to his servant, Go out quickly into the streets and lanes of the city, and bring in hither the poor, and the maimed, and the halt, and the blind. And the servant said, Lord, it is done as thou hast commanded, and yet there is room. And the lord said unto the servant, Go out into the highways and hedges, and compel them to come in, that my house may be filled. For I say unto you, That none of those men which were bidden shall taste of my supper."

9. The Great Supper

The parable before us this evening is extremely familiar. It is one of the great parables of Jesus Christ, one that touches every heart and home, and one that depicts humanity with amazing clarity. There is a lesson in this parable for both saint and sinner alike. It matters not whether we are members of the church, the truths in this lesson will reach into every heart; and all of us shall surely feel the need of coming to the Lord.

In this parable, we notice that "A certain man made a great supper, and bade many." We have no doubt that our Lord Jesus Christ is this man, the One who has both prepared and provided for the world a tremendous spiritual feast. He stands today inviting all to come to that feast. It is expressed so beautifully in Matthew 28:18-19:

> All power is given unto me in heaven and on earth. Go ye therefore, and teach all nations, baptizing them in the name of the Father, and of the Son, and of the Holy Ghost: Teaching them to observe all things whatsoever I have commanded you: and, lo, I am with you always, even unto the end of the world.

Jesus says the invitation is for all mankind. In Revelation 3:20, He says, "Behold, I stand at the door, and knock: if any man will hear my voice, and open the door, I will come in to him, and will sup with him, and he with me." Or the beautiful passage in Matthew 11:28, "Come unto me, all ye that labour and are heavy laden, and I will give you rest." He has, indeed, made for the world a tremendous feast, and He invites everyone to come.

160

The Invitation

You will notice that in the parable, the invitation is first sent to those who are within the city. I suggest to you that, laying aside the structure of the parable, what we have is the gospel call being first extended to the Jewish people. In Matthew 10:5-7, you recall our Lord saying, "Go not into the way of the Gentiles, and into any city of the Samaritans enter ye not: But go rather to the lost sheep of the house of Israel. And as ye go, preach, saying, The kingdom of heaven is at hand." In Romans 1:16, Paul says, "I am not ashamed of the Gospel of Christ: for it is the power of God unto salvation to everyone that believeth; to the Jew first, and also to the Greek." So, the gospel was first extended to the Jews.

This passage says they "were bidden." At what time were they bidden? It was the oriental custom to invite one to a feast; then at the particular moment of final preparation, a servant would be sent saying, "Come NOW for all things are ready." They were invited to come to a feast to which they had had a prior invitation. Certainly the Jewish nation was "bidden"—to use the Lord's words. They had been taught by the prophets, and John the Baptist had come on the scene saying, "The kingdom of heaven is at hand" (Matthew 3:2). They had every opportunity to know about Jesus, the Great Messiah, and the Kingdom that He came to establish. None of these people could say they did not know about the Great Feast. They had indeed been bidden.

As they go out to the people and invite them, they "with one consent began to make excuse," and they simply do not come. And so he said, "Go ... into the streets and lanes of the city, and bring in hither the poor, and the maimed, and the halt, and the blind." Notice, these people were still living in the city, but they were, in that distinction that we loathe to make, the poorer, lower class of people. These people would have nothing to preoccupy them. They weren't too busy with houses or lands or social ties to come to the feast.

You recall many of these came—"the poor, and the maimed, and the halt, and the blind." They came to the feast and yet the servant said, "Lord, it is done as thou hast commanded, and yet there is room." That is a beautiful thought—that the house of God is ever adequate. Regardless of how many come into His house, or how many come to the Great Feast, it is so commodious that there is always room. We sometimes sing, "There Is Room At The Cross For You," and that is so very true.

But notice, even as these people come, he says, "I want you to go into the highways and hedges, and compel them to come in, that my house may be filled." Now this time we are moving outside the city. Outside the "streets and the lanes." This time we are going out into the country, into the vineyards and the out-of-the-way places.

This picture so beautifully fits Acts 2:39 where Peter says the "promise is unto you, and to your children, and to all that are afar off, even as many as the Lord our God shall call." Moving out of the city and out into the country depicts an appeal being made to the Gentiles.

I would also point out that an appeal is being made to the poor and to the lowly. If the first ones who were invited had come, they would not have wanted to sit at meat with these, and yet the Lord wants them. This scene should always remind the church in every age that there is no room for a caste system or a system of partiality in the church. You recall that James had to write to rectify this problem that existed even in the day of Christ. Let's listen to his words in James 2: 1-7:

> My brethren, have not the faith of our Lord Jesus Christ, the Lord of glory, with respect of persons, For if there come into your assembly a man with a gold ring, in goodly apparel, and there come in also a poor man in vile raiment; and ye have respect to him that weareth the gay clothing, and say unto him, Sit thou here in a good place; and say to the poor, Stand thou there, or sit here under my footstool; Are ye not then partial in yourselves, and are become judges of evil thoughts? Hearken, my beloved brethren, Hath not God chosen the poor of this world rich in faith, and heirs of the kingdom which he hath promised to them that love him? But ye have despised the poor. Do not rich men

oppress you, and draw you before the judgment seats? Do not they blaspheme that worthy name by the which ye are called?

Here the Bible sets forth a problem of an ancient time; but, as I suggested, if this were a problem in that ancient time, what a problem it may well be in this time of affluence and sophistication. The church must ever be warned that such behavior will never be acceptable.

The Lord made an appeal to the poor and lowly. In fact, the scripture just flatly states that God has "chosen the poor of this world rich in faith, and heirs of the kingdom which he hath promised to them that love him" (James 2:5). May the church ever be reminded that the ground is level at the foot of the cross. It matters not who you are or what you have or what you do not have, if one is rich in faith, he stands high in the house of God.

So, at this point in the parable, the invitation is sent to everyone. All people are being invited. Notice that the last two classes invited, from the streets and lanes and the highways and hedges, would feel so unworthy that they would have to be constrained; he said, "Go out ... and compel" (or constrain) "them to come in." They were accepted, and they were wanted at the great supper.

They Began to Make Excuse

Notice the excuses of the first who were invited—not all three of these groups, but simply the first group, the prominent men of the Jews—the scribes, the Pharisees, the doctors of the law. Now notice, they were invited ahead of time, and again specifically at suppertime. But even though they had been invited—even though they had prior invitation—they went ahead and made their appointments of business and pleasure, with no regard for the time of the feast. They evidently placed no value upon the friendship of the Master or the feast that he had prepared. The excuses are excuses of disrespect. And I propose to you that they even progress in disrespect. They are familiar; let's listen to them again.

First, an individual is invited to the feast; and he explains, "I have bought a piece of ground, and I must needs go and see it: I pray thee have me excused." What an amazing thing! Few people would buy a piece of property without seeing it; but we shall give this person all the benefit of the doubt. Suppose that he did buy a piece of property, and he has not seen it. Parcels of land do not leave; it would not have gotten away. He could have seen it later, but he flatly states, "I bought it, and I simply must go and see it." And the Lord is not speaking to us only about a man who bought a field; He is rather talking about all those who, in all ages of time, allow the love of possessions to keep them from the Great Banquet Table of the King. The love of possessions was the problem of this individual as well as countless thousands through the centuries.

The man in our parable goes on inviting others, and he meets one who said he would really like to go to the feast but he couldn't make it because, "I have bought five yoke of oxen, and I go to prove them." Isn't this interesting? This man is in big business. He didn't say he had bought one—he rather said, "I have bought five yoke of oxen, and I go to prove them." Again we suggest, people do not usually buy even animals without seeing them. But suppose he did; he has made the transaction, the deal has been closed, and certainly the animals wouldn't have gotten away.

You notice a little difference in this case, however. While one said, "I have bought a piece of ground, and I must needs go and see it," this man has bought five yoke of oxen and said, "I go to prove them." In other words, the affairs of business are so pressing to him that they must come before an invitation to a feast. Jesus is saying that not only do men stay away from the Great Feast because of the love of possessions but also because of the affairs of business.

The third person, upon being invited to the Great Feast, simply states, "I have married a wife, and therefore I cannot come." With blatant bluntness he states that he has contracted a social tie; he doesn't even ask to be excused. Our Lord teaches us that social ties many times keep people from attending the house of God and doing the things they ought to do. Of all that may be said, and much could be said, of these three categories or excuses, one must conclude the excuses are steeped in hypocrisy. The fact is, they simply did not want to go, and so they offer their trifling excuses and say they won't be there.

I would like to point out quickly that excuses have never been accepted by God. Reasons, yes; but excuses, never! The excuses of Adam and Eve were not accepted. The excuses of Moses, the excuses of Aaron, the excuses of Saul, and many others on down through the stream of time, have just never been acceptable to God.

I would like for us now to listen to our modern day for a few moments. I would like to point out some of the excuses that I have heard over the years. These are not excuses that I have read about, but these are things that I have actually experienced. I have listened to people tell me, "I just can't make it. I would really like to be there, and I know it's a wonderful thing; but I can't attend the Great Banquet of the King. I can't come to the Feast because I still have this problem or that problem or this must be done or that must be done."

Too Young

One of the things that I have heard through the years is, "I can't come to the Feast because I am just too young." Have you ever heard that? Have you ever said that? Many people in this world feel that religion is for people who are so old and so decrepit that they can't do anything else, and that once they have reached that place, that's the time to begin serving the Lord. There are those who say, "I am too young, I have a lot of things I want to do yet." Many times I've heard young people of high school age say this. I remember being in Kansas City many years ago, and a young lady came forward one night as the invitation was extended. I shall never forget her words. She said, "I have been giving the Lord an excuse. I have been saying for a number of years now that I'm too young." She went on to readily acknowledge that the reason was, "I simply had other things I wanted to do. There were some wild oats that I wanted to sow, and I just wasn't willing to come to the Lord." I was grateful for her as she made the decision to serve the Lord while she was young.

We would do well to remember the words of Solomon in Ecclesiastes 12:1-4:

> Remember now thy Creator in the days of thy youth, while the evil days come not, nor the years draw nigh, when thou shalt say, I have no pleasure in them; While the sun, or the light, or the moon, or the stars, be not darkened, nor the clouds return after the rain: In the day when the keepers of the house shall tremble, and the strong men shall bow themselves, and the grinders cease because they are few, and those that look out of the windows be darkened, And the doors shall be shut in the streets, when the sound of the grinding is low, and he shall rise up at the voice of the bird, and all the daughters of music shall be brought low.

Solomon thus describes the life of man, beginning with youth and progressively moving into old age when his physical being becomes weaker and weaker until eventually "the dust shall return to the earth as it was; and the spirit shall return to God who gave it" (Ecclesiastes 12:7). I have always felt that this very first verse is so beautiful and meaningful: "Remember NOW thy Creator in the days of thy YOUTH" before those evil days come and before those years draw nigh in which you just don't care for things divine. I want to admonish you, tonight, to come to the Lord in your youth, and no longer say to Him, "Lord, I would serve you, and come to the Great Feast, but I'm too young."

I am well aware there are some who are too young; that is, if they haven't reached the age of accountability or if they don't understand these things, certainly they are too young. But I'll tell you, when people get to the place that they stand up and tell you, "I'm too young, and this is the reason that I am not coming to the Great Feast," I propose to you that what we have is not a reason. What we have is rather an excuse.

Too Old

Next, we move to the other extreme. I have listened to people say, "I would come to the Great Feast, and I would really like to serve the Lord, but I feel that I am too old now, I have wasted my life; I have burned the candle of life low and all that's left are a few ashes, and God wouldn't want me now." I remind you, tonight, that the Lord is "not willing that any should perish, but that all should come to repentance" (2 Peter 3:9).

The fact is, so long as you live and you are in your right mind, you can be born again. You can become a new born babe in Christ Jesus. It may well, indeed be the eleventh hour, but I remind you that the Lord went into the market place even at the eleventh hour calling workers into His vineyard.

Over this country I have seen many, many elderly people baptized into Christ Jesus. Of course, it is lamentable that one waits until those last years, having spent the best of his life; certainly that's lamentable. But the fact is, if you are here, tonight, and you have never obeyed the Gospel of Jesus Christ, you are still in "the land of beginning again," and you need so much to come to the Lord while there is time and opportunity.

I have often related the story, and it is still a pleasurable memory to me, of a dear lady up in Huntington, West Virginia. Many years ago, I was there conducting a meeting, and I remember this dear person beginning to attend the meeting. She was an elderly lady, 70 something years old at that time. I didn't get her to come to the meeting; some of the brethren had been out working in the community and found this person, and she began to come. I will never forget the first night she was there. She said, "I haven't been inside a church house in 50 years." Fifty years!!! ... she had never seen inside a church house, but that night she listened to the gospel preached, and the people of the congregation made her feel welcome, and she came back the next night and the next night and the next night. And before the meeting was over, I had the privilege of baptizing her in the flooding waters of the Ohio River. She was baptized into Jesus Christ. She became a new born baby; though she was old, she became new. What a wonderful thing it was to see this person become a Christian.

Perhaps there's one here, tonight, and you are saying to yourself, "I am just too old to begin." May I submit to you that that is just not true. The Lord is saying, "Come unto me, ALL ye that labour ... ." (Matthew 11:28). He is saying, "I stand at the door, and knock: if ANY MAN ... ." (Revelation 3:20). So we would admonish you, at this moment, to no longer give the Lord such an excuse.

Complacency

Another excuse that I have often found given for not coming to the Great Feast—and I think there are thousands and thousands relying upon this one—"I would come to the Great Feast, but I feel like I am all right as I am. I have always tried to be good; I've been honest, and I've always tried to maintain integrity. I pay my debts; I believe in God. I have never fought the church, never opposed it. I think I am good enough, and the Lord will save me anyway." My people, if there is any such thing as the peril of goodness, this is bound to be it!

There are those in this world, multitudes evidently, who feel they will in some way storm the gates of Heaven with their own goodness—that in some way, because they are good people, they will be saved. Now, let me hasten to add—and I'm reluctant sometimes to even mention this because I don't want anyone to feel that we don't believe that we must be good people—I want to submit to you, tonight, that unless we are good people and unless we are the best people on earth, I don't understand what we are doing here; and I don't understand the grand concept called Christianity. We must be good people, and yet what I am saying is that goodness alone ... goodness alone will never get you inside the gates of Heaven. Someone has said that it may keep you out of jail, but it alone will never get you into Heaven. Remember that in Luke 24:46-47 Jesus says:

> Thus it behooved Christ to suffer, and to rise from the dead the third day: And that repentance and remission of sins should be preached in his name among all nations, beginning at Jerusalem.

Jeremiah 10:23 still states that "the way of man is not in himself: it is not in man that walketh to direct his steps." Jesus says in Matthew 7:21, "Not everyone that saith unto me, Lord, Lord, shall enter into the kingdom of heaven; but he that doeth the will of my Father which is in heaven." And, "Man shall not live by bread alone, but by every word that proceedeth out of the mouth of God" (Matthew 4:4). I will suggest to you, tonight, that you will not even live by bread principally to say nothing of living by bread alone. And if it is true that we can be saved by our own goodness, then our Lord died in vain because there were some good moral people living before Jesus ever died on that cross. And yet, the fact is, He tasted death for every man, "that repentance and remission of sins should be preached in his name among ALL nations" (Luke 24:47). And if you are here and you are trusting in your goodness—your goodness alone to save you—I would be less than your friend not to tell you that just simply won't do. You cannot atone for your own sins by your own goodness. You must come to Jesus Christ.

Hypocrisy

Another excuse that I sometimes hear given for not coming to the Great Feast is this: "I would come to the church, and I believe in it, but I have decided that there are hypocrites in the church, and there's really not any point in my going because I am just as good as they are." I want to agree with you this evening that there are hypocrites in the church. Reluctantly ... however, I do agree with you.

I know there are those in the church who are just playing the part. They have the props; they have the costuming; they have the paint; they have the voice; they have it all. They are, indeed, good actors on the stage of life, but I do not agree with you that because there are some hypocrites in the church, that you ought to forfeit all the benefits and all the greatness and all the grandeur of that for which my Lord died.

If everybody in this world were to be lost and go to Hell, that is no excuse for your going. I know this, that anyone who stands between you and God just may be a little closer to God than you are. Whatever it is, or whoever it is, that is standing between you and God is bound to be a little closer than you are. Think about it. You know, we don't reason this way in anything else. We don't reason, "I am not going out to work tomorrow morning because I know there are some hypocrites out there in the business world." We have found some people who are not always what they say they are. We KNOW that that's the case. We KNOW that there are people out there who are not what they ought to be; and yet, none of us reasons, "Well, I'll never go back and work another day." We say, "We must make a living." That's true; but it is also true, my friend, that we must make a life that is WORTH living. And that will be only in Jesus Christ.

I've learned there's hypocrisy sometimes even in school systems. I have found there are a few people there who are not always what they claim to be. They are hypocrites in the fullest sense of the word. And yet, I don't know many people who reason, "Well, because I have found there are such in the educational world, I will never educate myself another day," or "I will never send my child to school again." Ah, but we say, "They must have an education." But, my friend, the greatest education on earth, in fact the only one that will endure for both time and eternity, is that education that is divine.

Society is full of hypocrisy, but I don't know a lot of hermits, do you? Married life even sometimes has hypocrisy, but I don't know a lot of bachelors. And I'll tell you a place that's full of hypocrites—Hell will be full of them. And we certainly ought to avoid being with all of them for all eternity. In fact, I want to suggest to you that Heaven is the only place I know that you can go and get away from them all. But I want to remind you that the church is the very gate of Heaven; you will never enter Heaven without it.

Don't let a few hypocrites rob you of eternal life. It would be better to be with a few of them here for a little while than to be with all of them in Hell forever and ever. You cannot reject the Christ just because there lived a Judas! Be it then or now, this is no excuse; it will not be acceptable to the Lord.

Fear of Criticism and Persecution

But again, another excuse I have heard is, "Well, I would come to the Great Feast and I would really live for the Lord, but it isn't consistent with my business." When a person says that, I think it is evident to them they are in the wrong business. And they really know they ought not to be there because it is inconsistent with the principles of Christianity. I hear this excuse every once in a while. It's amazing, people, that we make all of our plans; and then we try to find a religion to suit us and that will fit our plans, instead of obeying God and finding something that will suit Him and will fit our Christian living.

We are like those in the parable. We have already gone ahead, regardless of the invitation, and made our appointments of business and pleasure. We buy our land, and we get our oxen; we go right on; and if it fits in with the church, fine. If it doesn't, then we simply ignore the church. How many times have we all seen this happen? And we have seen many a soul made shipwreck.

We must admit that if we are in a business that is dishonest, there is only one thing to do and that is—get out of it. However, I often find that isn't the real problem. Many times I have found that those who offer this excuse are in a business that is all right, but they don't want to face the persecution they will have to bear—the ridicule and the scorn and the unbelief they must deal with day by day from some of their business associates.

Another excuse that I sometimes hear, "I would become a Christian, I would like to come to the Great Feast, but I know that if I do, my associates or my family will ridicule me." First of all, this fact I do not deny. I am very much aware that for you to become a Christian may involve your being criticized. You may find that people will do you a great deal of damage verbally. May I suggest to you, however, that this is no reason for your not living a Christian life or for your not coming to the Great Feast. I rather suggest to you that this is simply part of bearing the cross for Jesus Christ. And our Lord says in Luke 9:23, "If any man will come after me, let him deny himself, and take up his cross daily, and follow me."

Paul says, "All that will live godly in Christ Jesus shall suffer persecution" (2 Timothy 3:12). I do not know of any Christian, who has ever really lived for the Lord, who did not suffer persecution. In fact, you get ready for it—it will occur! Your associates may ridicule you. Some of your old friends may leave you. Some of those of your own household may turn against you.

What if the Apostle Paul ... what if Peter ... what if Stephen had said, "I would like to follow Christ, and I would like to do something for the church, but I am afraid that somebody won't like me." Where would the church be today? Where would the Cause of Christ be? I am very much aware that this is a very powerful tool of Satan. I have been through that.

I remember so well coming to a knowledge of the truth and then facing this very thing. I knew that I needed to be a Christian. I needed to obey the gospel, but I knew what it would be at home. I had fears of being persecuted and fears of people turning against me—of people really putting me down—and that did occur. But it can be done, and you will be the stronger Christian for having come through it. This is not a valid excuse in the sight of God. How would you like to discuss it with the Apostle Paul who suffered so many things for Christ? How would you like to talk with Stephen about it, a man who shed his blood standing for the cross and for what was right.

Waiting For Others

But maybe you're saying, "These things really don't bother me. The thing that's keeping me out of the church and away from the Great Feast of God is not that. I intend to come, but I am just waiting for a few other people. My wife, you see, has never obeyed the Gospel of Jesus; and when she becomes a Christian, then I am going to become a Christian, too," or "I am not a member of the church; my husband is, but he doesn't go to church; and what I have decided is that when he decides to make things right with the Lord and go back to the church, then I intend to obey the gospel and I, too, will sit at the Lord's Table."

First of all, may I remind you that in our text, Jesus did not accept this excuse. It mattered not that some said, "I have bought a piece of ground, and I must needs go and see it," and others said, "I have bought five yoke of oxen, and I go to prove them," or "I have married a wife and ... cannot come." I want to remind you that Jesus did not accept any of these. Service to God must come before anyone or anything! What if everyone did used these excuses? What if others were to say, "When somebody else becomes a Christian, I will." What if everyone were to adhere to such; no one would be a Christian. Our Lord expects you to be willing to deny yourself and to put Him before anyone in this world. It is then and only then that you can become a Christian.

Only One Reason

There are so many other things that might be said. Perhaps there are those in this audience tonight who are holding out with other excuses. I don't really know what all your excuses may be. But I want you to ask yourself how good it will sound before the Lord in the Great Judgment for all eternity and give Him that excuse that is keeping you out of the Kingdom of God tonight. Be honest with yourself.

Really, there is only one reason for you not to come to the Great Feast. You have been invited. You know you ought to believe the gospel. You know you ought to repent of your sins. You know that you need to confess Christ. And you know that you need to be baptized for the remission of your sins. You understand all that.

Do you know there is only one reason that—regardless of how many excuses you may be giving yourself and others—there is only one reason that you are not a Christian tonight; and that is that you have not fully made up your mind. You have not fully made up your mind to become a Christian and to take that great step because when you do, nobody—not all the demons of Hell itself—can keep you from doing it.

You can serve the Lord. You can become a Christian tonight. The only reason you are not a Christian is that YOU have not decided that this is what you need to do. You can ... if you will.

Plenty of Time

While we are singing this song, I would like to remind you that there is one excuse that seems to be universal. Out of all the others that may vary from individual to individual, there is one that has a note of universality about it. And that is this, "I still have plenty of time."

It doesn't matter how young one may be or how old he may be, for some strange reason everybody feels he has plenty of time. Opportunities are fleeting. The moments are passing. The hours are changing to days, and days are changing to years. We are chained to the chariot of rolling time and from it there is no release, but for some reason we keep saying, "There is plenty of time."

James says, "Go to now, ye that say today or tomorrow we will go into such a city, and continue there a year, and buy and sell, and get gain: whereas ye know not what shall be on the morrow ... . For that you ought to say, If the Lord will, we shall live, and do this, or that" (James 4:13-15). In 2 Corinthians 6:2, Paul says, "Now is the accepted time." When? NOW! "Now is the accepted time; behold, now is the day of salvation." I want to tell you, the cemeteries are filled with people who intended to obey God. Millions are unprepared who intend to obey God. Multitudes have moved into the great eternity since this sermon began—those who had every intention of changing their lives and obeying God.

Listen! The Lord is passing by. Do you remember that story given us by the Lord in Mark 10:46? The Bible says they came to Jericho; and as they went out of Jericho, there was a great multitude of people following along. There was a blind man by the name of Bartimaeus who was sitting by the highway begging. He suddenly became aware that it was Jesus of Nazareth who was passing by, and he began to cry out and say, "Jesus, thou son of David, have mercy on me." And you remember that others nearby told him to be still ... the Lord didn't have time for him. But he cried the more. Mark says, "He cried the more a great deal, Thou son of David, have mercy on me." And though the crowd had no time for blind Bartimaeus, Jesus did. Jesus stood still and commanded him to be brought to Him. You remember they went to the blind man and said, "Be of good comfort, rise, he calleth thee." Bartimaeus rose up, threw away his garment and came to Jesus. Jesus answered and said, "What wilt thou that I should do unto thee?" Bartimaeus cast those unseeing eyes upon Jesus and said, "Lord, that I might receive my sight. And Jesus said unto him, Go thy way; thy faith hath made thee whole. And immediately he received his sight and followed Jesus." (Mark 10:46-52)

I think that is a beautiful story. Old Bartimaeus knew that Jesus was passing by and though others told him to be still— that He had no time for the likes of him—Bartimaeus cried the more, "Lord, have mercy on me." Jesus said, "Bartimaeus, what is it … ?" "Lord, that I may see." I want to tell you tonight, the Lord is passing by. While the world and the devil are telling you, "Be still, the Lord doesn't have time for you" … or … "This is not the right time," I want to tell you, you had better cry out tonight, "Lord, that I may see." Why should you leave this place tonight rejecting a feast? Why should you walk away a hungering and a dying man? Why don't you come to the Great Feast tonight?

Sermon Ten

The
Parables
of
Jesus

"And He spake many things
unto them in parables"

Luke 13:1-10

"There were present at that season some that told him of the Galileans, whose blood Pilate had mingled with their sacrifices. And Jesus answering said unto them, Suppose ye that these Galileans were sinners above all the Galileans, because they suffered such things? I tell you, Nay: but, except ye repent, ye shall all likewise perish. Or those eighteen, upon whom the lower in Siloam fell, and slew them, think ye that they were sinners above all men that dwelt in Jerusalem? I tell you, Nay: but, except ye repent, ye shall all likewise perish. He spake also this parable; A certain man had a fig tree planted in his vineyard; and he came and sought fruit thereon, and found none. Then said he unto the dresser of his vineyard, Behold, these three years I come seeking fruit on this fig tree, and find none: cut it down; why cumbereth it the ground? And he answering said unto him, Lord, let it alone this year also, till I shall dig about it and dung it; And if it bear fruit, well: and if not, then after that thou shalt cut it down. And he was teaching in one of the synagogues on the sabbath."

10. The Barren Tree

The comparison of a man to a tree and his works to fruit is a common comparison in the Holy Scriptures. I think it is only natural that it would be so because it is both spiritually suggestive and appropriate. Fruit is the produce of the tree. It is the end for which the tree exists, and we expect fruition for our labors. If this is true of plants or trees, it is much more true of man. Man is much more the property of God than a tree is our property. God has spent so much on us, and we should expect Him to be disappointed if He finds no fruit in our lives.

This parable was occasioned by those who had an eagerness to tell something. On this day, the people came running to the Lord with a story. It seems that Pilate has committed a new outrage, and they are anxious to tell the Lord about it. They break in on His teaching and tell Him of a horrible situation. They tell him about blood that had been mingled with their sacrifices. It appears that while some were in the act of worship, a tide of soldiers swept over them. There was a horrible massacre; the blood of people flowed amongst the blood of animals, and they go on to describe this horrible situation. They seem to think, of course, that nothing could be worse. They saw those who perished as great sinners. They felt that because this had happened, those people were bound to be guilty of some enormous sin or of some horrible guilt. They felt they were so guilty it turned their very worship into sin; their propitiation became a provocation.

You remember that in that day—and I would suppose in any day—it would be considered a great curse to mingle the blood of the offerer with the offering, and they thus concluded that those people were bound to have been abominable sinners. But notice what the Lord does—and I am sure they considered His response surprising and shocking—Jesus turns to them and says, "Suppose ye that these Galileans were sinners above all the Galileans, because they suffered such things?" (Luke 13:2). Jesus bluntly says you're wrong; these men are no worse than anybody else. He does not deny that they are sinners, but He denies that they are sinners above all others just because they suffered these things. He says, "Suppose ye that these Galileans were sinners above all ... . I tell you, Nay: but, except ye repent, ye shall all likewise perish" (Luke 13:3). The Lord has an amazing ability to make people see themselves. So He turns the sermon around and applies it to them, too.

Robert Burns once said, "O wad some Power the giftie gie us. to see ourselves as others see us!" As humans, we would much rather discuss the death of others than discuss our own. We would much rather discuss the sins of other people than discuss ours. We would much rather react than act.

The Lord is saying to those who told the story, "Except ye repent, ye shall all likewise perish." A similar or worse punishment will fall upon you. The Lord is issuing a severe warning; we must listen to the lesson He is giving. There is always a lesson for us in the calamity of others. When we hear about some tragic things that occur to other people, it ought to be to every one of us a loud and an earnest call to repentance.

We must admit that whatever befalls another might justly have befallen us. I suppose we have all thought of such. A plane is down and two hundred seventy people are dead; sometimes it passes through my mind as to why I wasn't on board that plane. Why hasn't that ever happened to me? Or after having a bad dream, we wake up so grateful that it did not happen to us. It happened to someone else. You see, the Bible teaches that God is no respecter of persons (Acts 17:30). And this realization should remind us that when we hear of things that occur to others, it might justly have occurred to us.

The Lord continues His sermon. He asks, what about "those eighteen, upon whom the tower in Siloam fell?" Now concerning this example, I am not aware of what He is talking about, but I am sure His hearers were familiar with it. Over in Galilee, a sudden and swift catastrophe had occurred; and eighteen people perished. The Lord is saying that even in this incident, there is a call to repentance. The uncertainty of life, the ending of their world—all should awaken in us a sense and a consciousness of sin. The Lord has, as someone has so well said, given the invitation; and now He presents the sermon.

The scripture then states the Lord "spake also this parable" unto them. One of the interesting things is that Luke is the only writer on this parable. The discourse is severe and full of rebuke; now He brings up the great mercy and grace of God. He wants to talk to them about the longsuffering of God and His severity. He wants them to see the great guilt of man and yet the great grace of God. And so He speaks this parable: "A certain man had a fig tree ... ." All of us are familiar with this story. We, of course, are reminded that this man has a vineyard and evidently this fig tree is in his vineyard. The fig at that time was a native tree and much to be desired. It bore its fruit several times a year in that climate, in April and June and again in August, providing them not only fruit but shade; the fig tree was desirable.

Fruit is Both Expected and Required

This particular tree is growing in a sheltered field. It is protected, and cultivated. Evidently, the primary reference is is to the Jewish nation. Certainly, we can look upon this fig tree as being that Jewish nation. According to Isaiah 5:1-2 and 7, the Lord is setting forth the nation in this figure. The vineyard would suggest that the Jewish nation has been nurtured and blessed and guided. The coming of the master here is surely God Who, through the Old Testament years, looked and looked for Israel's fruit and yet found none. Through the "three years," He pictures the stubbornness and barrenness of these people. The warning is to "Cut it down"—impending destruction!

The fruit we are discussing is righteousness. The cutting down or destroying of Israel was due to unbelief and consequently lack of fruit. Although those things are bound to be in the background and the lessons are apparent, there are many,

many simple lessons to us for day-to-day living. Lessons of concern to Israel should be of concern to spiritual Israel. And we should see a universal application. Our Lord says in John 15:2, "Every branch ... " not just some but "Every branch in me that beareth not fruit he taketh away." So the basic principles are here.

The Bible states that the master of the vineyard "came and sought fruit thereon." I think it is so fitting of a man and his works. Let's turn to Psalms 1:1-3 and notice what he has to say regarding man and fruit bearing:

> Blessed is the man that walketh not in the counsel of the ungodly, nor standeth in the way of sinners, nor sitteth in the seat of the scornful. But his delight is in the law of the Lord; and in his law doth he meditate day and night. And he shall be like a tree planted by the rivers of water, that bringeth forth his fruit in his season; his leaf also shall not wither; and whatsoever he doeth shall prosper.

Now let's turn to Jeremiah 17:5:

> Thus saith the Lord; Cursed be the man that trusteth in man, and maketh flesh his arm, and whose heart departeth from the Lord. For he shall be like the heat in the desert, and shall not see when good cometh; but shall inhabit the parched places in the wilderness, in a salt land and not inhabited. Blessed is the man that trusteth in the Lord, and whose hope the Lord is. For he shall be as a tree planted by the waters, and that spreadeth out her roots by the river and shall not see when he cometh, but her leaf shall be green; and shall not be careful in the year of drought, neither shall cease from yielding fruit.

In John 15:1, Jesus says:

> I am the true vine, and my Father is the husbandman. Every branch in me that beareth not fruit he taketh away: and every branch that beareth fruit, he purgeth it, that it may bring forth more fruit.

Let's notice verses 4 and 5:

> Abide in me, and I in you. As the branch Cannot bear fruit of itself, except it abide in the vine; no more can ye, except ye abide in me. I am the vine, ye are the branches: He that abideth in me, and I in him, the same bringeth forth much fruit: for without me ye can do nothing.

And again that familiar passage in Romans 7:4, Paul says:

> Wherefore, my brethren, ye also are become dead to the law by the body of Christ; that ye should be married to another, even to him who is raised from the dead, that we should bring forth fruit unto God.

So in every case, the Bible sets forth the fact that we are people who are to bring forth fruit to the Lord.

Fruit is the natural outgrowth of inner life. Whether that be with a tree or with a Christian. A corrupt tree, the Bible teaches, will bring forth corrupt fruit (Matthew 12:33). A dead tree is going to have dead fruit or none at all. A good tree is going to bring forth good fruit. So fruit is the result. When the Bible talks to us about the "fruit of the Spirit" (Galatians 5:22), it is talking about results of the Spirit. And He said that all will bring forth after its kind. In every case, the fruit that we bear must be fruit that comes as the result of what we are. Fruit is not something that is to be tied on the tree. Alms that are given by us to glory in or prayers that are prayed to be heard of men are simply "tacked on" fruit, and they will never be acceptable.

Let's turn to an account that is given to us in the eleventh chapter of Mark where we learn that Jesus has spent the night in Bethany. He is on the way to Jerusalem; it is now early in the morning, and He is hungry. According to verse 12, he says:

> And on the morrow, when they were come from Bethany, he was hungry: And seeing a fig tree afar off having leaves, he came, if haply he might find anything thereon: and when he came to it, he found nothing but leaves; for the time of figs was not yet. And Jesus

answered and said unto it, No man eat fruit of thee hereafter for ever. And his disciples heard it.

Moving down to verse 20, he states:

And in the morning, as they passed by, they saw the fig tree dried up from the roots. And Peter calling to remembrance saith unto him, Master, behold, the fig tree which thou cursedst is withered away. And Jesus answering saith unto them, Have faith in God.

In this account, the Lord is discussing a fig tree that is by the road, not in the vineyard as in the parable that we're studying. He comes with expectation, and the tree promises much because it has leaves. On this tree, the fruit forms before the leaves form and the fact that it had leaves suggests it had fruit. But according to the account, He comes to the tree and finds no fruit at all. The Lord is not concerned, evidently, about the grace, the shape, and the symmetry of the tree or how beautiful or how abundantly its leaves may be; but what He is most concerned about is simply "Is it bearing fruit?"

Bear Fruit or Be Destroyed

The master comes and says to the dresser that he has been coming for three years and yet he has found no fruit. Over and over he has come, apparently more than one time each year, but he has found no fruit.

The master, of course, represents God, who is patient and long-suffering, having delayed judgment because "The Lord ... not willing that any should perish, but that all should come to repentance" (2 Peter 3:9). So God is patient, and He is longsuffering; but if He continually comes and finds no fruit in any season, we wonder how long He will bear with us. He comes, expecting to find fruit and finds nothing—nothing except utter disappointment!

Notice next that the master expresses himself clearly. He says, "Cut it down; why cumbereth it the ground?" This word cumber would suggest a reduction to idleness or inactivity. I want to point out that it implies more than just occupying so much ground. He said it's cumbering the ground. It's drawing off the life, the fatness, the fullness, the fertility of the ground and giving no return. The Lord is saying that a tree that is just there and a tree that bears no fruit is simply in the way: it is worse than useless! It is simply cumbering the ground.

Notice several things about this tree. First, it is useless. Why? Because it was bearing no fruit, there was no worth. In this passage, the Lord is describing so many today. He wants us to understand that some Christians are totally useless. They're not wicked people; they are not lawbreakers; they are not violent, revengeful, hateful. They are just simply of no use. They are there, but they are bearing no fruit. Herein is expressed for us one of the greatest tragedies of the soul. Jesus says in Matthew 5:13, "Ye are the salt of the earth: but if the salt hath lost his savour ... it is thenceforth good for nothing." Our Lord is saying that nature is useful. He is saying that salt that is salty is good. But unsalty salt is not worth a thing on earth. It is "good for nothing, but to be cast out, and to be trodden under the foot of men." In Matthew 25, He discusses the five foolish virgins. Why? They had no oil with them. He also discusses the one talent man. He describes this man as being wicked and slothful. Our Lord is saying that if you are fruitless, you are wicked. In Matthew 25:42, He is saying, "I was an hungered, and ye gave me no meat." So the true test evident in all of these passages is simple. Of what use are we? What are we worth to the Lord? Have we lost our worthiness to Him?

The Bible has never taught us that we have to be extra ordinary. The Bible has never said to us that we must speak with the tongue of men and angels. The Bible has never said that we must be sensational, but it does teach that we must be useful in the Lord's vineyard. We must accept the fact that the Lord's teaching in the first century is so current that it is true this very day. We must accept the rebuke. Our Lord is saying there are still Christians who are wasting space. There are those who are getting in the way of those who would serve Him. Like those in Matthew 23:13: "But woe unto you, scribes and Pharisees, hypocrites! for ye shut up the kingdom of heaven ... ." These were people who were standing in the door. They would neither go in nor allow others who would to go in. They were simply in the way.

Are You Cumbering the Church?

There are some people today who have been baptized, and they claim to be members of the church, and yet they seldom attend. They set a poor example; they give little to the church; they are perpetual critics and faultfinders. Nothing has ever been done right. The preaching has never been done as this person wants it. His life has become as uninviting as a desert, a life that is sterile and vain, a life that is a detriment to the church, a life that is an obstacle and a stumbling block.

There are those today who are simply cumbering the church, those who are not doing anything for God, those who are hearing no fruit for Him. Notice the Lord's mandate. He says, "Cut it down"! In this way, the Lord teaches that the useless tree invites destruction, and He proposes drastic removal. He is not interested in waiting any longer. As in Matthew 7:19, "Every tree that bringeth not forth good fruit is hewn down, and cast into the fire." Our Lord wants us to understand there comes a time and a place in which He expects fruit: and if it isn't there, there is no reason for us to continue.

You know, the law of nature says that whatever does not reproduce itself must die, whether it be trees or animals or men or the church of God. A family that does not reproduce itself takes its own life as a family. A church that does not reproduce itself takes its own life as a church. A Christian who does not reproduce himself—bear fruit and come forth in the lives of others—eventually takes his own spiritual life. And so the Lord teaches in Hebrews 6:7, "For the earth which drinketh in the rain that cometh oft upon it, and bringeth forth herbs meet for them by whom it is dressed, receiveth blessing from God: But that which beareth thorns and briers is rejected, and is nigh unto cursing; whose end is to be burned."

Where Does the Fault Lie?

Look at the divine mandate! Whose fault was it that it was cut down? One could never say that it was the fault of the soil or the sunshine or the rain or the owner of the vinedresser. The tree condemned itself by not doing the work of a tree. Fruitlessness is equated with disaster. "Cut it down"! God has the right to look for obedience in love. God has done more for us than any owner or caretaker of any vineyard has ever done. Do you realize that to spare you involves a great deal of difficulty and trouble? For you to be spared, providence must intervene—preachers must be preaching the gospel; prayers must be prayed; scriptures must be read and studied. To cut you down would be short and simple and just. It would be easy and effectual and efficient. There would be no more violating of the Lord's Day. There would be no more rejecting of the scriptures. There would be no more complaining. There would be no more bringing shame on the church. The Lord, however, wants to spare you, so He brings all these things to bear upon you. Indeed, there is the digging and fertilizing that is being done over and over again.

We raise the question, "Is it right to cut down?" We must answer, "Certainly." If you had a tree in your vineyard and it just never bore any fruit, regardless of how beautiful it may be, I think you would say that you could cut it down and never feel any qualm of conscience at all. I think the Lord is saying the same thing to us.

Is there one here who can say he has never had sufficient time to repent? Is there one here who can say he has never been dug about, he has never received the mercy of God, he has never known the fellowship of the saints, never had any afflictions, never had any trials, never had any pain, never walked in the valley of the shadow of death? Oh, I think we must all admit that we have been dug about, and we have been thus fertilized and helped. The gospel has been laid close to the roots of our lives. A Bible has been in our land and in our houses. Many of us have enjoyed the presence and the blessing of godly parents. We have been warned time and time again and yet with no improvement. We are older, but we are not wiser. We have given no service to God, no interest—a dead loss!

"My Spirit shall not Always Strive with Man"

"Cut it down"! This admonition still rings through the ages as a real warning. What if the Lord were to say of you, "Cut him down; he is filling a space where others might stand." If another mother had those children that you have, she might do a better job. If another man had the money you have, he might do more for the Lord than you are doing. If another sat in that pew where you are sitting at this time, maybe he would do more for God. If another had your talents, what wondrous things he might accomplish. If another had your health and your vigor and your strength, perhaps he would return more to God. "Cut it down"! Why cut it down? The Lord could say, "Cut it down" because your example is contagious. Somebody is following you. There is a dread disease in the vineyard, and the only remedy is to burn it out. The disease of sin must go.

Have you ever pondered why the Lord hasn't cut you down? I think all of us at some time need to sit down and think, "Why is the Lord letting me live? Why wasn't I one of those, as Jesus expressed to the people in that day, 'upon whom the tower in Siloam fell'? Why is the Lord letting me live?" Well, I know one thing, "The Lord is not .:. willing that any should perish, but that all should come to repentance" (2 Peter 3:9). There isn't any doubt but that every day that we live we're enjoying a beautiful period of grace; and the Lord is saying another year, another time for this person.

Think of the things that were occurring in that day. To those people, the prophets had come, and John the Baptist had preached, and Jesus was there. Yet, in spite of the prophets, in spite of John the Baptist, in spite of the greatest Man Who ever lived, it seems that the hearers were still the same. I wonder sometimes if this is not very true with us today.

We hear the gospel preached over and over and over, yet we continue in our sins. We're assured that "a greater than Solomon is here" (Matthew 12:42), and yet we pay no attention to Him. Rest assured, my friends, the Lord has not spared you because He is insensible to your sins. The Bible teaches that "God is angry with the wicked every day" (Psalms 7:11), and that sin is no trifle to God—however much it may be to men, it never has been to God, and it never will be. God isn't sparing you because He does not see. Your sins are like smoke in His eyes. Your sins and your iniquities provoke Him to His face. Your sins intrude into His very presence hour by hour and day by day. We might well question, "Why this long-suffering? Why hasn't God cut you down?"

May you rest assured today that there is One Who pleads for you. There is One "who is holy, harmless, undefiled, separate from sinners, and made higher than the heavens" (Hebrews 7:26), Who is pleading for you. There is, in short, a Man in Heaven; this is one of the most beautiful thoughts that ever occurred to me. I realize that it's wonderful to think about God the Son coming to earth, and that He did. "The Word was made flesh, and dwelt among us" (John 1:14). God came to earth! But I want to tell you a grander thought—one that is so beautiful—there is a Man in Heaven. "There is one God, and one mediator between God and men, the man Christ Jesus" (1 Timothy 2:5). So there is One in Heaven Who pleads for you today. You remember the gardener asked that the tree be spared, and I want to tell you the Lord pleads your case today. He pleads with mouth and with pierced hands and with wounded feet and with pierced side. He pleads your case that you might be spared.

I will remind you, however, that divine patience can be exhausted. There is a limit. There was a time, in the world that then was, that God stated, "My spirit shall not always strive with man" (Genesis 6:3). Men were no longer responsive to the Spirit of God. So then there was no reason that man should live, and so His Spirit no longer strove with man.

Even today we so misinterpret God's longsuffering. We decide, as the preacher said in Ecclesiastes 8:11, "Because sentence against an evil work is not executed speedily, therefore the heart ... is fully set ... to do evil." What is he saying? He is saying that we decide that because the Lord has not brought judgment upon us, it isn't going to happen, and so we can do as we please. The Parable of the Rich Fool should convince us that that's not the case. The tragedy of fruitlessness! The only escape is what the Lord states in Luke 13:3, "I tell you, Nay: but, except ye repent, ye shall all likewise perish." How very blunt and yet how very beautiful.

Our Lord is saying to us that we must recognize the presence of sin in our lives, we must confess those sins, we must repent of those sins, and it must be remedied in God's sight or we'll perish. Do you realize that you need to come tonight? You need to repent of your sins or you're going to die! We're nobody special; every person must repent or perish. Would you not come tonight believing in our Lord (Acts 16:31), and repenting (Acts 3:19)? Would you not confess His lovely name (Romans 10:10)? Would you not be baptized for the remission of your sins, as per the teaching of Acts 2 and so many other places? In view of this lesson tonight, I think we ought to listen to the old song that Charles Wesley wrote:

> "Depths of mercy, can there be
>   Mercy still reserved for me?
> Can my God His wrath forbear?
>   Me, the chief of sinners, spare?
> I have long withstood His grace,
>   Long provoked Him to His face;
> Would not harken to His call:
>   Grieved Him by a thousand falls."

Sermon Eleven

The
Parables
of
Jesus

"And He spake many things
unto them in parables"

Luke 16:1-13

"And he said also unto his disciples, There was a certain rich man, which had a steward; and the same was accused unto him that he had wasted his goods. And he called him, and said unto him, How is it that I hear this of thee? give an account of thy stewardship; for thou mayest be no longer steward. Then the steward said within himself, What shall I do? for my lord taketh away from me the stewardship: I cannot dig; to beg I am ashamed. I am resolved what to do, that, when I am put out of the stewardship, they may receive me into their houses. So he called every one of his lord's debtors unto him, and said unto the first, How much owest thou unto my lord? And he said, An hundred measures of oil, And he said to another, And how much owest thou? And he said, An hundred measures of wheat. And he said unto him, Take thy bill, and write fourscore, And the lord commended the unjust steward, because he had done wisely: for the children of this world are in their generation wiser than the children of light. And I say unto you, Make to yourselves friends of the mammon of unrighteousness that, when ye fail, they may receive you into everlasting habitations. He that is faithful in that which is least is faithful also in much: and he that is unjust in the least is unjust also in much. If therefore ye have not been faithful in the unrighteous mammon, who will commit to your trust the true riches? And if ye have not been faithful in that which is another man's, who shall give you that which is your own? No servant can serve two masters: for either he will hate the one, and love the other: or else he will hold to the one, and despise the other. Ye cannot serve God and mammon."

11. The Unjust Steward

This evening we turn your attention to a sermon of the Lord Jesus found in the 16th chapter of the Gospel according to Luke. I have long felt that this is a most unique story. I do not recall how many years ago it first caught my eye, but I can assure you that I have never read the book of Luke without its getting my attention again. I think that in no parable will we find the raw naked rebuke that we find in Luke chapter 16.

When we look at this occasion, we are looking at a time when Jesus was being criticized as He often was in His parables and in His other teaching. His criticism came because He sometimes used people who were scoundrels or people who were certainly less than desirable to set forth His lessons. There are those who propose that because Jesus spoke of such people, He really wasn't much Himself.

Jesus did sometimes choose some rather strange characters to set forth His stories, but I think the reason is apparent. For instance, when you look at Luke 18, the Lord tells the story of an unjust judge and an importunate widow. You recall the judge was a man who feared neither God nor man as evidenced by the persistence—or as we would say today, "constant nagging"—of this widow, the man finally consents to grant her request. Jesus says in His sermon that God is like that. That seems to bother us a little that Jesus would compare God the Father to an unjust judge. But He doesn't say that God is unjust. He is saying if that unjust judge, under persistence from this widow, would grant her request, how much more would a loving Father grant the request of His children who cry day and night unto Him.

Again, you recall that Jesus says that His coming would be like a thief in the night (Matthew 24:42-44). Now I don't think the Lord is commending thieves; He is just saying His coming will be like a thief—a thief's coming usually takes one by surprise, and that's the only point Jesus is making. On another occasion, Jesus says we ought to be as "wise as serpents, and harmless as doves" (Matthew 10:16). Certainly, the Lord wasn't commending everything about serpents. In fact, I find little about a serpent to commend itself to me. When I look at a snake, I see an animal that is slimy, and its mouth is sometimes full of poison. So I really don't see much to commend except still to this day, two thousand years later, I readily grant what Jesus said—that we do ascribe to them a reputation for being wise. They are crafty animals. In this parable, our Lord is doing the same thing. He is giving us a good lesson from a poor example. But I don't think anybody would ever charge Jesus with being unjust or that God is unjust because He uses this story. I think what God is really doing is hanging out a shingle for us, saying He wants some good men with as much business sense and as much regard for the future as this man in Luke chapter 16.

Now I want you to remember that this sermon was written almost two thousand years ago. That is a little difficult for me to keep in mind—that I am studying something tonight that was written long ago and yet is applicable NOW. Someone has so well observed that they know the church of Jesus Christ is divine because it has outlived us for two thousand years. The church has, indeed, outlived some shoddy business practices, so far as our really getting out and doing things for God.

The Picture of a Worldling's Heart

I would like for us to recall the occasion of this parable. The Lord has just finished preaching about the rich fool in Luke chapter 12. Then He comes to Luke chapter 15, and He talks about a lost coin and a lost sheep and a lost boy; I think there is a definite progression in those sermons. He is speaking to His disciples, to those who "heard him gladly." And I would hope tonight that He is still speaking to such disciples, people who want to hear Him gladly. Jesus one more time wants to draw back the curtain from a worldling's heart and let us see how people of the world operate. And it's amazing that it comes as no shock to us. I don't find it any shock at all when I look at a worldling's heart or the way the world operates. It is still going on tonight just as it was in that day.

The Lord begins by saying, "There was a certain rich man, which had a steward; and the same was accused unto him that he had wasted his goods." In that day, it was customary for a rich person to hire a steward or as we would say today, "a manager." He was the manager of that entire household. It was not his business to get the money together; it was his job to see that when it did come in, it was cared for—that is, properly spent—and that all the accounting was done as it should be. When we think of this steward, we think of others such as Joseph in the house of Potiphar (Genesis 39:1-6) and Eliezer in the house of Abraham (Genesis 15:2). These will give us an excellent background for what Jesus is saying in this sermon.

The rich man has learned that his steward was being unfaithful to him, the steward that he has trusted through the years. Possibly the man had come up through the ranks as a slave; and his master finally seeing that the man, like Joseph, could be depended on, placed him in charge of everything he had. With dismay, he learned that this man had been negligent, more than negligent—worse than that! This man was wasting his goods! It was a deliberate loss to him and was bringing pain to the steward. Certainly, you would expect him to call him and say, "You are fired," or at least have him give an account of what had been happening in his household. He accused him of wasting his goods. You will notice in verse 3 that the steward doesn't plead anything. He simply accepts it and says, "What shall I do? for my lord taketh away from me the stewardship." He got the message! When his master was through talking with him, he knew he had been fired; and he had no recourse. He had nothing to say in rebuttal. He just knew that it happened, and there really wasn't much point in discussing it: he was guilty.

Notice, first of all, he called him and said, "How is it that I hear this of THEE?" I think that that's the proper emphasis. He is saying, "I trusted you. I have put into your hands everything I have, and I just can't believe what I am hearing—that you are wasting my goods!" As we said, the man makes no defense. He admits no guilt; he only expresses a selfish anxiety in regard to the future. When the master said, "Give an account of thy stewardship; for thou mayest be no longer steward," I don't think he is proposing something that is going to occur in the future, He is saying, "YOU NO LONGER ARE ... ." The steward knew that he had lost his job; and as a steward, when you lost your job, you lost it all. You lost your house in that you lived in the household. You lost your food, you lost your livelihood, you lost it all!

The steward is suddenly faced with a world in which there is nothing for him. We watch him as he wrestles with his problem. It reminds me of Luke 12, and the rich man who counsels with himself saying, "What shall I do, because I have no room to bestow my fruits?" He counsels with himself, saying, "I cannot dig; to beg I am ashamed." I am not quite sure why he couldn't dig, unless perhaps a life of ease had made it impractical for him; indeed, it might be difficult for him. He said, "I cannot dig; and to beg I am ashamed." He found himself in a pretty bad shape.

I have noticed in the parables of Jesus that when the Lord lays an indictment against someone, it many times is because God is left out of that person's life; he is trying to make it by himself. When we come to the place where self becomes number one, and we are more concerned about MY fruits, MY goods, MY barns, MY house and MY soul, the Lord has a legitimate and serious case against us.

The steward in the parable under consideration tonight conceives a plan. He gets together with people who owe his master some tremendous sums. Evidently loans had been made, and he was in charge of them. He said, "How much owest thou unto my lord?" and each expressed how much he owed. Then he said, "Here is what we will do; we will just alter it." He cuts one of them in half, he alters the other one by a fifth. He doesn't say, "We'll just erase it." He is not the kind who is going to do away with all of it, but he is willing to alter it. I am not quite sure what He is saying to us here, except that there seems to be something basic in human nature that we feel that if we don't totally, radically change something, that it really doesn't matter. What you are looking at is just plain old out and out dishonesty. He is being dishonest about the whole thing, and these people enter into the bond of iniquity with him. Every one of them! The entire group is dishonest. These men know full well what's occurring. This man knows he is dishonest and leads them all into an evil collusion.

This is amazing to me. The Bible says, "And the lord commended the unjust steward, because he had done wisely: for the children of this world are in their generation wiser than the children of light." This is a most difficult passage; how do we explain it? We see dishonesty, and we see bonds of iniquity, and all of a sudden the Bible says, "And the lord commended the unjust steward." How could he possibly commend the man? The explanation has to be one of two things. Either He is commending out and out dishonesty ... or ... on the other hand, he is commending prudence, foresight, looking ahead, and the boldness of decision that must be made. It would appear that here is a case where dishonesty is at least momentarily disentangled from foresight. Here is a case in which energy is disentangled from evil ambitions. Nobody is going to commend the evil ambition of this man, but what is being commended is the energy that he is willing to expend to make preparations for his future.

The Children of this World and the Children of Light

The Lord, of course, is teaching a good lesson from a bad example. And the lesson? "The children of this world are in their generation wiser than the children of light." Now, I want you to think about these two groups. He said, "The children of this world are in THEIR generation wiser than the children of light"—and I think that is a beautiful expression. It's not only a beautiful expression, it's a unique expression—"the children of light." In fact, I cannot at this moment recall any other place in the Word of God where this expression is used in this manner. The Bible does say in 1 John 1:7 that "if we walk in the light, as he is in the light, we have fellowship one with another." But here He uses the expression that we are the "children of light." Now, in this same world in which we live, there are the children of the world—everybody surely at one time was a child of the world—but it is possible to become a child of light. Remember in 1 Corinthians 3, Paul says, "And I, brethren, could not speak unto you as unto spiritual, but as unto carnal, even as unto babes in Christ." He said, "For whereas there is among you envying, and strife, and divisions, are ye not CARNAL, and walk as MEN?" You "walk as men." What does he mean? Not just men of any kind, but he said you are still walking like men of the world, like people who have never been converted. So, it is possible for an individual to walk or order his life after the way of the world ... or ... he can walk in the way of the "children of light." What a beautiful expression! In 1 Thessalonians 5:5, Paul says, "Ye are all the children of light." In Ephesians 5:8, he says, "Now are ye light in the Lord: walk as children of light." It would seem to me that we are talking about children who are born of light, born in light, always being illuminated; the idea of truth and sincerity and integrity must be there.

You know, it's in light that you see things as they really are. I can still remember going to Temple, Texas, when I was a child. We made that journey about twice a year; it was a long trip. We would go down there and sell a few animals; it was clothes buying time. I can still remember going into the stores, and my mother would always go through a procedure that, when I became a teenager, became a little embarrassing to me. Before she would buy anything, she wanted to take it outside and that bothered me that she wanted to do that. But she always wanted to take it outside so she could see it in the light. I understand now what she was doing. It may look beautiful inside; but when you get it out in the sunlight, it may not look so nice. You can really see it as it is. I suspect the poorest time in the world to buy a used automobile is at night when the lights are gleaming off their shiny hoods. They are really beautiful. Wait until you see them in the morning light! How true this is in spiritual matters. The Bible is saying that we don't walk in darkness: we are "children of light." We ought to be able to see all the shades; we ought to be able to see it as it is, if we are children of light.

Let's listen to Him again. He says, "The children of this world are in their generation wiser than the children of light." Now, that's a little hard to take—even from the Lord. You would rather think that He would commend His own children and say, "My children are smarter than anybody else's." We tend to do that. But Jesus turns it around and just tells it as it is. He says, "The children of this world"—these people who have never been converted, who have never come to Me—"are in their generation wiser than the children of light." That's a rebuke, people, in raw naked form. Jesus is saying I want you to know that these unconverted souls are sometimes, many times, wiser than My own people—those who ought to know most about it, those who should see all the shades, those who should tell you what the colors really are. He is saying that we don't go to half the trouble to win Heaven as these people do to win earth.

They are Wiser in the Way They Operate

He said they are "in THEIR GENERATION"—He is talking about a collusion of men of the world, the way they do business and manage their affairs together. It is like the principle Jesus introduces when He says, "How can Satan cast out Satan?" (Mark 3:23). There are times when we will cast out one another, but Jesus says Satan doesn't do that; he is smarter than that—or as Jesus uses the word, "WISER." He is wiser; he knows that if he casts himself out, his kingdom cannot stand. And so Jesus wants us to know that "in their generation"—in their getting together, in the way they operate—they are "wiser than the children of light."

If there is anything that I have learned in what little dealings I have had in the business world—or, at least, in the business part of the world that I happen to function in (the public school system)—it is that there is almost no end to which people go to accomplish their purposes. And I am not saying that it's always wrong or it's always evil. In fact, sometimes I really admire the way the business world functions. They will pursue their business interests; they will lay out a fine product; they will totally learn the business. They will recruit men whom they feel will be most advantageous to their business and to their way of life. They will get them familiar with the prospect or the consumer; they will set up a campaign; they will get an artist; they will have television ads; they will have radio ads; all of this is brought down to a fine art. All these energies and moneys are expended to do one thing: to get that product of that company over to the consumer. THEY WORK AT IT! Sometimes we wonder why a certain company is so successful. I can tell you why. Somebody is spending a great deal of time, putting in a lot of late hours, and expending a great amount of energy.

If I may, I would like to inject a personal word at this point. Just this past week I was thinking if we had somebody working for the church and putting as much time and as much energy into that as I am spending every week—and you could say this about the business you are in, too, I'm sure—I really wonder what would occur in the church of Jesus Christ. About two weeks ago, we finished a plan that we have been working on for two years—an intricate plan that's to be submitted to Austin, Texas, a plan stating what we will do in our school for the next five years: cost projections, technical data, all kinds of things. And I am saying all that to say this—I just thought as we finally dropped that document in the mail: if we just had someone or someones that involved, working that hard every day for the church of the Lord, I really wonder what would occur. This is what's happening out there in the business world. It is true with many of the businesses of those who are represented in this congregation tonight. You know what it takes to make it go. It takes a lot of planning, a great deal of work, and substantial amounts of money.

Compare that with the way we sometimes seek the lost. Compare some of those things in which we are involved in our businesses with the way we rescue the perishing. It would make us ashamed, I think, of what we are actually doing for the Lord Jesus Christ. We give a man a tract, and we feel we have evangelized him. If we give him a book, we feel we have gone the second mile. If we set up a study and study two months with him, we have gone to the ultimate end; and if he's not saved at the end of that two months, we decide he is not one of those who have been predestined to be saved or that he is already guilty of blasphemy against the Spirit! We write him off at the time and place where a salesman is just starting.

I want you to think about this for just a moment. Compare the way we sometimes work for the church of Jesus Christ with the way that WE play a game—to say nothing of the way the world does it. We really get involved. We will spend our energies and really work to win that game. Or you think back for a little while about how much energy, time, effort, and money you spent to get that person that you wanted to be your wife or husband. It took you a while didn't it? But you got it done because you were really interested in getting it done.

Lay Up Treasures in Heaven

Our Lord is saying to us in this sermon that it's not enough to be good. It isn't enough to be dedicated. You must also be shrewd and calculating. In fact, He says, "Make to yourselves friends of the mammon of unrighteousness." Now, that's a scary thing isn't it? That's one of the reasons we pass this parable up. What He's saying is frightening. "Make to yourselves friends of the mammon of unrighteousness."

Do you remember what Matthew 6:19-20 states? Jesus says:

> Lay not up for yourselves treasures upon earth, where moth and rust doth corrupt, and where thieves break through and steal: But lay up for yourselves treasures in heaven, where neither moth nor rust doth corrupt, and where thieves do not break through and steal.

Now, that sounds good, but let me ask you something. How do you do that? How do you lay up treasures in Heaven? I am not in Heaven; I am down here on earth, and the Lord is telling me that I should lay up there while I'm here. I am not going to lay them up there after I get there. He is saying I must lay up my treasures in HEAVEN while I am still on earth. Now the question: How do I get it done? We learn in this parable how to do it.

First of all, the Lord states that we do so by investing in those who are going there. While I am here, if I invest in people who are going there or help get them there, I am laying up "treasures" in Heaven. Secondly, He is saying that I should use both my position and my possessions to help lay up treasures and make eternal friendships. Is this not what the steward did? When he was thrown out of his house, he had friends to take him in. Now, however unscrupulous his friends were and however miserable the prospect was in getting together with those kinds of fellows, the point is, he had a place to go. Jesus is saying one of these days you are going to move out of this old body, and you had better get some preparations made so that you have a place to go in the great eternity.

Even though we may not wish to acknowledge it, everyone in this room is like this man in at least two ways. One, what we have tonight is given us to use … listen to my words … to use, to invest temporarily. It is a trust that has been given us. We still think that when we make a dollar, it's MY dollar. Or if I have a piece of land, it's MY land. But I want you to know that this sermon teaches us that these things are given to us to USE and it's a temporary use. They are given to us to invest; this is the point Jesus is making.

Years ago I read about a little lad who was on his way to church. In one hand he had a dime his mother had given him to buy candy after church, and in the other hand he had a dime that he was supposed to give the Lord. He fell on the sidewalk; one dime got away and rolled into the sewer. He looked up and said, "Sorry, God, there goes YOUR dime." This is the way we are. What he needed to realize was that BOTH DIMES belonged to God. We are like him. We've got ours in one hand and God's in the other hand. What we need to realize is that what we have in BOTH hands belongs to God. "The earth is the Lord's, and the fullness thereof" (Psalms 24:1). Everything we have is to be used wisely—shrewdly—according to this parable; it has just been lent to us to use.

Let me tell you another way we are like this man. Everything we have is going to be taken away from us soon. EVERYTHING! We cannot keep it. You have heard that all your life. I've heard it for as long as I can remember, and I still find myself in need of hearing somebody say, "Look, YOU … CAN … NOT … KEEP IT!" We just can't do it. The only thing we can do—and this seems to be the word that comes back to me over and over—all we can do is invest it. If I have something, here it is. I am not going to keep it, but some things down the line of time are depending on it. You see, I am not going to keep it until I get down there—I am going to lose it in the interval. So the only thing I can do is invest it in view of things that are going to occur. Now, what's the best investment?

I guarantee you, in the morning about 8 or 9 o'clock, the wheels will be grinding, the computers will be running, and there will be determined men sitting in front of huge boards with lights flashing; they will be trying to decide on the best investments all the way from Wall Street to Tokyo to Sidney—that's their business. Some time ago I was talking with a man in Waco about some of our school business and the telephone rang. It was his investment counselor. This man was always calling him from some place in Waco where he in turn was on a hot line from somewhere else. They constantly fed information to him about what he should invest and what he should sell. They were intent on making the best possible investment.

Invest in Heaven

I think we need to realize tonight, as the Lord's people, that here is Somebody telling us what we need to invest and here's how to do it. The Lord is our Counselor. We are involved in something much greater than silver and gold. How do you invest in Heaven? Jesus is saying to lay up my treasures while here. How am I going to do that? I have learned one way that you can do it, and I would like to read from Philippians 4:10-19. In this place the Apostle Paul tells us one way that we can invest in Heaven:

> I rejoiced in the Lord greatly, that now at the last your care of me hath flourished again; wherein ye were also careful, but ye lacked opportunity. Not that I speak in respect of want: for I have learned, in whatsoever state I am, therewith to be content. I know both how to be abased, and I know how to abound: everywhere and in all things I am instructed both to be full and to be hungry, both to abound and to suffer need. I can do all things through Christ which strengtheneth me. Notwithstanding ye have well done, that ye did communicate with my affliction. Now ye Philippians know also, that in the beginning of the gospel, when I departed from Macedonia, no church communicated

with me as concerning giving and receiving, but ye only. For even in Thessalonica ye sent once and again unto my necessity. Not because I desire a gift: but I desire fruit that may abound to your account. But I have all, and abound: I am full, having received of Epaphroditus the things which were sent from you, an odor of a sweet, smell, a sacrifice acceptable, well pleasing to God. But my God shall supply all your need according to his riches in glory by Christ Jesus.

How did the Philippians invest in Heaven? They did it INDIRECTLY through a person who was preaching the Gospel of Jesus Christ; that person was the Apostle Paul. You see, the Philippians couldn't be in Thessalonica and in certain parts of Macedonia, preaching where Paul was preaching. But he said, "You sent once and again unto my necessity," and he said I want you to know that every soul I have reached in this place is your investment in Heaven. I want you to know that you have a little added to your account. In fact, he uses that word, did you notice? He said I don't "desire a gift: but I desire fruit that may abound to your account." Paul is saying the Lord is going to credit their account with an investment in Heaven. Why? Because they helped him to tell the gospel to somebody else. And so this is one way this kind of thing can be done.

That puts a new slant on giving! Giving on the Lord's Day should never be thought of as being a collection in which we are just taking up money for God. I realize we are doing that, and I think it's exceedingly important as our brethren have expressed over and over at the time we give. But we are not taking a collection for God as if we are collecting some old clothes. God doesn't need any money. You see, God owns the whole world and can you imagine what money is to God? However, he is telling us the collection needs to be done. It is a way to get souls saved. The Bible is practical. The Bible says Paul was writing that he needed to go preach the gospel to the lost, and he said brethren, "no church communicated with me as concerning giving and receiving but ye only." In this particular case, he said, "You sent once and again unto my necessity." He said you kept me going; and since you kept ME going, souls were saved, and this has been credited to your account. What a wonderful thought that someday, when they step through the pearly gates, they can meet people over there that they have never met on earth; and yet they meet them there because THEY had done something for them through the life of another individual.

You know, the same is true of all of us. I know that in this congregation, we have brethren who are not only supporting the Gospel of Jesus Christ by giving as they are prospered upon the Lord's Day but are sending money to preachers of the gospel in other places, and I think it's wonderful. That's a marvelous thing! "Fruit that may abound to your account" because you are willing to do these things; and there will be some souls that can welcome you to Heaven because of what you have done. It's a serious question: Is anybody going to be in Heaven because of you and your investment?

Some of those who operate in the business world carry with them their portfolio of investments. If you want to get a fellow like that started, you just talk to him about it a minute, and he'll tell you the whole story. He'll talk to you about his investments in stocks and bonds and oil and cattle or whatever he's in. What I wonder tonight is what does our portfolio of investments show in regard to Heaven. There may be some souls tonight in this place or perhaps some other state or down in Old Mexico or in Africa that you've never met—you don't speak their language, their culture is totally foreign to yours— but I want to tell you, there are some of those that you may meet in Heaven because of your investment. I thought of this some time ago as we were studying with some twenty or thirty men in Old Mexico. They will touch lives that we will never touch. They will meet people we will never reach, and it's because of brethren in this country who are willing to invest their money that those men are there.

You can do it DIRECTLY, too. You can make an investment in Heaven indirectly, as Paul said, or you can make it directly by putting money into His Cause, by talking to other people. There are so many ways to invest in others—through tracts and tapes and programs and books. The Lord is most practical. He said it's going to take some of the riches of earth to get some of the riches of Heaven out to the people of this world. And He said, what I want you to do, though, is not just invest,

He said I want you to invest SHREWDLY. I want you to really think about what you are doing.

Money is "Least" with God

Let's look at verse 10. "He that is faithful in that which is least is faithful also in much: and he that is unjust in the least is unjust also in much." Do you know what the Lord is saying? It did not first appear to me. He is saying that money is a little thing, it's least really. Money doesn't amount to much; money is a little thing. What a strange approach in a world where it's the biggest thing. We don't spell success in our world with S's; we spell it with dollar signs. When you go out in the morning and deal with the world, you know what you are dealing with. If you want to talk about success with a man out there in the world, you talk dollar signs. Jesus is saying here that with God, money is a petty little thing. He says if a person is "faithful in that which is least," God will count him "faithful also in much." He says if you are dishonest in that which is least, you would also be dishonest in much.

What is most with men is least with God. It is interesting that a fourth of all the parables of Jesus somehow dealt with money. He mentioned it somewhere, somehow. That means that about a sixth of the gospels deal with money. Now this doesn't mean Jesus was a fundraiser. What it does mean is that He said if you want to know where a man's heart is, don't ask him to get out his hymn book, ask him to get out his pocket book. You know what He said? That "where your treasure is" … now think what He is saying … "where your treasure is, there will your heart be also" (Matthew 6:21). He knew us didn't He? And that's why over and over again He deals with this matter that we call money—the thing we deal with every day of our lives. The truly spiritual person must be a person who sees money as a little thing except where it should be used in the Kingdom of God.

In verse 11, Jesus says, "If therefore ye have not been faithful with the unrighteous mammon, who will commit to your trust the true riches?" He says if the unrighteous mammon is what really matters to you, if that's the big thing in your life, it is going to lead to all manner of evil. You think what's going on out yonder tonight. Think what went on Saturday night for money. Have you ever stopped to look at a ten dollar bill or a twenty dollar bill and think where all that bill has been? For that little piece of paper, there have been those who have gone in and robbed a convenience store and may have murdered a person. Or some girl or some woman may have sold the only virtue she had for that little piece of paper. There are people tonight who will throw away a beautiful career for a moment as an embezzler. There are those who will lie on their income tax or do anything, you name it, they will do it, whatever it is, for money. What are we supposed to do if it's all that bad. Jesus didn't say go join a monastery. He didn't say for us to take a poverty oath. He didn't say, "Don't touch it!" He said He wants us to INVEST it. Take that same thing that can be used so wrongly and invest it in the Cause of Jesus Christ.

Listen to verse 13. He says, "No servant can serve two masters." This is His conclusion. "No servant can serve two masters: for either he will hate the one, and love the other; or else he will hold to the one, and despise the other. Ye cannot serve God and mammon." Listen to His words, "NO … MAN … CAN … " "YOU … CAN … NOT." Now that's pretty strong language for someone to speak two thousand years ago. Doesn't He understand that things may change and evolve through the years? But He is still right! "You cannot serve God and mammon."

Mammon is an old and a familiar foe. If you've studied the Word of God, you can hear the word "mammon" and it sends a chill through you; you know you are not supposed to have anything to do with mammon. It's something bad, and there is something wrong with it. Uncertain and unstable riches— mammon. Mammon was, the best I can gather from history on it, an old Canaanite deity, the god of money. Those who worshiped Mammon actually went into a temple and worshiped the god, "Mammon." They bowed at the altar of Mammon. Jesus is saying you can't worship in two temples at the same time. You can't bow your knee at two altars at the same time. It's impossible. You cannot serve God and Mammon. You can't be a full-time slave to two people. Oh, you might honor one and then the other; you might serve one more than you do the other; you might serve one in pretense and the other in fact, but you just can't march to two different beats at the same time. But, you can serve God and you can use—a you can INVEST—mammon, and I think this is exactly what He wants us to do.

The Final Audit

Let us never forget that we are stewards of the grace of God. Paul says in 1 Corinthians 4:1-2, "Let a man so account of us, as of the ministers of Christ, and stewards of the mysteries of God. Moreover it is required in stewards, that a man be found faithful." Peter states that we are "good stewards of the manifold grace of God." (1 Peter 4:10). To be anything less is to be accused of "wasting His goods" (Luke 16:1). There is no doubt that we will give account of our stewardship. The books must balance! The books will be opened. We shall be held accountable, accountable not only for the evil we've done but also for the good we could have done—as a good steward of Jesus Christ.

Sermon Twelve

The
Parables
of
Jesus

"And He spake many things
unto them in parables"

COUNTING THE COST

Luke 14:28-33

"For which of you, intending to build a tower, sitteth not down first, and counteth the cost, whether he have sufficient to finish it? Lest haply, after he hath laid the foundation, and is not able to finish it, all that behold it begin to mock him, Saying, This man began to build, and was not able to finish. Or what king, going to make war against another king, sitteth not down first, and consulteth whether he be able with ten thousand to meet him that cometh against him with twenty thousand? Or else, while the other is yet a great way off, he sendeth an ambassage, and desireth conditions of peace. So likewise, whosoever he be of you that forsaketh not all that he hath, he cannot be my disciple."

12. Counting the Cost

As we come to study the Lord's Word, I am made to realize that one must preach, several must listen. One does not have a Gospel Meeting by himself. I became aware of that many, many years ago. I have intended for this to be a cooperative endeavor so that when I leave this place, we can say we had a good meeting or that we had a meeting that wasn't so good. Now that can be my fault or it might be yours or it's probably both. We have been here to work and function together for good or ill. I believe we ought always to give the very best that we have. And if anybody can ever convince me that I can give less than my best, then I think that is the day that I'll stay home.

We are eternity bound souls, we are before the great Creator of the Universe, we are people who will never die. That surely ought to call forth the best from us. We have in our presence this evening no less than the King of all Kings; we have the God of all the Universe looking upon this assembly tonight. We have before us the possibility of becoming Christians or being better Christians, and that turns an otherwise drab evening into an important time.

We spend a great deal of time teaching people how to preach so they will know how to address an audience, and I think that is good. We need some people doing that. But I think sometimes we haven't spent a great deal of time teaching people how to listen. And you see, it takes both. It takes somebody preaching and somebody listening. Some time ago I figured up that if you go to church Sunday morning, Sunday night and Wednesday night and you attend a meeting like this one, in the course of one year, you're going to be listening to preaching for one week—one solid week, twenty-four hours a day, seven days a week. Some people are going to say that's a great deal of listening. If you're going to do that much listening, you need to know how to listen; and the Bible speaks to us about how to listen in James 1:21. We are told that we are to "receive with meekness the engrafted word, which is able to save your souls."

Some time ago I heard that in the Roman Empire, in the time of Christ, only ten percent of the people were literate. Only ten percent of the people had the capability of reading; and there really wasn't a great deal to read as far as the common masses of people were concerned. I suppose this is one reason that, in Bible times, when an epistle was delivered to a congregation, someone stood before that congregation and read the epistle to the people. I suppose this is one reason that Paul says, "Let your women keep silence in the churches: for it is not permitted unto them to speak … if they will learn anything, let them ask their husbands at home" (1 Corinthians 14:34-35). Not having a copy of completed scripture to read would necessitate a hearing in the assembly or an asking at home. The people in that day evidently did a great deal of listening. So I can understand why the Bible tells us that, first of all, we are to put away all filthiness of the flesh and spirit and to "receive with meekness the engrafted word" that is able to save our souls. And that is what we are going to be doing. I am going to attempt to speak, and you are going to listen, and I hope together that we can really accomplish something. I believe it can be done.

How to Live

Our brother has read you tonight from the words of Luke, really most of them are words of the Lord Jesus Christ. You are aware that in Luke chapter 14 Jesus is speaking to us on the subject of life. And that is what we are going to be talking about—how to live. If there's anything the people in this room should want to know how to do, it is how to live. Everyone in this room tonight is living. We're in the period that is called life, and the Bible has a great deal to say to us on the subject of living.

"What is your life? It is even a vapour, that appeareth for a little time, and then vanisheth away" (James 4:14). You know, I have learned that in living life a great deal of my life is composed of decisions. I have made a few big decisions in my life that really affected me—the time when I became a Christian, the time when I decided to get married and the person to whom I would be married, and the few times when I have made other decisions that were big in my life. But most of the decisions of my life have not been big ones; most of the decisions in my life are little daily decisions. Sometimes, I think, we feel that such really doesn't make much difference to God; I want to tell you that's not true. What you do from day to day—the decisions you make from day to day—are extremely important to the great God of Heaven. I know that because of what is stated here in chapter 14 of the Gospel according to Luke.

Someone has said that we shape our environment, and our environment shapes us. I have learned that the decisions I have made in life have had a way of turning around and making me and that's why it is so important that we make the right decisions. Whether you are young or old, the Lord will hold you responsible for the decisions you make because they are going to make you. When we look at some of the decisions we have made, we haven't always made the best decisions.

I would like to be able to stand before you and say that you are looking at a person who has always made the BEST decisions—they have always been the BEST ones that could have been made. I know better than that. All of my decisions have not been the best. And as I look back down the stream of time, I find that in some of those decisions I succumbed to the tyranny of the second best. They were not the best decisions. They were not necessarily evil decisions, but they weren't the best decisions that I could have made; and the Lord, according to Luke 14, wants us to make the best decisions.

They Watched Him

If you have your Bible with you this evening, you might want to open it to Luke 14; we will notice what Luke has to say and then what Jesus has to say. On this occasion, our Lord has been invited over to eat a meal with someone. I suspect, however, the Lord knows that He hasn't been invited because they are glad to have Him there. In fact, Luke so states:

> And it came to pass, as he went into the house of one of the chief Pharisees to eat bread on the Sabbath, that they watched him. And, behold, there was a certain man before him which had the dropsy. And Jesus answering spake unto the lawyers and Pharisees, saying, Is it lawful to heal on the sabbath day? And they held their peace. And he took him, and healed him, and let him go (Luke 14:1-4).

Now, I want you to think what's happening in Luke chapter 14. The Pharisees were people who ruled by influence, not so much by position. When Jesus was arraigned before Annas and Caiaphas and the Sanhedrin Court, you might well wonder why He was taken before Annas. Annas had at one time been High Priest in Israel; and if one ever occupied such a place of great prominence, he always held that place among the Pharisees.

The man who was inviting Jesus over on this Sabbath day was a CHIEF Pharisee. He wasn't just any old run-of-the-mill Pharisee, he was one of the big men among the Pharisees of his day, and he invited Jesus over on the Sabbath day, no less. You know, where I grew up down in Texas, you had everyday dinners and you had Sunday dinners. If you wanted to invite someone over to the BIG dinner, it was always on Sunday, without exception. That's just the way it was.

Among these people, it was on the Sabbath day. And the Bible says they invited Him over "to eat bread on the sabbath day," and "they watched him." I'm sure Jesus must have wondered— Jesus didn't wonder, but if I'd been there I would have wondered—why He was invited. Have you ever been in a situation like that? I have been in situations sometimes where I really wondered why they invited ME. I was so out of place. Nobody seemed to know what to say to me, and I really didn't know what to say to them either. I am sure the occasion of this parable was a similar situation.

By the way, have you ever thought about why the man who had dropsy was invited? Can you imagine a chief Pharisee inviting a man who has dropsy to eat with him on the Sabbath day? He really didn't want that man over there.

I suspect the man was a "plant." You see, they invited Jesus over there that day, and they planted this individual so they could watch what Jesus would do with him. They wanted to find some flaw in the Lord's character. They want to find some problem; they wanted to "put Him down" in some way. That was exactly what they were doing, and Jesus knew that. They were just watching Him.

I want you to notice what Jesus did. "Jesus answering spake unto the lawyers and Pharisees, saying, Is it lawful to heal on the sabbath day?" I want you to notice that He anticipated the question. They didn't even get a chance to ask it. He knew what they were going to ask. When He was invited over to the chief Pharisee's house to eat bread on the Sabbath day and there was a man with dropsy invited too, HE KNEW WHAT WAS COMING!

You know, you sometimes get asked questions you really don't know how to answer. I was supposed to know, but I just didn't. Jesus not only knew the answer, He knew the question. He anticipated it and turned it around and asks, "Is it lawful to heal on the sabbath day?" Of course, they couldn't answer that.

Jesus went on to ask another question. He asks, "Which of you shall have an ass or an ox fallen into a pit, and will not straightway pull him out on the sabbath day?" (Luke 14:5). He said you know very well if on your way to the synagogue you find one of your prize animals in the ditch, you're going to pull him out! You're not just going to walk on down the road when one of your best animals is in the ditch—an ass, an ox, whatever it is—you're just not going to walk on by. You're going to pull him out. And, of course, they got the point.

The point was, yes, they would take care of their animal; but they wouldn't bother with this poor man who was in this pathetic condition. But the point was if Jesus would answer and say yes, it's lawful to heal on the Sabbath day, they would accuse Him of breaking God's law. On the other hand, if He didn't answer correctly, then He was a person who was less than kind and very unloving.

"Whosoever Exalteth Himself shall be Abased"

Jesus continues to preach, and I think it's important in this study for our day for us to see what's happening. Jesus is at the house of the chief Pharisee. In that day, their tables were generally shaped something like a U. There were three places of prominence. One, at the closed end corresponding today to our head table. The other two were on either side. Any place other than these three places was considered to be less than the best. Servants would proceed into this U shape and would serve those who were reclining at the table. On this occasion, Jesus preaches:

> And he put forth a parable to those which were bidden, when he marked how they chose out the chief rooms; saying unto them, When thou are bidden of any man to a wedding, sit not down in the highest room; lest a more honourable man than thou be bidden of him; And he that bade thee and him come and say to thee, Give this man place; and thou begin with shame to take the lowest room. But when thou art bidden, go and sit down in the lowest room; that when he that bade thee cometh, he may say unto thee, Friend, go up higher: then shalt thou have worship in the presence of them that sit at meat with thee (Luke 14:7-10).

And here is His conclusion:

> For whosoever exalteth himself shall be abased; and he that humbleth himself shall be exalted (Luke 14:11).

The Lord wants us to understand tonight that the way up is the way down. And if you want to rise in the Kingdom of God, the only way, the ONLY way you are ever going to get there, is through a route of humbleness and service to God.

Jesus makes a promise to everyone, "Whosoever exalteth himself shall be abased." It's a promise from no less than the

Lord. He says if you want to be exalted, you humble yourself in My service, and YOU WILL BE EXALTED. I want to tell you, tonight, I sincerely believe that's true, though we're looking at it two thousand years later; it has never been more true.

He goes on talking to these people; He is still sitting in the house of the chief Pharisee. I guess by now they probably wish they hadn't invited Him; but He goes on talking with them: "When thou makest a dinner or a supper, call not thy friends, nor thy brethren, neither thy kinsmen, nor thy rich neighbours; lest they also bid thee again, and a recompense be made thee. But when thou makest a feast, call the poor, the maimed, the lame, the blind: And thou shalt be blessed; for they cannot recompense thee; for thou shalt be recompensed at the resurrection of the just." And all of a sudden, in the midst of this "one of them that sat at meat with him heard these things, · and he said unto him, Blessed is he that shall eat bread in the kingdom of God" (Luke 14:11-15).

Have you ever noticed this passage? I really don't know what it means. I don't even know why he says it. He is sitting around, and it just seems that he felt he ought to say something. Have you ever been in a situation like that where people feel as if they have to say something? I sometimes get into situations where people who don't know preachers well feel as if they must say something appropriate; and they come out with all kinds of things. I don't understand why he says it. I do know that Jesus doesn't seem to be impressed. The Lord was never impressed with platitudes and show. He goes on to tell us a story. I want us to hear the story. And I'm not going to preach a sermon tonight on the story that follows because it illustrates our behavior many times.

They Began to Make Excuse

Jesus goes on to say:

> A certain man made a great supper, and bade many: And sent his servant at supper time to say to them that were bidden, Come: for all things are now ready. And they all with one consent began to make excuse. The

first said unto him, I have bought a piece of ground, and I must needs go and see it: I pray thee have me excused. And another said, I have bought five yoke of oxen, and I go to prove them: I pray thee have me excused. And another said, I have married a wife, and therefore I cannot come (Luke 14:16-20).

There is not a child in this house tonight who doesn't know that story. We KNOW that story. We know about this man. He evidently is well off, he is a rich man, royalty, no doubt. He is living in this city, and he decides to make a great supper. He said I want you to go out and invite the people in. Go "say to them that were bidden, Come; for all things are now ready." They did that, and yet the house was so commodious that he said go out "into the streets and lanes of the city." And, of course, this is done; and he said, "Go out into the highways and the hedges, and compel them to come in." I think you know what the Lord is saying in this lesson; however, we often fail to make the application. The problem with us tonight is that we know what the Lord is saying; but we, like they, are not making the application.

When I look at this lesson, it's so familiar to me, so simple and yet I find it's so rebuking. One man, when approached, said, "I have bought a piece of ground, and I must needs go and see it." There is nothing wrong with that; in fact, I think I could take the Bible and defend a Christian's right to hold property. I can take the Bible, I believe, and show that it is perfectly within the Christian's right to buy property, to own that property; and while it is within his power—as the Bible puts it—he may do what he will with that in accord with Christian principles. He may sell that piece of property; he may not only sell that piece of property, but he may sell it for gain. So, there is nothing wrong with land. We look at this and wonder, "Well, what's the problem? This man 'bought a piece of ground,' and he says, 'I must needs go and see it.'" I guess many have known the thrill of buying a little piece of ground and the joy of walking over it. Of course, that isn't the lesson the Lord's giving us. The lesson is that this man was in love. This man was in love with his possessions to the extent that he couldn't be bothered with a feast regardless of who made it or how grand it might be. What a privilege he missed. You know, there was nothing that said he couldn't buy a piece of ground and still go to the banquet. He could have done so. But he chose not to—and this is why I called it at the beginning—the tyranny of the second best. There is nothing wrong with land; there is nothing wrong with buying land; it's just that it was second best. What was best? Sitting at the King's banquet table was best. He could have had them both. Instead he chose the one that was worth the least. His priorities were not in order, to use a modern term.

Another man said, "I have bought five yoke of oxen, and I go to prove them." I want you to "have me excused." Now, when he says, "I pray thee have me excused," it's evident that he had heard about it; he knew about it; he knew he really ought to be there; he just had an excuse. He was in big business. He had bought five yoke of oxen, and he went to "prove them." I would suspect he might have seen those oxen before he bought them, but suppose he didn't. He's bought them; they're not going to get away. He could have gone to the feast and then come back and still have done all these things. There wasn't anything wrong with proving the oxen that he had bought.

If you want to put it in a modern setting, when one of you farmers goes out to buy a new tractor and you finally get it home, you can't wait until you can get out there and try out the horsepower and see what it is like—you'd like to tinker with it. This man just simply wants to check out the "ox power." He wants to know what he's bought. Jesus is saying there is nothing wrong with that. What is wrong is putting that before MY ways and the things that I have invited him to do.

The other man just said, "I have married a wife." He had contracted a social tie—a real social tie. "I have married a wife"—he just wouldn't be there! There is nothing wrong with marrying a wife. There is nothing wrong with a man caring for his wife; that's what he is supposed to do. In fact, in Old Testament times, when a young man married a wife, he was exempt from going to war for a year. But this man is not being invited to a battle. This man is being invited to a feast, and there is nothing that says the wife couldn't go along. I haven't heard of many wives who wouldn't enjoy a night out. The wife wasn't the problem. He is just saying to us that he really could

218

care less about the man or his feast. How current that is tonight. How true it is in the times in which we live.

Did you ever notice the element of newness in this lesson? This really hadn't dawned on me before—new land, new oxen, new wife. What did he have? He had something new. Now, of course, land is not new. It has been around for a long time; it was around before the feast. But it was new to him. He had five "new" yoke of oxen. He had a "new" wife. So many of the things of this old earth seem so new to people in comparison to the age of the Gospel of Jesus Christ, when the fact is, these are just some of the things that have always been around.

The Lord Must be Number One

That man missed the chance to secure a part of Heaven in order to get a part of earth. This man missed the chance to get the world's greatest Business Partner on his side in order to go out and see how good his oxen were. But I think the point the Lord made is obvious. He said sometimes you let the trivia of life get in the way.

I would like to think that the more educated we become, the more sophisticated we become, the longer we live on the earth, the more accumulated knowledge we have, and the more of this Book we have to study that we wouldn't make the same old mistakes—we just wouldn't let the trivia of life get in our way. But we still do. And the lesson is still so applicable to us. I guess the best place to see that is in other people. It's easy to see in others. We sometimes see this in our own children, don't we? We don't see our children necessarily making EVIL choices, but we sometimes see them making choices that aren't the BEST choices. We sometimes look at our children and see them buying things that aren't really wrong, but it's not the best. They are not engaged in some evil activity, but sometimes they miss the BEST activity. That's the point in Luke chapter 14. Don't ever think these are insignificant; we call them little things, but don't think the Lord's not concerned. He's concerned with what's number one to you tonight.

We sometimes sing "Is it business, is it pleasure, is it money or friends?" Does my life show that Jesus really matters to me? I can stand here tonight and tell you that the Lord and the church are NUMBER ONE in my life; but if you could just be around me and live around me a while, you'd REALLY know. The fact is, all of us sitting in this room tonight know one another pretty well. We know OURSELVES pretty well, and we know that our lives show what is number one to us. I guess that's why this lesson is so important to us because it's here that we best demonstrate—not with our mouths, but with our lives—our love for Him and for His Cause.

I want you to look at verse 25. He is still talking to these people. In verse 25, He says, "And there went great multitudes with him: and he turned, and said unto them." At this point in the life of Jesus, there were some great multitudes. I don't think that means there were three or four or ten or fifteen people. There were some great multitudes following Him.

Now, you might suspect that if Jesus really wanted to gain all those people, He would have told them just to come on in and that all the details would be figured out later. He looked at those great multitudes and saw souls that needed to be gained—souls that were lost, people who needed to be taught. He looked at them and said, "If any man come to me, and hate not his father, and mother and wife, and children, and brethren, and sisters, yea, and his own life also, he cannot be my disciple." Now, you think of that. How would you have felt if you had been along with that great multitude following this Man. After all, He is a pretty spectacular Man; He can do things other people can't do; He can do some things the Pharisees claim to do, but we all know better than that. We like what He is doing, but we don't understand all about it. All of a sudden, He turns around and says, I want to tell you something. If you don't hate your father, your mother, your sister, your brother and your own life also, you "CANNOT BE MY DISCIPLE." Now, that is pretty blunt. What would have been your response? Would you have decided, "Well, look, if it's that way, I don't want any more" ... OR ... would you have risen to the challenge and said, "Here is a life that requires total commitment and that is meaningful to me."

You know, that is a difficult word. He says, "If any man come to me, and HATE not his father, and mother, and wife, and children, and brethren, and sisters ... ." I'm sure preachers have come your way who say that means to "love less." They're right. But I think we must not blunt the edge of this sword. Remember, Jesus is looking at that great multitude of people, and He wants them to understand that just following along after Him doesn't make a disciple. He said you must "hate" your father and mother and sister and brother. What does He mean? Does this mean that we are to harbor hatred in our heart for these people? I want to tell you tonight, I don't believe that passage teaches you are to harbor animosity in your heart toward people who are near and dear to you. I don't even believe you are supposed to love your relatives with a diminished love. In fact, the scripture says, "Husbands, love your wives, as Christ also loved the church and gave himself for it" (Ephesians 5:25). This is intense love that is seeking the best for that individual. Jesus loved little children and said, "Suffer little children ... to come unto me: for of such is the kingdom of heaven" (Matthew 19:14). No man loved like Jesus, so He isn't saying that you need to love your dear ones with a diminished love, and He certainly isn't saying you need to have malice and animosity in your heart toward loved ones.

Something that has always bothered me, people, is that sometimes we treat the people who are closest to us—that we ought to love the most—in a way that we wouldn't think about treating people who are totally of the world. Now explain that. We will never find any justification for that in Jesus' words, according to Luke. He didn't say love them with a diminished love, but what He is doing is using an oriental hyperbole, a deliberate exaggeration. According to outward appearance, or speaking from appearances, it would appear that you hate your relatives. Let me give you a current example. We all get involved with family reunions. You know ... all your family is getting together for something and you're never there. "You're never here when we have any 'get togethers'; and when you are here, you never show up until after church is over." You've been there, too, haven't you? You get there sometimes, and they have had to wait lunch on you or go on without you. I suppose they think that we really don't love them—our fathers and our mothers and our relatives and our family; but that's not true. We love those people very much, but I want to tell you tonight, there is Someone Whom we love better. We love those people a great deal, and we don't know just where they are on the scale of things, but they are pretty high. But they cannot be number one.

I guess the best way to understand such is to learn what Jesus said, "Yea, his own life also." He doesn't say you are to become some kind of psychotic individual who hates himself. What is He saying? Even when it comes to your own life, the scripture says, "No man ever yet hated his own flesh" (Ephesians 6:29). But here He is saying that you hate your "own life also." He is saying even your own self must come second to Jesus Christ and His way of life. It is here that we learn that Christianity is not something you do on Sunday morning and Sunday night and Wednesday night. Christianity is a way of life. It is total commitment; it can never be anything other than that.

Count the Cost

Look at verse 28. Jesus says:

> For which of you intending to build a tower, sitteth not down first, and counteth the cost, whether he have sufficient to finish it? Lest haply, after he hath laid the foundation, and is not able to finish it, all that behold it begin to mock him, Saying, This man began to build, and was not able to finish.

He uses the illustration of the king. He says, "WHOSOEVER ... ." I want you to take that home with you tonight; I want you to let it drive home in your heart. "WHOSOEVER ... ."— that's me, that's you—"doth not bear his cross, and come after me, CANNOT be my disciple." It's impossible. You must be following and imitating Jesus even to the point of death according to this and other passages. He uses this parable to illustrate it. He said that in that day they built towers. Now, we don't build such towers down in Texas; I don't think they do up here either. In that day farmers, and people who were in the grape business, would build a tower in the midst of their vineyards—even the Old Testament speaks of it—from which they would be able to view marauders and those who would destroy; towers in vineyards were the common practice.

Jesus wanted to teach something those people would understand, and they did understand Him. He says if a man is going to build a tower, what does he do? First of all, he should sit down and count the cost "whether he have sufficient to finish it." What is the point? The point is that before we begin, we ought to have some contemplation of completion. Are we going to be able to finish?

Let's put the idea into a current setting. Think about the elderly gentlemen sitting down on the courthouse square whittling and discussing and solving the problems of the world. Some fellow is coming down the street, and one asks, "Who is that?" "That is old Sam." "Who?" "He is the fellow who is always starting towers. He started a tower over on Johnson's old place; he bought another place and started a tower over there, but he has never finished one." Jesus so beautifully points out that such has always been looked upon with disfavor—even in worldly goods.

Between Waco and Fort Worth, there is a house that somebody began to build many years ago. It's a nice house, beautiful location; some of you may have seen it. It still has only the tar paper on the outside. It could have been a beautiful house. I don't know what happened, but they stopped working on it. I don't know what the problem was, whether there was a death or a divorce or what happened, but that house stands as a monument crying out to all who pass by. Through all these years it has stood there as one big black monument. Someone began to build, and for some reason they were unable to finish.

Jesus says this was true in towers, but His point is that most of all it is true in the lives of men and women. He is saying that all over this world are unfinished lives. Think of that! If we could see people as we see towers, this world would be dotted with thousands who have heard the gospel story, they've heard about Jesus Christ, they began to build, they at one time received with meekness "the engrafted word," for a while, they began to live for Him, but they didn't finish. All over this country there are tragic stories of unfinished lives. Indeed, we need to count the cost. We need to think it over before we ever begin.

Now, you think how that struck the multitude. Jesus' philosophy was not—and I think, brethren, we need to listen to this—Jesus' philosophy was NOT to engulf a great number of people who were willing to say, "We're willing to head your direction," and later down the line somewhere we'll talk about salvation—we'll grow into Christians. That isn't what He proposed. He turned around to that crowd and let them know that what He was doing was no playful extravaganza. He let them know that crowding along after Him did not constitute discipleship. And I want to tell you tonight that just because we congregate within a church house does not mean that we are what we ought to be.

When I go into a store and see something that I want and I am convinced that I just must have it, I ask, "What does it cost?" If the sales person tells me, "I don't know," that really bothers me. Why doesn't he know? He is working there; and if he's working there, he ought to know. I am not debating with him. If someone is working there as a salesman and he doesn't know, I don't really think there is much point in discussing it any further. I will find somebody who does know; how am I to pay the cost if I don't know the price? Someone must be able to tell what the price is. That is one of the marks of a truly great leader. Jesus Christ, our Leader, knew the cost, didn't He? He knew what it would cost.

One thing you will never ever say about Jesus Christ, about the church, is that all these people just got me into something that they didn't know what it was and now they can't get out of it. I want to tell you, tonight, that wasn't true of me. In fact, when I first began to hear the gospel preached, I was approaching 18 years of age. I never had heard the gospel preached prior to that time; the bare word irritated me just a little. Some of the things preached made me angry. But you know, I am indebted to those men who came into that community down home and who preached the gospel and told me exactly what it cost. No where down the road have I ever had to look back and say, "Well, I've gotten into something that I just didn't know what it was going to be like—if only I could just get out of it!" I want to tell you, it's worth it all. Oh, there's a cost. There's a price to be paid; we must "love less" our father and our mother and our sister and our brother and our very life. Otherwise, there is not much point in even starting. That's pretty blunt, but that's what He's saying—count the cost, whether you shall have sufficient to finish.

Well, the challenge is there. The Lord is uncompromisingly honest about it. I hope tonight that two things are apparent. Number one—am I willing to deny myself to be a Christian? I don't think there are a lot of people who really are ready to give up what they must give up to BE a Christian. I am not talking about THINGS necessarily. The biggest thing I have ever had to give up is this thing right here—self. I have found that when I get THIS straight, I don't have many problems about places where I am supposed to go and places where I am NOT supposed to go, and things I am supposed to do and things I am NOT supposed to do. You see, those are the branches; when we get down to the real root of the matter, it's this matter right here. And that's why Jesus says if you're not willing to "love less" your very self, you cannot—that's what He's saying—you CANNOT be my disciple.

It's impossible unless you make up your mind that you owe your allegiance to HIM, Jesus Christ, the Son of God. Killing off self as Paul says, "I am crucified with Christ: nevertheless I live; yet not I ... and the life which I NOW live in the flesh, I live by the faith of the Son of God, who loved me, and gave himself for me" (Galatians 2:20).

The Lord is not so much interested in what you've BEEN doing as He is in what you are doing NOW. What are you willing to do? What are you willing to be? Are you willing to pay the price for being a real, genuine Christian? The Lord is not interested in some of your money; He is in interested in ALL of your money. The Lord is not interested in some of your time; He is interested in ALL of your time. He's not interested in some of you; He wants all of you. If you're going to become a Christian, that means all of your time, all of your talent, all of your money, all of your life! It is a total commitment to Him, to Jesus as King and as Savior—with no strings attached. He wants a life with no strings and no angles. That's the cost! Have you really counted the cost of a life without Christ? Have you really considered eternity in Hell?

Do you remember the old song that was based on this parable? It was titled, "Have You Counted The Cost?"

"There's a line that is drawn by rejecting our Lord,
     Where the call of His Spirit is lost,
And you hurry along with the pleasure mad throng,
     Have you counted, have you counted the cost?"

"You may barter your hope of eternity's morn,
     For a moment of joy at the most,
For the glitter of sin and the things it will win,
     Have you counted, have you counted the cost?"

"While the door of His mercy is open to you,
     E're the depth of His love you exhaust,
Won't you come and be healed, won't you whisper, I yield,
     Have you counted, have you counted the cost?"

Then he gives the chorus:

"Have you counted the cost, if your soul should be lost,
     Tho you gain the whole world for your own?
Even now it may be that the line you have crossed,
     Have you counted, have you counted the cost?"

I want to tell you, tonight, what we are talking about is so important. Have you ever counted the cost of falling into the hands of the Living God? Or ... have you ever counted the cost of falling OUT of the hands of the living God? Either one.

If you are here tonight, and you are not a Christian, I want you to count the cost of walking out that door and still not being a Christian. You can do that. I don't know how many in that great throng of people that Jesus preached to that day turned and walked away. I do know that John states that many of them "walked no more with him" (John 6:66). They couldn't face that commitment. They couldn't give up; they wouldn't pay that kind of cost.

But I believe there are people in this room tonight who are willing to pay that cost. I know some of you are paying it. If you're here tonight and you're not a Christian—you're a young man or a young lady, whoever you are-you can pay the cost. You CAN believe the gospel. You CAN repent of your sins. You know, it's not so hard to believe, I think it's a lot more difficult NOT to believe.

But I am not going to stand here tonight and tell you that it's simple to pay the cost of repentance. It is difficult to repent (Acts 2:38). You CAN confess your faith in Jesus Christ (Matthew 10:32-33). You CAN be immersed in His name for the remission of your sins (Acts 22:16). You can become a Christian—you can become a follower of Jesus Christ.